D1506501

The Three-Wall Nick and Other Angles

The THREE-WALL NICK

and Other Angles

A Squash Autobiography

Frank Satterthwaite

Holt, Rinehart and Winston   New York

Copyright © 1979 by Frank Satterthwaite
All rights reserved, including the right to reproduce this book or
portions thereof in any form.
Published by Holt, Rinehart and Winston, 383 Madison Avenue,
New York, New York 10017.
Published simultaneously in Canada by Holt, Rinehart and
Winston of Canada, Limited.

Library of Congress Cataloging in Publication Data
Satterthwaite, Frank.
The three-wall nick and other angles.
1. Squash (Game)   2. Satterthwaite, Frank.
3. Squash players—United States—Biography.
I. Title.
GV1003.62.S27A37   796.34′3   78-14173
ISBN 0-03-016666-7

First Edition

DESIGNER: *Joy Chu*
Printed in the United States of America
10 9 8 7 6 5 4 3 2 1

To My First Coach, My Dad

CONTENTS

ILLUSTRATIONS

ACKNOWLEDGMENTS

One of the perils of writing a book is you may discover that many of the "brilliant ideas" that you were just bursting to share with the world are not your own.

It wasn't until I started writing this book that I began to realize just how much my thinking on the game has been shaped by the thoughts of others. Now, as I read over the final manuscript, it has become obvious to me that my principal contribution has not been to come up with the great ideas, but simply to pass some of the good ones along. And so I must give a very unoriginal, but heartfelt thanks to the many wonderful people in the world of squash who provided the inspiration.

Even the idea for this book was not my own. It came from my agent and squash buddy, Mel Sokolow, whose only stipulation was that I mention he is the National Veterans Doubles Champion of both the U.S. and Canada. I must also give a special thanks to my editor, Tom Wallace, even though he threatened to break my squash arm if I missed another deadline.

Finally, many thanks to S.R. for the many distractions that substantially delayed the completion of this book.

Frank Satterthwaite
October 1978

The Three-Wall Nick
and Other Angles

COURT AND GALLERY

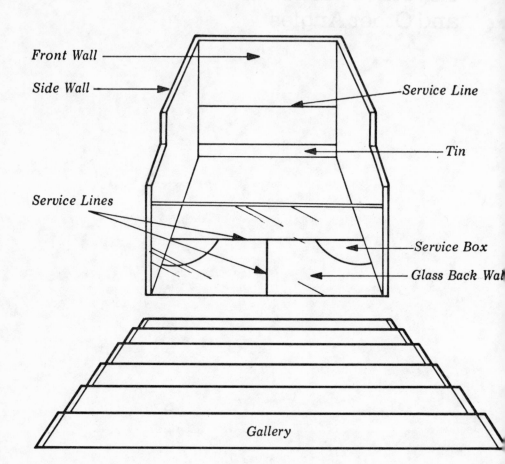

Front Wall

Side Wall

Service Line

Tin

Service Lines

Service Box

Glass Back Wall

Gallery

Prologue
MATCH POINT!

"Keeping It Interesting" for Sharif Khan

Ordinarily I don't figure to beat the world champion. But when I'm up 2-love in games in a 3 out of 5 game match, the thought of victory does cross my mind.

That Sharif Khan was the world champion of hard ball squash was at the time indisputable. Just one month earlier he had defeated Australian Geoff Hunt in a dramatic finals of the 1977 North American Open. Dramatic because the squash world is divided between those who play with the zippy North American "hard ball" and those who use the squishy English "soft ball." And Hunt who, as perennial British Open champion, is the acknowledged king of the soft ball version of the game, was for the first time going after the North American Open title, which is considered the world championship of hard ball squash. Hunt had nothing to lose, but Sharif, who had won this tournament seven times before, was not only defending his title, but his entire record as well. For if he lost, people would start saying the only reason he won all those previous titles was because Hunt wasn't entered. After all, Hunt had always beaten him in the soft ball game, and they'd never played before with the hard ball.

Well, Sharif rose brilliantly to the challenge. Sometimes by overpowering Hunt, other times by changing the pace, Sharif dominated the play throughout most of the match, and, though he dropped the second game, he seemed to have the match all wrapped up in the fourth when he led 2-1 in games and 13-4 in points.* But then Hunt started coming on. He won 4 points, lost 1, and then saved 5 straight match points to make it 13-14. To most of us in the gallery, it looked like Sharif, who was obviously tiring, had blown the match, for Hunt, who'd won 9 out of the last 10 points, now needed only 1 more point to tie the game up. And if Hunt could win this game, his superior fitness would no doubt tell in a fifth game.

But Sharif in the next exchange showed his champion's courage by going for a bold but decisive putaway. And when the ball, which he angled into the crease where the side wall meets the floor, rolled unplayable, there was nothing Hunt could do but shake Sharif's hand, for Sharif had just won the Open title an unbelievable eighth time.

Now, one month later, Mr. Hunt having departed, Khan was expected to coast to his eighth North American pro title. True enough, he made it to the semis of this tournament with little difficulty, but there he encountered a very unexpected problem. Me.

I'd be less than honest if I said that going into this semifinal match I'd had that funny feeling that somehow this was going to be my day. The truth is, I felt I'd already had my day. When I got up in the morning, all I wanted from squash was to win my morning quarterfinal match. Making the semis of the pro championships, that would let them know I was on the scene. At each stage of my squash career—in the juniors, in college, and in the amateur ranks—I'd made my presence known. Not the top player, but a player to be reckoned with. Now, I was trying to prove myself in the pro ranks.

That I at age thirty-three should be in my rookie season, trying to make it as a pro, says something about me and about the game. I'd always been where the action was in squash, and now the action was in the pro game, and I didn't want to call it quits just yet. I wanted to be part of the game as it "opened up." I could see it coming. In Australia, Britain, and Mexico, with pay-and-play courts as the vehicle, the game had taken off. Now suddenly in Canada and the U.S., commercial courts were popping up all over. This game that was once played almost exclusively in private

*Readers unfamiliar with the method of scoring and rules of play may find it helpful to consult Appendix A, "The Game, How Played, Scored."

schools and private clubs was "going public." Entrepreneurs were discovering that squash, here as elsewhere, is an easy game to sell. All you had to do was put up courts and the game sold itself. And companies with products to sell were starting to think that squash might be a good way to sell them, so commercial sponsorship of tournaments was becoming a factor in the game.

What this meant was the best players in the game were now pros, and the pros would be the ones who'd be introducing the game to the public. I wanted to be there. Which explains why I had traveled to the Southfield Athletic Club on the outskirts of Detroit in March 1977 to play in my first North American Pro championships, a tenderfoot in the pro ranks at the not so tender age of thirty-three.

I was seeded in the tournament, but I wasn't expected to beat my opponent in the quarterfinals, Rainer Ratinac. A superfit Australian, now teaching squash in the U.S., Rainer had been to the finals of both this event and the North American Open. I was something like 1 and 4 with him. The one time I'd beaten him was in a minor tournament, several hours after he'd received news that his first son had been born. If I could beat him here, and make it to the semis of this major tournament, that would really be something.

So when I got up in the morning, all I wanted from squash was to beat Rainer. And my wish was granted. Though I started off shakily, losing the first game, I suddenly caught fire and ripped through him the next three games, 15-10, 15-5, 15-8. Everything came together, and I just couldn't miss. I wouldn't have wanted to play myself that time. I don't think I've ever been happier than when I won that match, and I certainly felt like I'd done my day's work. All that was left was a match against the world champion, Sharif Khan.

Just before we entered the court for that afternoon match, I said to Sharif, "I'm sorry. I know you were planning on playing Rainer, but I'll try to keep it interesting."

Picking up on the jocular tone of my apology, Sharif responded in a humorous, mock British accent, "Ah, splendid. Shall we have a little hit?"

I was pleased to hear that. I didn't want him to take this match too seriously. The last time we'd played, three months before, I'd just pulled a big upset over Toronto pro Clive Caldwell. I'd gotten hot and blitzed Clive 3-zip. When I played Sharif the next day, he went after me like I was out to steal his title. If ever a cannon were rolled out to kill a gnat, it was on that day. I was just happy to have beaten Clive, who was rated number three in the pros at the time, but Sharif got it in his head that having played so well against Clive, I might now be going after bigger game, and he wanted to set me straight. Ordinarily we have exhibitiony four-game matches, but that time he jumped on me early as if to prove a point. He hammered me into the ground. I'd never seen him play so hard against me. Taking everything early, he gave me no time to think. The pace, the gets, it was incredible. But I was stunned more by the fact he was taking me so seriously than by the play itself. This was just a little pro round robin in Los Angeles that didn't count for anything.

But that's the way Sharif maintains his dominance. It doesn't matter who he's playing or where, if someone seems to be getting hot, he goes after him. If he senses someone's tracking him, Sharif immediately turns and becomes the hunter. Like a sheriff in the Old West, he doesn't want anyone to get the idea he just might be able to pick him off. If one gets through, they'll all be taking shots at him. So the better the opponent, the worse he beats him. That way everyone backs off. On that day my good friend Sharif had played like he had a personal grudge against me. The offense? I'd stepped out of line by beating Clive.

I didn't want him taking my win over Rainer too seriously. No, I wanted him in a more playful mood. That's why I made light of my morning's victory before we stepped into the court.

A warm-up against Sharif is the damndest thing. Ordinarily your opponent positions himself on the other side of the court, about a foot behind the service line; you hit him a cross-court, he sends it back. As the ball starts to warm up, you try a few shots. All the while, carefully, tentatively limbering up, you gradually get reacquainted with the game. Not Sharif. One moment he's 6 feet from the front wall volleying your cross-court. The next he's behind you somewhere, blasting the ball into the back wall so that his return goes whistling by your ear en route to the front. When you're warming up with him you never know where he's going to be next. He's constantly in motion. This may be his second match of the day, but it's as if he's been away from squash too long and has all this pent-up energy he has to release.

Sharif has this incredible gusto for the game, and like a kid digging into his favorite dessert, he can't seem to get enough of it at once. It's obvious that squash is more than a business for him. It is, as he puts it, almost a religion for him and his family. Certainly he's never so alive as when he's on the court. Off the court with his black hair and mustache, his swarthy complexion and pearly smile, he's nice looking, but no Omar Sharif. But when he enters the court, his expressive face takes on a striking intensity. His alert eyes bug with determination, and as he leaps about, in his form-fitting clothes, with his swashbuckling strokes and derring-do, he becomes handsome indeed.

But there's more to his warm-up than just love of the game. He's also showing off—to the gallery, to the opponent, to himself. As he hotdogs around the court, he'll set himself up with a couple of lobs so that he can smash a few overheads, his entire body jack-knifing into the follow-through. You get the feeling it's a psych. He's like a basketball player showing off a few slam dunks just before the game to intimidate the opposition. Smashing the ball around the court is his way of psyching himself up and getting himself into the match. His way of building up a head of steam that will carry him into the first game.

It's an awesome display of speed and firepower. With the ball flying every which way and Sharif everywhere, you feel like there's a lot going on in the court that you're not part of. It can really put you off. But I've played him enough times to be used to it by now. And I know that sometimes he gets a little carried away with all this stuff. What I'm hoping is that's what will happen this time. That he'll continue to showboat around in the first game.

True enough, that's what happens. Apparently not taking the match or me too seriously, he clowns around during the first game, playing to the gallery. It's not that he plays the clown, but he's just very flamboyant, giving the paying customers a show. How dull if he were always the grim competitor, making mincemeat of his opponents. It's good for the game to have a champion with a little life and a spark of humor in him.

He affects the air of a man having a grand old time out there. He makes it seem like a playful romp. He hams it up, exploding in mock anger at a call or an error, popping his eyes in disbelief, like a Pakistani Harpo Marx.

The gallery ooo's with appreciation as he blasts the ball into the back wall. (He didn't have to hit the ball into the back wall to make that get, but he knows those back-wallers are guaranteed crowd pleasers.) He rallies himself with a cry of "Come on Pakistan" just before he serves. The gallery snorts its appreciation; I smirk, for I've heard that line a thousand times.

The crowd is loving it. They think it's all a playful romp. A lot of laughs. That Khan fellow has a great sense of humor. But I'm out there on the court, and I know better. I know he's not just playing to them, he's also trying to convince me that he can win in a breeze. Bluff me out of the whole thing so he doesn't have to work too hard.

The challenge is to tune him out. And to pay no attention to the gallery's enthusiasm for his antics. And the thing is, he's playing it a little loose. Those blasts into the back wall may look and sound impressive, but often as not the ball rebounds right into the center of the court. He's dashing about the court all right, but he's not really taking the ball as soon as he might. He's overhitting a little so the ball's coming well out off the back wall. And he's hitting a few more tins than he might ordinarily. If I can tune him out and keep plugging away, there are plenty of opportunities to pick up points here.

He's not focusing in 100 percent on the match, and I know even when he has me down 14-12 in the first game, I can still win that game if I really hustle. And I do win it, 17-15. I don't so much win it as steal it when he's not looking. Well, it serves him right for taking me a little too casually. But that's the way he usually plays at the start of matches.

It's not all that tough to get a game off Sharif if he's not gunning for you. But winning 2 games is an entirely different proposition. I knew when I got that first game he was now going to get down to business. No more freebies.

I stole that first game by outhustling him in a wide open game. I like to play an all-court game, with lots of shots, counterpunching, and scrambling. That's what I'm best at. And playing this freewheeling style, I can work Sharif, make him sweat, make him suck air. We always have exciting points and I usually pick up a game. I can keep it interesting this way, but I can't beat him.

I'm a good scrambler and one way or another can get my racquet on almost anything, but while I have to work to make my gets, Sharif doesn't. We're the same height, 5′8, but at 160 I outweigh him by 10 pounds. If I lost that 10 pounds, however, it still wouldn't make any difference; I would still be a heavy-footed, herky-jerky runner by comparison.

I run, I set up, I hit; but with Sharif running, stretching, and hitting meld into one continuous motion—an elastic-limbed flow that cannot be broken down into discrete movements. Most of the time he walks, and when rushed, he doesn't so much run as pounce, like a leaping panther. I, alas, am a lunging panter.

I like to mix it up and scramble, but I'm not going to beat Sharif that way. What it comes down to is you can't make it an athletic contest against a superior athlete. That wide open play with lots of probes and initiatives works fine against Sharif so long as the match has an exhibitiony feel to it, but now that I've got a game, and Sharif's going to get serious, I've got to come up with something else.

The only way to beat Sharif (and here we enter the realm of theory, for he loses a match maybe once every two years) is to delimit the field of battle. Instead of an all-court game, you have to find one thing you might be able to do better than him and get him to play you on your terms.

Toronto pro Gordie Anderson has a bigger forehand than Sharif, so he tries to get the play over to the right side. Ratinac attempts to get Sharif into long points and beat him on fitness. And Caldwell will try to keep the ball snug along the side walls so that Sharif can't get a good clean hit at it. He tries to frustrate Sharif by keeping it going up and down the wall, up and down the wall until Sharif finally makes an error from impatience. But it's not in my nature to wait, wait, wait. I have to attack.

The way I attack is to hit deep and then try to put the ball away short in the court. But these short shots can backfire if my opponent gets to them in time, because a loose ball, short in the court, can all too easily be counterpunched for a winner. And nobody's better at getting there in time than Sharif. Furthermore, his eye is so good, even if he only just gets his racquet on it, he'll likely redrop the ball or angle it out of reach for the point.

With most players, you can take them short just to move them around and work them, but you can't fool around with Sharif short in the court. He's poison up there. Which is useful to know, but the problem remains, how am I going to score points against him when he's bearing down?

My answer on this day was to hit short shots—three-wall nicks, drops, and corners—that were so good even Sharif couldn't handle them.* It was one of those days when I just couldn't miss.

---

*These shots are described along with other technical definitions in the glossary at the end of the book.

I could have been out there blindfolded with a Ping-Pong paddle and still putting the ball away. But the key was this, I was not compromising on my short shots. I wasn't tentatively half-hitting floaty little dinks in an experimental way. No, I was hitting them like I meant them. There was no indecision on my part. I accepted the fact that the only chance I had was to take some chances. When I'd go for the point, it was either my point or into the tin. But I didn't leave him anything short to fool around with. I made some errors, but I was making more winners. It was like I was shooting a pair of dice that were loaded in my favor. This feeling that I couldn't miss—I don't know whether it was the heat of creativity or the glow of a hot streak—either way, it sure felt good.

There was one shot in particular I was driving him crazy with, the reverse corner. In theory it would seem to be the worst shot to use against a fast man. After all, you're hitting the ball diagonally across the court in such a way that it ricochets around the far front corner and rebounds right out in the middle of the court. Unlike a drop shot that hugs the side wall, it ends up right in the center of the court. If your opponent is on it, he can do whatever he wants with it—the whole court is open.

Sharif, of all players, would seem the worst guy to use it against, except for one thing: he grew up playing the English version of squash, first in Pakistan and then when he was in school in England. And in the English game they rarely, if ever, use the reverse corner, because the English ball is so soft, it doesn't squirt out of the corner, and so is too easy to catch up with. The reverse corner is effective only if it is unexpected and it happens so quickly your opponent doesn't have time to recover. I learned all too well how useless the reverse corner is in the English game when I played in the world soft ball championships. But that experience also tipped me off to the fact that the English ball players are vulnerable to that shot when they play our game, because they don't look for it.

Sharif, who is now based in Toronto, has been playing our game for over ten years, but he still doesn't see that shot as well as he sees all the others. It's the most un-English shot in the American repertoire, and even when he's looking for it, he doesn't move for it instinctively. As fast as he is, he can be in trouble like anyone else if he gets a late start, because so much of squash retrieving is a matter of anticipation.

Even so, the reverse corner is an iffy proposition against him.

It's effective only if you hit it hard and low, otherwise it hangs or comes off the second side wall. And against someone as fast as Sharif, even though he's not always on it as fast as he might be, still, you have to punch the shot closer to the tin than normal or he'll get it. And I don't like shooting several inches above the tin these days.

There was a time when I thought hitting the ball a shade above the tin was a display of great finesse. But when you're a pro with a few bucks on the line, you learn pretty quickly to play the percentages. The past year I'd more or less stopped using the reverse corner because it seemed too risky going so close to the tin. I never practiced it and I tried to refrain from using it in matches. But there was something about the construction of these courts at the Southfield Athletic Club that made the ball squirt out of the corner and die quickly as it skidded along the floor. And since Sharif didn't cover that shot as well as the others, I got into using it. I hadn't practiced it for a long time, but there's something about the way I cock my racquet that makes that shot a natural for me, and I got into one of those moods where I was popping reverse corners anywhere, anytime, and making them. They were coming off my racquet so automatically, I was as surprised as Sharif, really.

I'm sure Sharif thought he was playing a madman. How can you protect yourself against a guy who's not afraid to try any shot, and, what's worse, is making them? I had him off balance because he couldn't predict when I was going to go for another winner. Maybe the percentages were against these shots, but I was making them.

But the best memory of that game was the way I won the final point. Up 14-11, I found myself short in the court with a loose ball. The temptation was to go for another corner or maybe a drop, but I knew from experience that when it gets down to the final points of a game he wants, there's nothing Sharif can't dig out short in the court. So I cocked my racquet early and held it there as if I was about to go for another corner, and then I smacked a drive. He was nowhere near it. I'd caught him cheating forward in anticipation of another short shot. Even more satisfying than hitting a shot perfectly is faking an opponent out with your shot choice. And to catch the world champion going the wrong way on game point, that's the ultimate.

All of a sudden this match had taken on a new look. Even though I had the initiative and was outplaying him that second game, I didn't really believe I could win it until the referee said, "Game Mr. Satterthwaite, he leads 2 games to love."

I had gone into this match determined to give it my best shot. After all, you don't get to the semis of the pro championships too often, at least I don't. And who knows, anything can happen. But it's pretty tough to persuade yourself you can win when you've played someone maybe ten times and never done better than take a game off him.

But now I'm up 2–love and starting to think, my god, I can win this thing. Well, it's one thing to pop shots willy-nilly when you've got nothing to lose; it's quite another to keep them coming when you're up 2–zip. My lead has become a factor in the match.

Probably the worst thing you can do when you've got a lead is to sit on it. The only way to protect a lead is to try to increase it. If you don't press forward, you go backward. File that thought under twenty-twenty hindsight, for, as I see it now, where I went wrong in the third game was to get too conservative. Whereas in the second game I was out front, on the attack, going for it, in the third I was hanging back in the court, playing conservatively. Instead of playing to win, I was playing not to lose. And the result was I lost the momentum. I no longer had Sharif off balance, trying to guess what I was going to do next.

Of course, you never know about these things. Did I let up the attack, or was it more a matter of Sharif seizing the initiative? Sharif is a champion and he wasn't about to hand over a match just because he was down 2–love.

It became obvious that Sharif's plan for the third game was to pick up the pace. He lets you know when he's going to pour it on, because before serving, he rocks forward, bounces the ball a few times, and then looks over at you, still bouncing the ball. He looks at you hard, and then a little smile comes across his lips, as if to say, "Are you ready for this?"

The way I handle that look is to frustrate him by not letting him find my eyes. As soon as I see him lean forward, I fix my gaze on the front wall, giving it as cruel a look as I can muster at the moment. I pretend not to notice him, but out of the corner of my eye I can see what phase of the service delivery he's in, and so I'm ready for his serve.

I can handle that look, but handling the pace is something else. When he decides to turn on the heat, he moves forward in the court and starts cutting everything off. He camps out in front of the T, even, and with full-bodied, slashing strokes, starts "King-Khanning" the ball. He's an explosive athlete, and when he gets himself pumped up, nobody can hit the ball as hard as he can, as soon as he can. A couple of other players are possibly as quick to the ball (I'm thinking of Mike Desaulniers and Stu Goldstein), and Gordie Anderson, when he has time to set up, can hit a bigger forehand than Sharif. But what Sharif can do that no one else can is blast balls that other players can only just get their racquets on. That's pace. And pace nullifies all. If you don't have time to set up, it's all you can do to get the ball back. You can't hit hard, you can't hit shots. You feel like you're tending goal.

When Sharif first came on the scene, he used to play entire matches area bombing the front wall at close range. Bang, bang, bang. Not the most accurate of shots, but he'd get the ball flying around so fast, you couldn't think. An incredible display of speed, strength, and stamina. The essence of physical squash. He soon took over from his older cousin, Mohibullah Khan, who had more finesse, and at one time had been, in the opinion of many veteran observers, the fastest man ever in a squash court. But Mo, approaching thirty, was starting to burn out, and couldn't take Sharif's heat.

But now Sharif is himself past thirty—thirty-two at the time of our match. Which seemed pretty young to me, since I was thirty-three, but what it means is he no longer can keep up this wild man stuff for an entire match. Like Muhammad Ali, he can get up on his toes for a couple of rounds, but he can't fight an entire fight that way. In recent years, though, Sharif has compensated for the decline of his physical prowess by developing his skills. He's much more accurate than he used to be, and he knows how to control a point without working too hard. Sometimes he lets his opponent punch himself out, lets the challenger throw everything he has at the champ, while he himself bides his time pushing the ball down the side wall and lobbing it cross-court.

He knows he can't go flat out for more than a game or so; therefore, he waits for the right moment to throw a "full court press" at you. And here he's a great psychologist. What he's trying to do when he picks up the pace is not just win points but also break you. He wants to so overwhelm you, you think there's no way you can beat someone like that. When he gives you the treatment, it's hard to realize that he's punishing himself as well. He once told me that it hurts when he pushes himself like this, but he tries not to let on; and it helps to remind himself that if he's hurting, his opponent must be hurting even more. What he's trying to do is get you to back off. The thing you have to do, as Caldwell once explained to me, is ride it out without letting it get to you. Batten the hatches, reef your sails, and try to keep from capsizing, for the gale will pass.

Still, it's hard to keep up your spirits when you're getting shelled something awful. I had begun that third game too tentatively, and pretty soon he was on top of me and I couldn't get out from under. He won the game 15-8.

I was pretty discouraged at the end of that game, but as I came out of the court for the five-minute break, I noticed there were four Khans waiting for Sharif, two of his brothers and two cousins. This is a Khan emergency. A Khan has won this tournament for the past fourteen years. Sharif's dad, Hashim, won it in 1963 and 1964, his cousin, Mo, won it from 1965 through 1969, and Sharif has won it every time since then. Cousins Mo and Gul and brothers Aziz and Charlie had played in this event, but they were out now. Sharif is the only Khan left in the tournament. If Sharif loses, it's no longer a Khan tournament. There's tension between Sharif's side of the family and his cousins, they seem to play rougher against each other than against anyone else, but at a time like this they pull together. They all speak fluent idiomatic English, but right now they're jabbering excitedly at one another in Pakhtu, obviously urging instructions on Sharif.

Funnily enough, this bucks me up. The tension in their pleadings reminds me that I'm the one who's leading. I know they're telling him to keep up the pace. But I also know that, even with this five-minute break, he can't keep it up forever when we get back out there.

The locals are urging me on while I towel off, but there's no one around to coach me. However, I remember something a sparring mate of mine back in New York told me the night before. I was staying with Dave Linden's dad in Detroit, and Dave had called to find out how things were going. When he learned I'd made the quarters, he told me, only half in jest, "Don't think too much." And it's true. You get in a big match, and you can start thinking so much, you think your way right out of it. You worry too much about what you should be doing, instead of just doing it.

Remembering Dave's comment also reminded me of some good advice I'd received right before I played my semifinal match in the national amateurs the year before. Bob Hetherington congratulated me on finally having cracked through to the semis of that event. Reverend Bob had himself played in a number of these pressure semis and, since it was Sunday, he couldn't resist giving me some counseling. "Just do one thing," he told me. "Go out there and have fun. Do that, and good things are bound to happen." Well, it almost worked. I lost that match in overtime in the fifth game.

That had been a very disappointing loss. I was the number two seed in the tournament and over the years had had a winning record against the top seed, Peter Briggs, who went on to win the title. I knew I was going to turn pro later that year, so when I lost in that tournament I knew it had been my last chance to win the national amateurs, and in all probability my last chance to win a major title. But now, here I was, a year later, in the semis of the pros, an infinitely tougher tournament, leading the world champ 2 games to 1. One more game and I'd have a win that would more than make up for not just that disappointment in the nationals, but for every other loss I'd ever had as well.

Not that I'd had a career of losses. I'd been playing the game long enough to have had my moments. At one time or another I'd managed to beat every major player in the game, except Sharif. But no matter how well you do, you always wish you had done a little better. I'd made it to the semis of the national championships at each stage of my career—the juniors, the intercollegiates, and the men's amateurs—which was pretty good, but it would have been better to have made it to the finals and possibly to have won one of these titles.

Well, maybe it was all leading up to this. Maybe this was going to be my big pay day. I returned to the court resolved to go for it. No holding back, no dithering over strategy. Just play from instinct and go for the game.

As soon as I got the serve, I blasted it right at Sharif's head (via the front wall, of course) just to let him know I was back on the scene and not intimidated. He doesn't like to field a fast serve any better than anyone else, and he tinned his return. I then proceeded to throw everything I had at him, and it worked. I regained the momentum. Once again I had him guessing and off balance. If he was meaning to pick up the pace again, he wasn't doing it. He was playing a madman who was popping shots anytime, anywhere, and making them. It's very tough to defend yourself against a guy who won't do the sensible and expected thing. I got into one of those crazy moods where I was defying the odds, and it was all he could do to try to keep up. But he wasn't keeping up. Sure, I made a few tins, he made a few gets, and so he picked up points here and there; but when I knifed another tin-defying backhand into the far corner to make the score 13-9, I knew I had it. And so did Sharif. Ordinarily he struts about the court with a "Khan-do" swagger, carrying his shoulders high. But after failing to get that last shot, as he returned from the front wall I could see him literally drop his shoulders. I'd only seen him do that twice before, the two times Vic Niederhoffer beat him. Both times it was late in the fourth game, with Vic leading 2-1 in games and well up in points. Now I'd brought him to the point where he was trying to think what to say when he loses. I could see from the sullen look of resignation on his face he'd given up and was now preparing himself to take defeat like a champion. Telling himself to be a gracious loser at the end of the match. He was going to play it out, but there was no hope now, not with the score 13-9.

The next point, he gets badly in my way in the center of the court. He fails to clear as I set up to go for a winner. I stop play, turn around, and ask the referee for the point.

There's not that much room in a squash court to begin with, but in a tense match like this, we're playing each other as close as we can get away with. We know the rules, you're supposed to get out of the way when it's your opponent's turn to hit, but neither of us is going to give an inch more ground than we think we have to. It's not like we're on opposite sides of a net. We're vying for control of the same space, the center of the court. This has not been a push and shove match, but we have had our share of collisions. Most of the time, they couldn't be helped, but this time I figure I deserve the point.

The referee pauses for a long time to consider my request. He decides to award me the point. Sharif, of course, appeals the decision to the two judges. They, too, pause, but they both think we should play it over. So the referee's decision is reversed. Ordinarily I'd get the point in a case of interference like that. But evidently, when you're 2 points away from victory against the defending and seven-time champ, they're not going to hand over points on technicalities.

So we play the point over, only now I'm starting to think about the score, about how it was almost 14-9, but now it's back to 13-9, and I better not blow that lead. That break in play has disrupted the flow. Sharif must sense I'm faltering, for suddenly he's back on the offensive, out front, King-Khanning the ball, and the next thing I know, the score is tied 13 all.

Since I got to 13 first, I have the option to extend the game, but I choose "no set." This way all I need is one point and I've got him match point. That call ought to put the pressure back on him. But I lose the next point and now he's one point away from tying it all up, 2 games apiece.

Just a moment ago I had the thing seemingly all wrapped up, but now I feel like I'm losing. I'm still only two points away from victory, but now I'm thinking about how I just lost 5 points in a row. I have that sinking, panicky feeling that comes when you lose the momentum. Even when you're ahead, if a guy has a streak going, you can feel like you're losing. You hear that big train coming around the bend, and there you are tied to the tracks, too panicky to do anything about it.

Then I remember something Ralph Howe told me about playing in the finals of the North American Open. The match slipping away from him late in the fifth game, he told himself, "You'll never get here again, so you better win it now." And he did.

I tell myself, "This is it. You'll never get here again. Just 2 points and you've beaten Sharif."

The next point I'm back on the offensive, and I catch him flatfooted with my trusty backhand reverse corner. I've snapped his streak and I've got him match point.

Match point! I pause for a long time before serving to him. I want him thinking about the fact that this is match point. The more time he has to think about it, the more likely he is to tighten up. And I want to consider carefully what serve to throw at him.

The first thing that comes into my mind is how nice it would be to ace him right now. I picture a slow serve that creeps around the walls high and out of reach and then drops dead, deep in the court, for point and match. Sharif just standing there, unable to even take a swing at it. But I don't trust my slow serve. I don't hit it well consistently, and if I don't hit it just right, he gets an easy volley that doesn't put any pressure on him. A more likely ace would be with a sidearm slice serve. I'm pretty good with that one. There's a real chance I can catch the crease with it, where the side wall meets the floor, just behind the service line, and the thing will roll unplayable. But what if it doesn't nick? The damn thing could bounce right out in the center of the court, and Sharif would be sure to take me out of the play by backing me into the side wall. No, the slice serve could backfire.

Another possibility for an ace would be a fast serve hit close to the wall. He lets it go, thinking it's going to rebound off the side and back walls, but instead it catches the nick on the back wall and is unplayable. But what if it doesn't catch the nick? Again, it's likely to come out in the center of the court and he's got a chance to take me out of the play.

Maybe now's the time to do the totally unexpected. Surprise him with a fast serve hit to the wrong side of him. Or how about something really wild, like an around-the-corner serve that ricochets around a front corner and comes at him diagonally? If he doesn't volley that one, he'll have to chase it around the back of the court, and it might get away from him. Then again, if I mix it up too much, I might inadvertently open up the court. He's such a good scrambler, if I try to fool him, he might surprise me with an unexpected, improvised response.

No, going for an ace is too risky. These serves can backfire too easily. This is the time to load the pressure on, but without taking silly chances.

I decide to come at him with a fast, "criss-cross" serve, a hard serve that will break in front of him off the side wall. I've used this serve a number of times throughout the match. He doesn't seem to like it. And he never hurts me with his response. The beauty of this serve right now is it will force him to make a quick decision, to volley it or let it go. Since a fast ball breaking into him is a tough volley, he'll want to let it go if he thinks it's going out. But if he lets it go and it lands in court, he might not be able to catch up with it. The odds are, at match point, he'll volley it, even if he thinks it's likely to land out of court, for fear that if he lets it go and it's not a fault, it will get away from him. So if I angle it right, I'll make him play a tough volley he's not sure he should be making. Because it's a tough volley, it should put him a little off balance, and I know he can't hurt me with his response, unless he lucks out with a fluky mishit. And I like the fact that the criss-cross is a fast, overhand serve, because it will force him to think fast under match point pressure, and because the act of smacking the ball hard will get me into the point aggressively.

In choosing which serve to go with on match point, it takes a couple of seconds to think through what it later takes several minutes to explain.

So criss-cross it is. I hit a good one, but Sharif's able to get it back all right. The point goes for several strokes, then we get tangled up in the center of the court. It's nobody's fault really, we're just playing each other incredibly close. So the point stops and we have to play it over.

Again I go with a criss-cross, varying the angle a little, and again he makes a respectable return. We get into a very careful exchange. Match point is no time for speculative shots or unforced errors. It looks like we're settling into a long point, but suddenly a routine forehand cross-court catches the crease where the side wall meets the floor. It doesn't roll unplayable, but it takes a low, skidding bounce and is not returned.

I can't believe all the clapping and cheering. All match long, I've felt the gallery with me. The gallery's not that big. A hundred and fifty, maybe two hundred people, fill the seats that look down from behind the court. But it seems big. When you turn around and look up to address the referee in the one part of the court that's not walled in, all you see is a crush of people. There are never enough seats to go around for a big match, so the overflow of spectators is always in every conceivable posture of fire code violation. And the acoustics of the court are such that when one hundred people go wild, it sounds like one hundred thousand. Because of the limited space for the gallery, people sometimes say squash is not really a spectator sport. But when you play a match, even though the gallery is small in numbers and you're faced away from them, you certainly know they're there.

Anyway, they've been whistling at my winners, and cheering for me with each game won. I'm the underdog and I'm showing them something wholly unexpected. But this time Sharif has the underdog's applause. They're cheering now because he's come back from a seemingly hopeless position to tie the match up 2-2 in games.

Obviously, losing that match point hit me hard. But I've been competing for so many years now, I've learned how to control myself in these situations. When I lose a game by 1 point, or even blow a match point, if the match is still on, I'm not going to let my opponent know I'm upset. You've got to be like a boxer, the more his punch hurts, the bigger the smile you give your opponent. I'll show my displeasure when I make errors and lose lesser points, but if I lose a game I really wanted, I give my opponent a big smile and say, "Nice game." I'll be damned if I'm going to give him both the game and the psychological boost of seeing I'm upset about losing it.

There's plenty of time after a match to worry about missed opportunities, but while the match is still in progress you've got to force yourself to think about the business at hand. And so, though my once bright chances were now clouded over, I went looking for silver linings. I'd been on the winning and losing end of enough upsets to know that frequently what happens is the favored player gets himself in trouble, gets himself out of trouble, and then he lets up. And that's when he gets himself in trouble he can't get out of.

I knew it would be almost impossible for Sharif not to let up a little right now. Having just put everything he had into saving a match he'd thought he'd lost, he had to be relieved that the score was now all tied up. He also had to be thinking that he'd broken my spirit, that he'd just proven once again that any time he turns it on, he can beat me.

I knew if I really went after it at the start of the fifth game, I had a good chance of getting a quick lead. And any time you're leading in the fifth game of a match, you've got a chance to win that match.

I was right. Playing with the abandon of someone who has nothing to lose, I got off to a quick 8-3 lead. Once again Sharif's got "bad loss" written all over his face. I'm physically exhausted by now; it's been a long match and I put everything I had into the start of this game, but if I can just hold on, I've got him. But he wins the next point, and then steams a serve at me, which as I'm falling back, I mishit for a lucky winner. If ever I needed a lucky shot, it was right then, for that breaks his momentum and gets me back the serve. But Sharif thinks my ball hit the tin, and appeals to the judges, who both agree with him. I don't know if they're right or wrong. I was so off balance at the time I hit the ball I couldn't tell for sure what happened to it. So I don't get the serve, and Sharif gets the point. Instead of 9-4 it's 5-8, and I can feel him coming. I can see he's getting himself all pumped up. He knows I'm hurting. I'm doing everything I can to look like I'm not tired between points, but I can't disguise my heavy breathing. Like all competitive squash players, I'm programmed to run after the ball, and no matter how tired I get, I'll never quit on it. The will power is there. But when the lungs start screaming and the legs get to feeling like mashed potatoes, you no longer get to the ball with time to spare. You can still make great gets when you're exhausted, but you can no longer control the play. When you're fresh you're looking for chances to take the ball early and impose your style of play. But when you get tired, all you can do is respond. You lose your alertness. And when you get fuzzy, you can't hit your shots with sharpness. Your attempts at putaways hang or are into the tin. And you give your opponent lots of opportunities to take charge.

Enough of these "explanations"! What I'm trying to say is Sharif won 10 of the next 12 points to take the last game 15-10.

It's all I can do to keep from throwing my racquet, and I'm not by nature a racquet thrower. But the gallery is being so appreciative, I tell myself, don't spoil their moment. Don't do something ugly while they're giving you a standing ovation. They're thanking me for having staged a remarkable challenge. And they're congratulating Sharif for his champion's performance. Someone who can win when he's not having a good day and his opponent is playing the match of his life is truly a champion.

I manage a smile, a handshake, and an arm around Sharif's shoulders as I lift my racquet to acknowledge the gallery's enthusiasm. But I don't share their enthusiasm. Nor is Sharif exulting. His face is totally drained. He looks like he's just been revived from a near drowning. The expression on his face brings home to me just how much I had him beat. Always gracious, he says to me as we leave the court, "I really respect you." For Sharif to say those words to me and mean them, which he obviously does, is like being a young physicist and having a Nobel Prize winner tell you he really likes that paper you just published. But at the time, though I appreciate his telling me he respects me, I'm thinking, "Yeh, and you'd respect me a lot more if I'd just beaten you."

But I don't say anything; I just nod. I do a lot of nodding right after I lose a match. People come up to me and say, "Too bad. I just want to tell you, you played a great match." And it's all I can do to keep from snapping back, "It's never a *great* match when you lose." If I say anything just then, I know I'll regret it later. So I just nod.

It takes a minute or so to cool down from the "snapping-back stage," and then I can say nice things about my opponent's play and handle the compliments on my own losing effort with a measure of grace.

And, frankly, once I'd cooled down, though I didn't like being reminded that I'd lost, I did enjoy the celebrity of having come so close. Everyone seemed to know about my match that weekend. Even the towel boy the next day asked me, "Are you the guy who almost beat that Khan fellow?"

I enjoyed the fact that the spectators thought I was one hell of a player, but most important to me was to win the respect of my fellow pros. I had wanted to prove that I could compete seriously at the top of the game, and that's what I had done that weekend. Sharif's brothers, Aziz and Charlie, told me that, except for his match against Hunt, my match against him was the most pressure they'd seen Sharif under in a long, long time. And Sharif's dad, the legendary Hashim Khan, said to me, "Sharrrreeef lucky to win today. I thought you beat Sharrrreeef." Serious recognition from the grand old man, what more could a squash player ask for?

Well, to have won that match point against his son Sharif, that's what I would ask for.

I remember asking Jay Nelson, a friend on the circuit, what it was like getting over a match he'd blown in the semis of the national amateurs—a match in which he'd led Peter Briggs 2-1 in games and 12-3 in points and had gone on to lose. He said that he kept replaying that fourth game in his head. He'd get to 12-3, and then instead of losing the next 3 points, he'd imagine himself winning the next 3 points. He'd enjoy his "victory" for a moment, but then suddenly wake from his reverie, remembering, dammit all, he'd lost.

It had seemed like a strange trick to play on oneself, but for a long time after my loss to Sharif (a longer time than I'd care to report) I found myself doing the same thing . . . It's match point, only this time my cross-court is the one that catches the crease! . . . It's match point and Sharif hits a cross-court to my backhand, I'm on it like a flash and smack a three-wall nick that rolls! . . . It's match point and he guns a cross-court into the tin! . . . It's match point, and I return his serve for a perfect winner into the corner! No, that's not right, I was serving and he was receiving. What am I thinking about anyway? I lost the point and he won the match. Dammit . . .

I'm afraid there's no changing the outcome of that match now. But I can find victories in that defeat. In addition to the respect of my fellow pros, the other important thing I won that weekend was the knowledge that on a given day I could play better than I ever dreamed possible. Well, maybe not for an entire given day, but for several games against Rainer and in long streaks against Sharif I was virtually unbeatable. Proof that every dog has his day.

Seriously, though, perhaps the greatest weakness that most players have, at all levels of the game, is the tendency to underestimate what they can achieve. Most players set their sights too low. I wish I'd known earlier in my squash career that someday it would be possible for me to play as well as I did against Sharif in this match. If I had known I had that ability in me, I would have played a lot better, a lot sooner.

The president of our pro association at the time, Jim Mc-Queenie, who has seen a lot of squash and whose opinion I respect, told me after the match, "Well, now you know you can do it. Everything's there. If you just don't let losing that match point bother you, it's all ahead of you."

I appreciated his saying this, and I like to think I look young, but did he know I was thirty-three? Oh well, Hashim Khan didn't win his first major title until he was thirty-five, maybe older. And he went on to compile the greatest record in the history of the game.

No, even in the Walter Mittyest of my squash fantasies I don't dream of doing that. But I can see myself in the court with Hashim, locked in a classic confrontation . . . the capacity gallery hanging on every point . . . will it be Satterthwaite, will it be Khan? . . . it gets a little rough in the court, but that's the way squash is when two tough competitors go head to head . . .

I can see it all so clearly, because that match actually happened!

Then there's Heather McKay, at age thirty-seven still so superior to the competition that the number two women's player in the world would consider it a great victory to take a single game off her. And the rest consider themselves lucky to win a point or two. There's another example of an athlete who's getting on but still has it. Imagine what it must be like to dominate the field the way she does. Imagine what it must be like to go into the court against a player like that. Knowing that she's been undefeated in formal competition for fifteen, sixteen, years. Knowing that sportswriters have called her just possibly the world's greatest athlete. What do you do against a player like that when the gallery's packed and everyone's there to see how you're going to do against her?

As it turns out, I have a pretty good idea what it's like, from firsthand experience! You see, it's been my lot to compete at the top of the game in its many forms. I've been so hooked on the game for so long, I've had the chance to stick my head into virtually every phase of it—the club game, the prep game, the college game, the amateur game, the pro game, the soft ball game, the Khan game, the women's game, the seventy-plus game. I don't believe anyone else has ever gotten himself so involved in so many different areas of the game. And because I've worked hard at it, studied the styles of the great players, and listened to the great coaches, I've been lucky enough to have been able to compete at the top of the game in its many forms and phases. I've had the experience of going head to head in serious competition against all the great players. Yes, even against the world's top woman!

This is how it happened.

Chapter 1
THE CLUB GAME

"Gentlemen are expected to wear white . . ."

Squash began for me in the mid 1940s in the New Jersey C league at the age of three. No, I wasn't a prodigy, but neither were they. C was the lowest rating awarded by the New York Metropolitan Squash Racquets Association, which held sway over the New Jersey league.

These were "the happy hackers," and Dad was one of the hackiest (and happiest) of them. My mother dutifully attended the Saturday afternoon matches at the Short Hills Club and frequently had me in tow. She recalls that the first match I saw so fascinated me that if she hadn't thought fast and grabbed me by the seat of the pants as I was going over the railing, my career might have ended then and there on the floor of a squash court.

Though the C league didn't have the best squash, it certainly had some of the best matches for the simple reason that each player, whether or not he had any real strengths, had some very real weaknesses. If you get two first-rate players in the court, there may be some contrast in style, but there will be no obvious Achilles' heel. And really, the styles tend to converge at the upper registers of the game. Not so in the C league, which in terms of handicapping is a little like the contests the Romans used to arrange for the Christians. Bring on a man with a sword and shield and let's see how he does against, say, a warrior with a net and trident.

In Dad's league you had Herb "Twig" Bush, all 6'7, 280-plus pounds of him, a little slow to the front wall, but then so were his opponents who had to take a detour to get there. There was Somebody Hoover who developed a blistering, hard serve to compensate for a stiff knee. He'd get the ball so heated up and bouncy that he could limp to a drop shot.

There was the kid, Don Smith, who was very fast but had an equally quick temper. The strategic question was how to get him to blow. And how do you handicap Stu Auchincloss, a former B player who severed something in his right hand and was now entering the C's as a lefty?

There were players moving up in the squash world like Dick Leinbach, who had a German wife who ran both him and his dog every morning. Training was considered almost unsporting among these weekend athletes and prompted the unkind question, "How far can just legs carry you?" The answer in Leinbach's case was the A league.

There were also players moving down like Seymour Perkins, a onetime Met B League champion, who, pleading age, managed to get the association to move him back to the C league. Just how much had he slowed down? Or was it really a matter of geographic convenience since there was no B league in New Jersey?

Off the court Perkins had the most genial of smiles and the gentlest of manners, but down in the pit, he had the foulest mouth I'd ever *seen*. Always a gentleman, as a courtesy to the ladies in the gallery he never said out loud what was on his mind; but you didn't have to be trained in lip reading to get the drift of his thoughts. As I write this, I suddenly realize that when I have need of verbal spontaneity on the court, my mixed-company-under-the-breath-but-very-articulate swearing routine is modeled after Perk. And giving credit where credit is due, I guess I must have picked up my expertise in the postures of fatigue watching "club" squash.

They all claimed that they played squash mainly for exercise—"just to keep in shape"—but from all the gasping and groaning and doubling over that went on in the court, it was more like they were doing penance for not being in shape. They seemed to feel that so long as it hurt and they sweated a lot, they could cleanse their bodies of the martinis, the cigarettes, and the expense account lunches that they had been meaning to cut back on. Many of them, like my father, were commuters and family men, which left only weekends for squash. This meant that rather than making any real progress in their conditioning they were at best on a "maintenance program," i.e., they'd total their bodies on the weekend with the result that it would take a week of Epsom salts and infrared lamps to get their traumatized systems back to where they were the weekend before.

Dad was always a good, solid C player. A good runner, he had trouble with his volleys and only so-so ground strokes. But as he got older he got pretty good at breaking up his younger opponent's style by throwing him "junk"—mixing in seemingly "nothing balls" from funny angles that disturbed his opponent's timing and concentration. It worked on me, anyway, long after I thought I should be beating him.

Perhaps in reminiscing on these idols of my youth I am getting a little carried away, but at the risk of romanticizing the C player, I would suggest that it is in this league that you find some of the best strategists (some of the most ardent ones, anyway) because every opponent at this level has a chink or worse in his armor (else what's he doing in the C league) and so the game is to find his and protect yours.

The better you get, the more you simply impose your game, you almost play by a formula and your opponent be damned. But not in the C league.

C leaguers are also some of the best slow servers,* simply because there's a real chance that a good one won't come back, whereas A players get sloppy in this department because a first-rate serve is unlikely to win them the point outright. Sloppy when they shouldn't be, for a good serve could force a weak return and establish good position.

So, some of the C players weren't bad, but they weren't all that good, either, and Dad wanted something better for his son. A nut on tennis as well as squash, he wanted me to become the racquets man that he wasn't. The racquets man he might have become had he been properly trained and encouraged as a youth. Dad was a happy hacker, yes; but he would have been a happier one if he'd made B. Dad never made B; I never made national champion. (Not yet, that is.) The Goddess of squash isn't a jealous mistress; she's A Big Tease.

Dad would now and then review with me the names of some of the people who might be moved up to the B league the next season. And then he would add, not wholly convincingly, that he hoped he wouldn't get moved up as this would mean having to play his

*The basic serve in squash is a soft lob, hit underhand.

matches week nights in New York, since there wasn't a division of the B league in New Jersey.

Today, in his retirement, Dad finds some solace in the fact that with the growth of the game, D is now the entry level. This improves his status as a C player.

Squash at the Short Hills Club was a men's sport. This was true at most clubs that had squash courts back then, and those of us who were to become good squash players started off in tennis as kids. So to tell you how I came to be a squash player, I must tell you something about my "career" as a tennis player. It began formally at the Short Hills Club.

Short Hills, located in northern New Jersey, was (and is) a well-appointed bedroom for New York. The club was your basic suburban family club sans golf. A place where kids could be dropped off for a summer's day of tennis, club sandwiches, and swimming.

At the club, tennis was considered a basic social skill. Group lessons, accordingly, were offered to boys and girls starting at age seven or so. The club pro, who we all called Tommy, ran this program with the assistance of some interested mothers. My mother, who was more skilled as an organizer than as a tennis player, took time out from her PTAing, Junior Leaguing, and New Eyes For The Needying to do her bit for the tennis program, and continued to help out until my sister, Sally, who is three years younger than me, graduated from it.

Each year Mrs. McBride, who as Nip Anderson in the twenties had been a top tenner on the national ladies circuit (in what you might call the pre-Billie-Jean-King-era-and-then-some), set the tone. "Tennis is a polite game. You shake hands with your racquet and that's the way you should hold it. At the end of the game you shake hands with your opponent . . ."

While Tommy, in his long flannels, drilled one set of children on basic strokes, the rest awaited their turn at one of several backboards set up in the platform tennis courts. If you could keep the ball going ten times against the backboard, it was worth one lollipop, fifteen times was worth two.

On the theory, I guess, that candy is dandy, but sex won't rot your teeth, we were soon graduated to mixed doubles competition, in which each team of a boy and girl (paired so that the competition would come out as evenly as possible) would play four games against every other team.

It was much like dancing school, which was also held at the club and after school. The major differences being that for dancing school we wore all black—suits, shoes, and socks—but for tennis it was all white.

All white, indeed. Before the trophies were presented to the boy and girl who over the spring had accumulated the most games in round robin mixed doubles, a retired admiral would get up on a cement-topped tree stump and from this pulpit deliver his annual sermonette on "While it is nice to win, more important are the friends you make and most important is the sportsmanship . . ." And in making these points, he somehow worked in his recollection that at the club where he learned to play tennis as a child, there was a sign which read, "Gentlemen are expected to wear white, all others must."

The point behind both dancing school and the children's tennis program was that we should learn to be at home in this social milieu.

But Dad made sure my tennis instruction went beyond group lessons on form and etiquette. Unlike most of the other fathers, he cut into his own playing time to take me out on the court to hit. Some of his practice sessions with me were a bit embarrassing because of all the commotion and big dealing that attended them. We'd spread out over several courts because of all the balls we had coming and going, but these outings were fun because he was taking an interest in me and was so enthusiastic, and because before long I was hitting the ball better than the other kids my age at the club.

Dad prided himself on knowing good form and being able to teach it. It is true he could grasp things intellectually, but in the descent from principle to practice he frequently landed with a thump. He was no craftsman. In home "repairs," after elaborate designs, it was even odds which nail he'd strike with the hammer. Not a bad athlete from the waist down (he was pretty quick), he did not have superior hand-eye coordination. Like most club players, he had a jerky stroke. But he never quit. Like a golfer in quest of the perfect putter, he was always on the lookout for the gimmick that was going to put some steadiness in his game. At one point he sent away for a huge net device that was sort of like a trampoline. Stood on end, depending upon how it was tilted, it would throw back lobs, shoulder-high volleys, drives, whatever you wanted. That's what it said in the catalog, so he cleared and leveled a little area in our backyard, had a macadam surface put down, and set the thing up. That net contraption proved no more governable than his forehand, and no matter how he thought he set the thing, the balls would be returned with all the predictability of popping corn. But he seemed to enjoy the struggle, and though he couldn't claim much improvement in his game, he was rather cocky about the solution he came up with for the winter days when it was so cold the ball wouldn't bounce right and he didn't have a squash game on. His solution: heat up a batch of balls in the oven and store them in a thermos until just before using.

I got my interest from Dad. But, with all due respect, I got my style from Tommy. And deep down Dad realized this, for deep down he dug to shell out for my many private lessons with Tommy. And so I learned Tommy's topspinny tennis strokes that traced a figure eight. Big loop-de-loop flourishes that attracted favorable attention from other members at the club. I was known as having "good form." Though most of the members didn't have good form, they would have liked to look nice on the tennis court. I fulfilled that club ideal.

Tommy was great with kids. The first thing a little kid should learn is not strokes and strategy, but that racquet sports are fun. A Mexican pro once told me the way he starts little tots off in squash is to just put them in a court with racquets and balls and let them do whatever they want. If they want to play field hockey, fine. The important thing is that they associate a racquet and ball with fun. When they're ready, they'll start trying to imitate the adults, and at that point he starts working in a little instruction. Taking a page from his book, I had my niece hooked on squash before she could say the word. It was easy. All I had to do was cut a couple of old squash racquets down to the size of Ping-Pong paddles by sawing off the necks about 5 inches from the heads and rewrapping the leather grips on the stubs. Then I started pushing a tennis ball around on the floor with my little racquet, and pretty soon she wanted to do that too. Before you knew it, we were pushing the ball back and forth, and heaven help you if you wanted to quit or tried to take the racquet out of her hand. The point is kids will reach for a racquet, if you let them.

The great thing about Tommy is that he made it fun. Like all good club pros, he kept us entertained. He would sing in a mock operatic voice when stringing racquets. And he knew how to lighten a lesson with a few balls hit behind his back, an exaggerated imitation of a misstroked ball, or a little poem: "Sally, don't rally in the alley." And after his failure to return a well-hit ball by a pupil he would wail, "Oh, Jelly Belly," a takeoff on his real name, Iannicelli.

There weren't many balls Tommy couldn't return, if he wanted to. He had the quickness and coordination of a shortstop, which is what he was in his early years for the "Brooklyn Crandalls," a semi-pro baseball team of the twenties that played around the corner from where he grew up. But in those days, he was considered too small for the big time, and so he turned his hand to racquet sports, which he learned apprenticing to several club pros in the New York area.

He was 5'5, only because he had a long forehead, but his right forearm would have done nicely for a blacksmith who was 6'5. He had the trickiest wrist of anyone I've ever seen in any racquet sport, at least that's the way I remember him. In squash and tennis he would hold his shot until you committed yourself, then flick it wherever you weren't at the last instant.

Squash and tennis were united in the person of Tommy. He had, in fact, been world champion for seven or eight years in the game of "squash tennis." Squash tennis was literally just that, squash played with a small tennis racquet and a tennislike ball. It was big in the New York area in the twenties, bigger than squash racquets, I am told. (Told by the occasional elderly remnant of that era who corners me at a squash racquets function to tell me what a great game squash tennis was.) With practically no indoor tennis and no platform tennis in those days, squash tennis was a way for tennis players to while away the winter months waiting for the thaw. But if you can imagine trying to sustain a rally in a squash court with tennis racquets and ball—considering the reaction time, the angles, the caroms, the cramped conditions—it seems a very untennislike activity.

Actually, the squash tennis court that evolved is, curiously, a foot narrower than the squash racquets court, which explains why in New York you sometimes find yourself playing a squash game in a court that is too narrow, but does not explain why some people thought squash tennis was a winter substitute for tennis. The rubber ball that was used way back then was about the size of a tennis ball, but much bouncier because it was under higher compression (and kept so by periodically pumping it up with a hypodermic needle) and much spinnier because it had a fine net covering, which accentuated whatever "English" was put on it. Because of the shortage of rubber, the ball wasn't made during World War II, and after the war, according to the aficionados, the manufacturer never made it right again. They argue that's the reason the game died out. But the game had already faded by then and I am inclined to believe that the critical juncture was in the thirties when, for whatever reason, squash racquets, not squash tennis, caught on in some East Coast colleges, colleges that stocked the New York clubs where squash tennis had once flourished.

The handful of diehards who still play squash tennis now and then are reduced to using a regular tennis ball, which breaks after several minutes of play, making the game a rather expensive outing. And they must use children's tennis racquets since squash tennis racquets are no longer manufactured. Squash tennis, alas, is a lost art.

Several years ago, Joe Holms, who has played the game a little bit, carried a complete novice to the finals of the National Squash Tennis Doubles championships. The next year they got serious and practiced once with the happy result that they won the "nationals" before a crowd of six people (if you include the referee and two judges). Look it up in the almanac, you'll see *our* names there.

But Tommy, apparently, was something else in that game. Admittedly, the world championships that he had won could as easily have been called the "New York Open"; nonetheless he could keep the amateur champion, who used to stop by the Short Hills Club to tune up for his nationals, under 5 points a game. Dad also recalls that sometimes in the heat of a point, Tommy would yell "Breadbasket," and then slam the ball around the court with such speed and accuracy that after hitting its third or fourth wall it would invariably land in his opponent's stomach. A blow felt more in the ego than the solar plexus. But it was accepted that Tommy was the best, so it was all in good fun. Because of his wins in squash tennis, Dad and some of the other men at the club called him "Champ."

By the time I was ready for squash instruction, Tommy, fortunately for me, was no longer pushing squash tennis and had made the transition to squash racquets. Now in his late forties, he was well past his prime, but in the few open and professional squash racquets tournaments that he played in, he could hold his own against most of the top players. He had that tricky wrist, and squash racquets for him was squash tennis in "slo mo."

There was no organized program at the club for kids in squash. Dad wanted him to give me some lessons when I was about nine, but Tommy said I was too young and my wrist wasn't strong enough yet for a proper stroke. So Dad proceeded to teach me himself. That was enough to get Tommy to start working with me.

He taught me the basics, beginning with the grip. Again, as with tennis, it was a matter of shaking hands with the racquet. But this time a little more on top of the racquet so that the same grip would serve for both backhand and forehand.

Getting a good grip on the racquet is much more important than most players realize. The only way to compensate for a wrong grip is with a wrong stroke.

Most good players appear to use one grip for both sides, a grip that is midway between the conventional backhand and forehand grips used in tennis. To find this midway position shake hands with the racquet and then adjust your grip so that the clump of flesh at the heel of your hand is almost on top of the racquet but a little to the right. Centered, say, at one o'clock if you look at the butt of the racquet as a clock, with twelve at the top. (Or centered at eleven o'clock if you are a lefty.) Tennis players will recognize this as the "continental grip."

Conventional wisdom has it that in squash one grip is preferable to two because most rallies are so fast there isn't enough time to switch your grip. This isn't so. It might be so were the handle of a squash racquet as big as that of a tennis racquet, for then the only way to change grips would be to rotate the racquet in the hand. But in squash you can change grips simply by letting the butt of the racquet slide toward the little finger for backhands and toward the base of the hand for forehands, so that the clump of flesh is on top of the racquet (12 o'clock) for backhands, and behind the racquet (2:30 or 3 o'clock) for forehands. The adjustment is at the heel of the hand; the position of the fingers hardly changes at all because the handle is small. The switch is accomplished by loosening up on the grip as you flick the head of the racquet back in preparation for a stroke. It's easy enough to change grips, the question is do you want to?

The one-grip system keeps the face of the racquet open, which makes it easy to impart underspin. Having the face of the racquet open is particularly important for handling low balls, of which there are many in squash, and for making "gets," since this involves reaching and scooping under the ball.

Proponents of the two-grip system argue that the one-grippers don't get the hand behind the racquet enough to develop a good forehand, that a forehand is hit most powerfully and accurately if the hand is in the same plane as the face of the racquet. I hope this isn't so, since I'm still a one-grip man myself. At least I think I am. I may be a crypto-two-gripper and not realize it because the shift is so subtle and automatic. Such was the case with veteran Diehl Mateer of Philadelphia, who in his day had a pretty good handle on all the major squash silverware in North America. He told me he figured he'd been playing all his squash life with one grip until a few years ago he tried putting some sticky stuff on his hand to prevent his racquet from slipping and found his shots went haywire. It dawned on him that the sticky stuff was preventing him from making subtle adjustments in his grip, and it was only then that he realized he was a two-grip man.

Whether you go for the one- or two-grip system, there are two common errors to be avoided. The first is getting the hand too much behind the racquet on the forehand side. Some players, perhaps because they were never properly introduced to the game, instead of shaking hands with the racquet, hold it as if they found it lying somewhere and just picked it up. They fit a side of the handle into the hollow of the hand so that the clump of flesh is at four or five o'clock. This is what is known as the "Western grip." It works fine for Bjorn Borg hitting heavily top-spinned tennis forehands, but makes the slice difficult, in fact, well nigh impossible on low balls, and leaves the racquet face so open on the backhand you can't get any power off it. The power in Borg's tennis backhand comes from his left hand, but the two-handed backhand doesn't work in squash because it takes too much time.

If you are lucky enough to come across an opponent who uses the Western grip, you'll find that the only shot you need be concerned about is his high forehand volley, which he can meet squarely with this grip. But he will give you errors aplenty on low forehands since the racquet face is directed right at the tin, and he'll send back cripples on his backhand.

The other common error is holding the racquet as if it were a club or a hammer, that is, making a fist around it with the fingers bunched together. True, this is the firmest of grips; nobody's going to take the racquet away from you when you hold it like this. But making a fist tightens the wrist, thus preventing the desired suppleness and snap. And, furthermore, you can't "feel" a racquet that is held primarily in the palm rather than in the fingers.

You want to grip the racquet increasingly with your fingers as you move up the handle, as it is the fingers, particularly the thumb and forefinger, that provide the touch and control. The way to get the handle properly into the fingers is to hold the racquet not at right angles to your forearm, as you might a hammer, but diagonally, so that while the butt is near the heel of the hand, as you move up the racquet, the handle is increasingly off the palm and onto the fingers.

The thumb and forefinger should be separated a little from the rest of the fingers and slanted forward, though the forefinger still hooks around the handle and the thumb runs diagonally, not straight, up the handle. The thumb and forefinger are used to guide, not to grip. The gripping is done primarily with the third and fourth fingers. The little finger does what it can, but not much is expected of it.

Some people use the thumb as a brace for their backhand, putting the pad flat against the back of the handle. A few coaches even encourage this, but since it tightens the wrist I don't think it's such a good idea.

The racquet is like a bird: hold it too tightly and you choke it; hold it too loosely and it flies away. No, Tommy didn't put it quite that way. I picked that up from Errol Flynn instructing one of his comrades on how to hold a sword. Actually, you should *not* maintain the same pressure on the grip throughout the stroke. Most of the time you should hold the racquet very loosely, with "spaghetti fingers." It's only when you are about to make contact with the ball that you should squeeze the racquet. If you squeeze too soon, you will lock your wrist and reduce the snap, too late, and you'll lose the racquet.

Of course, Tommy didn't go into all of the above with a little kid; he just said "Hold it like this. No, like this. That's it." Children learn best by imitating and that's the way I learned from Tommy. But the most important thing I learned from him was that squash is fun. Tommy had a lot of exhibitiony shots, adapted from squash tennis. The one I remember in particular was the "double boast." He'd wind up like he was going to hit a drive, but instead he'd blast it into a side wall. It made a hell of a sound as it ricocheted off that wall. He hit it at such an angle that it would go side wall, side wall, and then just kiss the front wall so that despite all the commotion, it had the effect of a very delicate drop shot. So delicate, you could break your nose on the front wall trying to get it back. But the angle going into the first side wall had to be perfect or the ball wouldn't graze the front wall. I used to practice it hours on end. I now know it's a totally nonpercentage shot, except for Tommy. But it was fun.

The play off the walls was the fascination of squash for me. It is a great adventure to slam the ball every which way and see what happens, and like a kid set loose in a toy shop, I ran around trying everything out. Which is not a bad thing to do when you first start out, since the only way you're going to learn how the ball rebounds off the walls is to fool around in the court for a while.

Playing with Dad and Tommy on the club's two courts, I got the feel of the game—of the racquet, the ball, and the walls. The hand-eye coordination that I had developed through tennis was helpful, but my tennis stroke, I soon discovered, wouldn't do. I had to learn to use a shorter backswing so that I could get my strokes off quickly and in cramped conditions, and to tame my follow-through so that I would be ready to play the next shot, and my opponents would be ready to play the next time I called—what opponents I could find.

There were only a handful of boys who fooled around with squash. Dad organized a ladder for us, or I should say for me, but the big after-school winter sport was hockey. This meant that when the club's pond was frozen, so was the juvenile activity on the squash courts. I dabbled in a few pickup hockey games myself, but didn't get into it to the extent of forcing my parents to buy me a Short Hills Rangers uniform.

There were no squash tournaments in those days for kids my age. My introduction to the real world of racquet competition came not in squash, but in tennis, in the regional junior tournaments sponsored by the Eastern Lawn Tennis Association (ELTA).

I started playing the circuit around New York when I was eleven. It was in these events I learned that "Fancy Dannery" wasn't what it was all about. Around the club the competition wasn't all that stiff among kids my age, so my idea of squash and tennis was showing off fancy shots. True, the successful country clubbers on the junior tennis circuit had stylish strokes, but they also were involved in serious junior development programs and, unlike me, knew something about winning matches. But the kids with the club monograms on their shirts weren't always the ones who came up winners on the circuit, for the public parks players, some of whom showed up with the damndest looking strokes, would eat a pound of clay before they'd give up a point.

The older boys on the circuit would have me home for an early lunch with a serve-and-volley game. But what really got to me were the "pushers"—pat ball artists who, like defensive Ping-Pong players, would keep the ball in play by pushing back half lobs until you made an error. I was always going for the big shot, they for the point.

Some of the boys had coaches who took a half dozen or so of them around, advised them between games, and supervised their practice sessions between matches and tournaments. But what I remember best were the mothers. Not all the moms there like mine limited themselves to chauffeuring duties.

My most vivid recollection of stage mothering was the "lady" who, on seeing her son get what she thought was a bad call from his opponent, commenced taunting "their" opponent with the chant, "If you can't beat, cheat; if you can't beat, cheat . . ."

It's true that when I started out most of my opponents were older than me, since in those days the lowest age bracket was fifteen and under. But even against kids my own age, I showed up with no concept of how to win points other than a knowledge of the rules. I had no idea of strategy, of how to move my man around so as to bring out the worst in his game. What were the percentage shots? What were the pressure points? I didn't even know these were the questions.

So I'd get beat, throw my racquet in the back of the car, flop down in the front seat, and be returned home to the club, where I'd practice my serve and challenge the backboard (in between swimming and club sandwiches) until it was time to go off on the next foray.

It was a mystery to me, my parents, and many at the club why I didn't do better in these tournaments those first couple of years. Still, my parents were very encouraging, and, results notwithstanding, they kept pumping my head full of you-can-do-it notions. But self-belief and the winning attitude don't come from just love, interest, and encouragement. You need concepts on how to win and a steady flow of good competition. And you need a few wins.

I would get blown out of these ELTA tournaments in an early round and then get no good competition until the next event came along. I'd play in four or five of these tournaments and then head off to our summer place in Canada, where I would again cut a dashing figure on club courts. So I'd net about ten days of tough competition in a summer. That was no way to get "tournament tough."

My big moment back then came when I was thirteen. At Forest Hills, no less, where thirty or more clay courts were turned over for a week of Eastern junior championships. This was the first time a thirteen-and-under championships had been held. Since this was a new age category, they had scant win/loss records on which to base the seedings. The guy who was in charge of the junior tournaments apparently was impressed by the style I had displayed when going down to defeat against older players, for I found my name on the draw in capital letters, meaning that I was SEEDED. (My heart pounds, even today, at the recollection of seeing my name in caps on the draw—SATTERTHWAITE.) Not only was I seeded, I was the number two seed. Some ace from Baltimore was the top seed, and we had been paired as the number one seeds in the doubles. It turned out that my first match would be the next day, so I had a whole afternoon and evening to gloat over having made it.

The next day, when I returned to the West Side Tennis Club, there was some good news and some bad news. The good news was that the top seed had defaulted, leaving the field to me, so to speak. The bad news was that since he hadn't made the trip, we were out of the doubles. My thoughts, therefore, turned to singles. But only briefly, for in the first round the top remaining seed went down love and one.

I learned from that tournament that a SEEDING is not the same thing as a tournament victory. It took a while to recover from that one. Five years later I did make it to the quarters of the Eastern eighteen-and-under championships at Forest Hills; but first, I had to learn how to compete.

Chapter 2
THE PREP GAME

"Squash Head"

I learned how to compete at the Phillips Exeter Academy in Exeter, New Hampshire. Going to Exeter was like going off to Harvard at age fourteen. There was the same weather—crisp New England. Same architecture—collegiate Georgian. Same kind of student body—seventy students each year went on to Harvard. And the same sink or swim academic pressures. There were no tutors (save for exceptionally advanced students), no study halls, and no excuses. It was "liberty tempered with expulsion," as one master put it. Though many of the masters were warm and caring individuals, as teachers they saw their primary function to be the setting of standards, and it was up to the student to figure out how to measure up. Most prep schools tried to establish a warm, family atmosphere to the extent that this was possible on an all-male campus. Not Exeter.

The school never feared for the welfare of its students, confident that:

a) Exeter isn't for everybody, and

b) There are any number of places that would warmly embrace an Exeter casualty.

Exeter had a sizable endowment and a substantial national reputation, which enabled the school to compete for talent up and down the socioeconomic scale, all across the country.

My getting in there was not quite the accomplishment I'd have you believe, for, to tell the truth, my father and an uncle had preceded me, and in those days, if the admissions committee thought the son of an alumnus had a reasonable chance of keeping up, they let him in. But once you arrived on campus, the question of "Who are you?" translated to "What can you do well?"

But everywhere you turned, you were more than likely out-classed. Everywhere I turned, anyway. I had been a pretty good student at Short Hills Country Day, but my first day of classes at Exeter I found myself in morning assembly sitting next to Peter Salk, son of the doctor who had recently discovered the polio vaccine, and in church Arthur Schlesinger's son signed the attendance card right below my name.

I had sung the lead in a Short Hills Country Day Gilbert and Sullivan, but there were no parts for a boy's soprano in the Exeter Glee Club, a cracking one at that. I read some lines for a play given by the French Club, and was awarded a walk-on part. I had played football at Country Day, but at 5'3, 115 pounds in my first year, I was assigned to a peewee intramural league, in which the first day of practice they said, "OK, all the backs over here," and everyone lined up over here, nobody that size had ever played in the line before. I got to play in the backfield and to wear "42," the number of Dick Kazmaier, Princeton's Heisman trophy winning tailback of the early fifties; but that was about it for football my first year. Things started to look up, however, when we got to winter sports.

I remember my first day of squash at Exeter. I was hitting with a friend and about half way through the session there was a tap on the door, and in walked Mr. Bennett in what looked to be his underwear. Up till then I knew Mr. Bennett only as my English teacher. A mild-mannered teacher of prose and poetry, who wore leather patches on his sleeves and crepe-soled shoes on his feet. A gentle soul who didn't seem aggressive enough to be an athletic sort, and who was well into his fifties anyway. But there he was in the squash court, with a racquet in his hand, looking surprisingly lean in a plain, collarless T-shirt and what turned out to be, not boxer underwear, but pale blue gym shorts.

No frills for Mr. Bennett. He was so shy and soft spoken I underestimated him at first in English class. That was until I saw what his red pencil could do to my attempts at English composition. He was no friend of the run-on sentence, and a sworn enemy of the passive voice, but he liked nothing better than to come across a dangling participle or any other form of ambiguity, for this would provide him with the opportunity to feign the most absurd and humorous of misinterpretations. When I wrote in my first story for him, "The young boy approached his father, hoping for a raise in his allowance," Bennett asked in the margin, "Did the old boy deserve it?"

This was a private joke between just the two of us, so the point was as well taken as any criticism can be taken. But I quickly learned that the only fluff he would tolerate was the gray hair that puffed out on both sides of his head.

Back in the court that first day, he nodded vaguely to each of us, hit with my friend, then hit with me, asked us a few questions—I explained I'd played some squash at the Short Hills Club—and then he nodded again to each of us with a little smile and was gone. My friend kidded me about Mr. Bennett having spent most of his time with me, but I hadn't noticed. I was just trying to figure out what Bennett, who always moved with quiet suspense, was up to. My friend was right, though, because Bennett started giving me lessons, about once a week.

I learned he was the varsity coach, in fact, had been the coach since the thirties. I didn't get this out of Bennett, but it turned out that he was very much the athletic sort and at Harvard had been a crackerjack baseball player in the twenties and I think a hockey player as well. At any rate, he didn't take up squash until he came to Exeter to teach, right after graduating from Harvard. But he made a real study of it, and became the greatest coach in the history of the prep school game. Certainly he was the best at teaching the fundamentals, and, though I don't have the statistics on this, I'm sure that over the years he had by far the best win/loss record of any prep school coach. But there were two other things about Bennett, the coach, that I particularly remember, qualities he had that are sadly lacking in some so-called "great coaches" in squash and other sports: he was very fair and he had a sense of fun about him. He never lost sight of the fact that it was a game we were playing. Squash under Bennett was fun, and perhaps the greatest tribute to him as a coach is the fact that Bennett players always continued playing squash long after they left school. With his wry sense of humor he communicated what I consider to be a healthy attitude toward winning and competition, namely, that win or lose, the game is fun, but it's more fun when you win.

Maybe I remember him as particularly fair because he singled me out as a young prospect. The way he built strong teams was by not only coaching the varsity, but also working with some of the younger boys who looked like they might have potential.

His genius was for stripping things down to their essentials, including himself in those gym shorts. He set an example of how to do more with less. He spoke softly, so you strained to listen to him. He didn't talk much, so you paid attention to the few words he chose. In English class his message was, "Say it in plain English in as few words as possible." And in squash he was no less a stickler for concise expression, for he taught a stroke that was simple and direct, one that delivered a punch without taking much room or time. He was my *Strunk and White* for the fundamentals of squash.

Bennett taught the simplest, most basic of squash strokes. A stroke that is quick, compact, flexible, deceptive, safe, and accurate. It's also a stroke that I no longer use, or, at least, I've modified it somewhat. But it stood me in good stead in those days, and provided the foundation. Since it's an effective stroke, and the easiest one to learn, and since once you understand this stroke it becomes a reference point for all the others, it's worth looking at for a moment.

To visualize the Bennett forehand, think of someone trying to skip a stone on water with the elbow tucked into the belly, perhaps roped in. And the backhand is like tossing rings at a stake, with the body low and turned sideways to the target and using the arm, rather than the wrist, to toss the ring. I'm not sure if that does it; what I'm trying to convey is the image of a short, low, and level swing—a swing that couldn't be any simpler.

Bennett had us turn sideways to the ball and get down in a crouch like an elderly hunchback leaning forward on a cane the height of the racquet. Getting down to the ball like this enables you to get a good look at the ball and a good line on where you are aiming. Most of the action in squash is quite low, say, at about knee height. This is because the ball is not particularly bouncy off the floor and because, with the tin only 17 inches high, the aim point is pretty low. In tennis most ground strokes are hit at hip height; the tennis ball is twice as bouncy as a squash ball and the net over twice as high as the tin. If it's important to get down for tennis shots, it's twice as important to get down for squash strokes. Getting way down enables you to execute a level transfer of weight through the ball so that your weight is going in the direction you want the ball to go. No matter what type of stroke you use, getting down to the ball is a good thing. It takes a little more effort, but it's worth it.

We were taught to keep the swing short by keeping the arm in close to the body so that the elbow practically rested on the right hip for forehands. On backhands, since the arm swings away from the body on the follow-through, the elbow needs a little more leeway. Using a stroke that's in close to the body also helps hide the ball, thus adding deception to your shot.

A short stroke is quick and flexible. If the ball comes faster than expected, or takes a funny bounce, you don't get caught in a big windup. And a short stroke can be executed in cramped quarters, which is what a squash court is. A problem that all beginners have, until they learn to limit their backswings, is that their racquets are always running afoul of the back wall. And their high, tennisy follow-through is usually a problem for their opponents. A wild backswing or wraparound follow-through is not only a "discourtesy" to opponents, it is also inaccurate and takes too much time.

Bennett preached slice. This is perhaps the most important concept in the squash stroke. We were taught to slice the ball by tilting the racquet head back and leading into the stroke with the butt of the racquet so that the racquet face draws down and across the back and inside (side toward you) of the ball. The racquet face is kept tilted back or "open," not by adjusting the grip, but by cocking the wrist and laying it back with a rotation of the forearm.

Slicing increases the time that the ball is on the racquet, and makes the strings "grip" the ball. Both factors enhance your feel and control. But most important, slicing puts some underspin on the ball, which makes the ball rebound downward off the front wall. If you impart top spin, by closing the face of the racquet and pulling up and over the ball as you hit, you can actually see the ball climb on the front wall. And when it climbs, it takes higher and longer bounces off both the front wall and the floor, with the result that top-spin drives tend to come off the back wall before bouncing twice on the floor. A ball that comes off the back wall is easy to retrieve and, if it comes way out, it's a setup. And top-spin touch shots have to be hit perilously close to the tin to keep them short. Underspin permits you to clear the tin by a safe margin—of, say, 6 inches, at least—and still get the ball to lay down.

So Bennett taught us to keep the face of the racquet open throughout the entire stroke. It's interesting: in tennis you get the ball safely over the net and drive your opponent deep by using top spin, since a top-spin ball will loop over the net and take a long bounce; but in squash you get the ball safely above the tin and buried deep in the court by using underspin. This is something that many tennis players who take up squash never learn.

For finesse shots—shots in which you want to be particularly accurate and make the ball slow down and really sit down—slice is accentuated by keeping the wrist well in front of the racquet head throughout and curling under the ball as you stroke it. (Leading with the wrist increases the sidespin; curling under increases the backspin.)

For power strokes, you want enough underspin on the ball to keep it off the back wall, but not so much spin that the speed of the shot is cut appreciably. The more direct the blow, the more power. A spin shot is a glancing blow, and, therefore, less powerful. So for power shots you want the racquet face tilted back some to get underspin, but to get that extra umph, you want the racquet head to have caught up with the wrist at the moment of impact so that you apply a maximum of snap and a minimum of power-attenuating sidespin.

I said power stroke, but, alas, that was the one weakness in the Bennett stroke, as I was later to learn. A short, level stroke does not produce super power. (To get power, you must take the racquet back high, which is what I do now with a big golflike windup.) But Bennett taught us to meet the ball perfectly at the moment of impact. And since the stroke was quick, compact, flexible, deceptive, safe, accurate, and easy to learn, I don't have a whole lot to complain about.

In teaching me the stroke, Bennett would feed me a setup and have me paste it down the right wall on the forehand and down the left wall on the backhand. It wasn't just some place to hit the ball, it was the basic shot in the strategy he taught. A strategy known as the "straight up-and-down" game (or simply, the "up-and-down" game), which means hitting the ball up and down the side walls. The basic shot is variously called the "down-the-wall," the "alley," or the "rail" shot (see Figure 1).

You try to keep the ball as close to the side wall as possible without touching it, because if it catches the side wall, it slows down and bounces toward the middle, which makes it easier to play.

But if the shot is really tight along the wall, the only safe response is to use the racquet like a brush and try to gently sweep the ball off the wall, keeping the wrist limp so that it, rather than

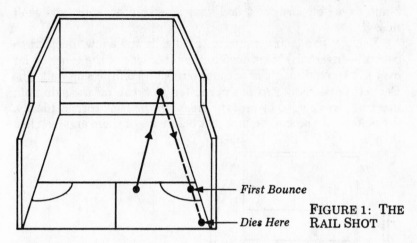

First Bounce

Dies Here

FIGURE 1: THE
RAIL SHOT

the throat or head of the racquet, yields as you scrape the shot off
the wall. The problem is that when the ball is really close to the
wall, you sometimes panic and take a stiff-armed swipe at the ball,
just the opposite of what you should do. But after a few $45 prac-
tice strokes, you learn.

When you hit your "rails" really well, they not only hug the
wall but also take their second bounce just before reaching the
back wall. This is known as good "length." If it's hit too short, it
doesn't drive your opponent deep; if it's too long, it comes out off
the back wall.

But when a rail is glued to the side wall and hit with perfect
length, your opponent only gets one chance at the ball, can't get a
clean hit at it because of the side wall, and has to use a restricted
backswing because of the back wall. Very nasty.

You get good length by using slice and hitting the ball the right
speed and the right height above the tin. And what's the right
speed? Well, not too hard and not too soft. The first bounce should
be somewhere back of the service line on the floor. You have to get
a feel for the way the court and ball are playing on that particular
day. The less lively the ball and/or the court, the higher you have
to aim above the tin, and as the ball heats up in the course of play,
you have to adjust accordingly. Length is something you can never
take for granted. It's not something you learn once and for all time
and can then forget about. It's something that has to be continually monitored throughout every match. When you lose a string of
points, the chances are it's because you're not hitting to length.

Some days you just can't find your length; other days you can't miss it.

Bennett had us programmed to hit rails and a few "deep cross-courts"—inverted V's hit deep to the other side of the court, as far over as we could hit them without a rebound off the side wall. The Bennett cross-court was not permitted to break off the side wall; instead it was angled toward the crease in the back corner. Ideally, it would take a second bounce just before it got there and look like this:

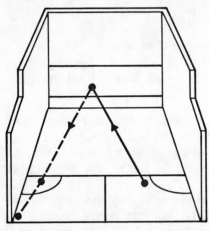

FIGURE 2: THE DEEP
CROSS-COURT

These cross-courts were used to keep our opponents "honest." If we hit a rail shot every time, our opponents would move over to the side we were on in anticipation, so the occasional cross-court kept them from "cheating over."

Sure, we hit a few other shots, the occasional drop and a rico-chet around a front corner every now and then, but Bennett kept returning us to the basic ground strokes.

In essence, what Bennett did was wean us from the walls, which may sound a little funny since squash is obviously a wall game. But most people overuse the walls. Some, in fact, go "wall crazy," as I did when I first started out. It's a natural thing to do. You step into the court and you discover you can hit the ball most any direction you like and it stands a chance of staying in play. And you find you can totally discombobulate other novices by knocking balls into walls so that they come out at crazy angles, angles which beginners haven't learned to read yet. It works great, except when you hit yourself with your own shot. These multi-walled wonders work so well you get the idea that nothing is quite so creative as angling a shot so that it takes in an extra wall or two.

The problem is this: when a ball hits the back wall or a side wall, either on the way to the front wall or coming back from it, it usually rebounds toward the center of the court, easy prey for an alert opponent. And the more walls the ball hits, the more likely it is that the ball will come out in the middle. Now that's not always so. In fact, in learning to become an advanced player you learn to use the walls so that the ball doesn't come out in the middle. But most of the time, when people hit the ball so that it rebounds off a side or back wall, they really shouldn't. Just watch a couple of non-A players, or even low A players, and you'll see that most of their two- and three-wall shots rebound toward the center. Or, go out in the court yourself and slam it into an extra wall or two, and see if in most cases it doesn't end up in the middle.

Most players overuse the walls not only in their attempts to hit "creative" shots but also in the process of making gets. There are lots of times when it's easier to get the ball back by poking it into a side or back wall, and again, when you first discover this, you think it's quite a clever thing to do; it makes you feel like you're making full use of the court, but these returns more often than not rebound to the middle.

Most players would move up at least one notch, anyway, if they'd treat squash as the art of keeping the ball off the walls, front wall excepted. Hit to length and keep it off the walls. The up-and-down game is not squash in its most advanced form, but it's a good basic game and one I frequently return to.

Even today, when I'm clicking, I set up a lot of points and score a number of winners with my rail shots. And when I'm looking for a safe place to put the ball, I send it up and down a side wall, until one of us decides to make a move. And this is the way it is with all the top players.

Nelson Gidding, the screenwriter, who was a Bennett pupil twenty-five years ahead of me at Exeter and is a scrappy veteran squash player, observed with great excitement after watching me pull out a match I almost lost in a Los Angeles pro round robin not long ago, that "in extremis" I returned to the basic, Bennett up-and-down game. Bennett, who passed away several years after I graduated from Exeter, would have been very pleased to hear this. I know I was.

Bennett provided not just the basic concepts, but also the basic competitive environment. The ladder was the organizing principle of the whole squash program. Everyone was assigned to a fifty-minute time period during which fifteen boys under the supervision of one or two instructors would play. Each section had a ladder and there was a hierarchy of time periods. So if you moved to the top of one ladder, you got to challenge onto the ladder of the next highest section. This meant I was continually practicing with and competing against people who were as good as or better than me. Very different from my early experience with ELTA tennis.

Each ladder had biweekly challenge matches. The rules were simple: if you won, you challenged the man above you; if you lost, you accepted a challenge from below. Our names were written on both sides of circular white tags with an arrow pointing up on one side and down on the other. The tags were hung on hooks, and depending upon whether we were due to challenge up or accept a challenge from below, the heavenly or infernal arrow was showing. If you were sick, your tag was set aside, and when you returned, you were inserted back into the lineup at the number at which you had been when you left. No further clarifications were necessary, but as a rookie, I once asked Bennett the typical niggling sort of question that ladders and rankings seem ever to invite, to wit, "What if I beat A badly, but lose to B, and then I get sick and A challenges B and beats him, but just barely? What then? Shouldn't I go ahead of both A and B?"

To which he responded with a twinkle in his eye, "We've got a very simple system here. To move up, all you have to do is win your matches." We didn't discuss that again.

Seeing my arrow mostly skyward gave me a big lift those first couple of years. It was my first experience of real success at Exeter.

On the one hand, squash was an escape from the pressures of Exeter into a world that was fun and familiar. Yet, on the other hand, a little world in which name tags were arrayed in a ladder of relative success was pure Exeter.

In doing well on the ladder, I was succeeding in Exeter's terms, even if only the squash players knew about squash. Around the courts I was recognized by the coach and other players as someone with a talent, as someone who could do something that other people couldn't. In that little world I was someone special. It didn't matter that it was a small world, for it was a totally immersing one.

I don't know what Exeter would have been like for me without squash, but with it, I had an early experience of success that gave me the confidence to tackle other areas, so things worked out pretty well for me there, and I remember Exeter as a happy time.

My first two years I was the best in my class in squash, except for Terry Robinson. He was always one or two slots ahead of me as we moved up the ladders; and he lettered his lower middle (sophomore) year, while I didn't. Our challenge matches must have been amusing to watch (though I saw little cause for mirth at the time) since while he was big for his age and I was small, stylistically, we were reversed. I was the physical player; he took the mental approach. But he looked like a big bear—round shoulders, round back, hair everywhere. And like a bear, he was surprisingly quick. He tiptoed around the court on the outside of his feet, as if to deny his size, but this only made him sway like a big bear. That tiptoeing routine was his way of saying "I'm thinking all the time." As a rule, the big fellows who play squash tend not to throw their weight around nearly as much as the little guys. This was certainly the case with Terry. In the ninth grade he was already full grown, about 6'1, 185, and because of his combined size and speed, he looked like quite a football prospect, but after a year of football, he switched over to soccer, in which he became very good.

Terry was a brilliant student, particularly in math and science, and this showed in his squash game, for he loved to throw in funny little angles. His pet was the "around-the-corner" hard serve, in which he would take a giant step toward the center of the court to get the angle from which he could fire it sidearm back toward his side so that right after hitting the front wall, it would hit his side wall, and then come at his opponent diagonally. This is what it looks like:

If receiver does not volley it, he should pivot this way to follow the ball around.

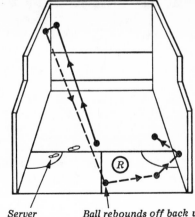

FIGURE 3: THE
AROUND-THE-CORNER
HARD SERVE

Server   Ball rebounds off back wall

It's frequently tough to volley the return, but if you let it go to the back wall, it can get away from you. If you decide not to volley it, the easiest way to handle it off the back wall is to follow it around by pivoting 270 degrees (in a counterclockwise direction if you are receiving on the right side of the court, clockwise if you are on the left). Once you learn how to turn for the shot and how it plays off the back wall, it's no big deal to return. But this serve is confusing to a beginner, and if used sparingly, it can sometimes catch even an advanced player off guard.

Whenever he needed a quick point, Terry would throw that little serve in, and I'd panic. He didn't overuse it, so it took me a long time to figure out how to handle it. And in the meantime, the threat of the serve was almost as bad as the serve itself. That serve sticks in my mind, but the real reason he won those matches was because he was physically much more mature than me. We were wary of each other since we both wanted to be number one in the class, and we spent the whole time being excessively polite and formal to one another. He was too serious for me to kid around with anyway.

My third year, I finally cracked through against Terry. We were still in different phases of the maturation cycle, which is to say, while my acne was still in full bloom, he was starting to comb his hair forward; but by then I had done most of my growing, and was pretty close to my adult speed and strength.

That year I also made the varsity football squad. Squash players, as a rule, didn't play football; many of them weren't big enough, and those who were, like Terry, seemed to gravitate toward the finesse rather than the grunt sports. I didn't really like football that much, and as the last-string quarterback I became rather more expert at our opponents' offenses than our own, since in practice I was frequently called upon to run them against our defense. But I got to suit up for games on Saturday and playing football seemed like the manly thing to do. I played tennis in the spring, and didn't want to be just a "racquets man."

Football was a duty; squash was fun. And squash was particularly enjoyable my third year, for I finally made the team, playing as high as number two in some matches. Louis Williams, a senior, was our captain and our number one man all year.

At 6'3, 185, Louis would have made a great end, but instead he was the high scorer on the soccer team. Unusual for a squash player, instead of playing tennis in the spring, he played lacrosse, in which he was again top scorer. Many considered him the best all-around athlete in the school. Actually, he was Exeter's Mr. Best

All Around Everything. Your basic tall, dark, and handsome honor student, athlete, and soloist in the school singing group; he was the college placement officer's dream. And beyond that, he was a genuinely nice guy. Disgusting! When I shot up to number two, he seemed like the natural limit to my rise. Which was a self-fulfilling prophecy, since in our challenge matches, whatever the score, we both knew he was going to win. We'd play even for a game or two, and then that was it. One thing's always for sure: if you're sure you're not going to win, you're right. Anyway, he had a long reach and with little effort was always out in front and in control, which is the way he was in everything he did.

The other senior on the team that year was Johnny Thorndike, who was the captain of the soccer team. At 5'7, 130, max., he was Mr. Hustle. About halfway through a match his pants would start sticking to his little rear end, from all the sweat there. Sometimes he hustled too much. He'd get so excited, he wouldn't get set for shots. He was, like Louis, on the academic high honors list, but he had to work for it. All this pep earned him the presidency of the student council as well. He was my best friend on the team that year, though I've never been a pep club type myself. But Thorny could laugh at himself, and I've always been a comment maker, and I guess that was the fit. We had some great battles. He was the Steady Eddy while I was streaky, in and out. Our rivalry never got in the way of our friendship. We had our jokes, and whenever I lost to him, though I didn't like it, I figured, Well that's OK, he's an upperclassman, I'll have my day.

I waxed somewhat less philosophical when I lost challenges to classmate Terry Robinson. Our arrows were shooting back and forth on the ladder that year, but unfortunately, he didn't have any unpleasant characteristics around which I could build up a good hate, and so our relationship remained excessively polite and formal. He did have a bad temper, but it was turned inward. He tried very hard to keep it in check, but he was a perfectionist and if he made a couple of bad errors, he'd explode at himself, and, with nobody at the controls, his game would go into a tailspin.

One of the best pieces of advice I ever got on keeping my head came from Bennett's assistant coach, Donald Dunbar. He was new to racquet sports but at college had been a pro prospect as a pitcher, and so he knew something about the importance of composure; in baseball, after all, the game is to try to rattle the man on the mound. One time, when Dunbar and I were playing, I was really down on myself, and every time I made a mistake I made a comment about how poorly I was playing. Afterward, I observed that I was in a terrible slump, and he responded, "Look, if you don't mind me saying this, you'd play a lot better if you'd just keep your mouth shut. When you talk to yourself like that, all you do is become more and more negative. You start looking for errors and, sure enough, you make more errors. And, furthermore, your whining is music to your opponent's ears. Keep your mouth shut, and you'll be surprised how fast you pull out of that slump."

Time and again, in the heat of competition, that piece of advice comes back to me. The fact is there's a lot of scrambling and craziness in squash points, and it's inevitable that you will make some dumb mistakes. But squash is not like gymnastics or figure skating, where one slip and you're out of contention. Or, as Dunbar would say, you don't have to throw a strike every time you get your man out. So, part of learning to compete in squash is learning to accept your mistakes; so you only lose one point per mistake. And learning, like the man on the mound, to keep your mouth shut.

I discovered that if I could just hang in there against Terry, eventually he'd make some bad errors, get mad at himself, and come undone. Of course, the problem was hanging in there long enough. Sometimes he'd blow me off the court; other times, himself. I was far from a fully developed player, but by then I had a good grip on Bennett's basics. I wasn't a super power player, Bennett's boys never were, but I was now quite sturdy and could hit pretty hard. But my biggest asset was my quickness to the ball.

Thinking back on it, the top prep school players all covered the court particularly well. Some were better at this than others, but if you wanted to isolate one factor that set the really good players apart, it was the ability to keep the ball coming back. And the same holds true today at the top of the game. Whether a player is known as a "shooter," a "slugger," or a "getter," if he's near the top, one way or another, he covers the court exceptionally well. The thing that's interesting is the way different players use different abilities to get that job done. Louis wasn't particularly fast on his feet, but he had good reach and anticipation. Thorny didn't have that reach, nor was he super fast, but because he was small, he could change directions quickly. He also was very fit, so he appeared to get faster as the match wore on, since while most of his opponents would tire and slow down, he didn't. Terry had not only good reach but also very fast hands. He also had excellent speed once he got started. I didn't have his reach or top speed, but had better acceleration and could turn faster. I also had particularly good balance when stretched out and twisting. By my upper middle (junior) year I was probably the best on the team at covering court.

I can't remember who was the fifth member of the team that year, but the principal competition was between Thorny, Terry, and me for the number two and three spots. I could continue to describe the differences in our styles, builds, and temperaments, but the most interesting thing was the similarity in our games, for we were all very much products of the Bennett system.

With the Bennett stroke and strategy, Exeter teams were usually the best in New England. The competition involved five-man teams with our number one man playing their number one man, our number two playing their number two, and so on down the ladder. Other schools might from time to time inherit a more outstanding individual at the top, but we always had more depth. The other schools that we played, "St. Grottlesex" sans Groton—that is to say, St. Paul's, Middlesex, Deerfield, Andover, Brooks, and there must have been others but they don't come to mind—were not as well coached, and so the prevailing style at these schools was what I call "Go Fetch" squash. Like young pups with boundless energy and enthusiasm, they liked nothing better than to run after the ball and return it right back to you.

The Harvard frosh was the only team we usually lost to, but they beat us with our own graduates.

My first year on the team we won the New England Interscholastics, placing three men in the semis and two in the finals of this knock-out event. Which was great for the Big Red, but not quite as satisfying for me, personally, since I didn't make the trip. I stood number four on the ladder at the time and only three players could enter from each school. But I have a happy memory associated with that tournament because as soon as Thorny and Louis got back, they rushed to my room, racquets and bags still in hand, to fill me in on everything that happened. Not just the results, but also the moves and "psychs" they put on the opposition. It took a while to make sense of what happened because they kept interrupting each other to tell anecdotes within anecdotes.

Being on the team was fun. True, squash is a sport for individuals, and we didn't get the experience of teamwork except in the sense that we rooted for each other during the matches (clapped hard for our own man, begrudgingly for his opponent), and at the 2-1 break* we clustered around our man while Bennett urged him to hit the ball down the wall more.

But if there was not the experience of teamwork, there was, nevertheless, a team experience. We shared the high adventure associated with getting off campus for away matches. But the thing that was most fun for me—aside from the pleasures of the game itself—was the continual nothing-is-sacred banter that was the language of the team's esprit de corps. Though I can't say as I provided any leadership in this area, the squash team had, on average, the brightest students in uniform. The teams were always very verbal, which meant that win or lose, we always had our "wits" about us.

Bennett used to say whereas most people complained about the approach of winter with all its bad weather, he always looked forward to it because of squash. I felt the same way. And, for that matter, unlike most members of the human race, I never had much use for spring back then, because in those days it meant the end of the squash season. So I was very happy to discover at the end of my third season at Exeter that there was yet another interscholastic event, this one held over spring vacation at New York's Racquet and Tennis Club. I think it was called the "Scholastic Singles." Whatever it was called, it proved to be an even stronger tournament than the New England "interschols" because it attracted the top school boy players from Philadelphia as well as New England, which made it the top interscholastic event. Since I returned home to Short Hills for spring vacation, the tournament was easy to get to, and it worked out well, for I got a good draw, one that permitted me to get to the quarterfinals without much difficulty. A good draw for getting to the quarters, but then I came up against the top seed, Maurice Heckscher.

It was enough that Maurice was the top seed, but did he have to look like him as well? A handsome, 6-foot blond, he had one of those golden boy confident smirks as if half-smiling into a perpetual sun. Indeed, basking in the reflected glory of his squash background. Though listed on the draw as representing Episcopal

---

*There is a five-minute rest between the third and fourth games, during which players can leave the court and coaching is permitted.

Academy, like all top players from the Philadelphia area, his base was the Merion Cricket Club. I'd never been there, but I'd played enough squash to have heard of Merion, and I'd seen a picture of it in the yearbook put out by the national squash association. The clubhouse was the backdrop for a group picture of the winners that past season of the national singles, doubles, open, intercollegiates, and juniors, all of whom were members of the club. The winner of the juniors was a freshman at college and so was ineligible for this interscholastic event. Maurice's older brother, Ben, was the national champion in the picture.

Maurice was the first Merion player I'd ever played or even seen in action. As a general rule it's a good idea to scout your opponent. Watch him play; take measure of his strengths and weaknesses before you take him on. As a general rule, but in this case it was just as well that I had not gotten a chance to see Maurice play until we warmed up for our quarterfinal match. When I saw him stroke the ball during the warm-up, I got a shock comparable to the jolt a little child might receive when, having recently and proudly mastered stick-and-ball-print script, he catches a glimpse of an older child's tracebook and discovers the superior aesthetics of longhand. The pleasing, flowing, rhythmical, natural loops and slopes render his simple stick characters scratchy and awkward by comparison. Just when he thinks he's mastered the art of writing, he discovers there's another way and it's better looking.

I had thought I had learned *the* squash stroke at Exeter: get down to the ball in a crouch that resembles a hunchback looking for a contact lens; tuck the elbow into the belly and keep it there so the backswing is short and follow-through checked at knee height, take a level, open-faced cut at the ball . . .

All of which seemed fine until I caught a glimpse of the top seed taking his racquet back, head high, and next swooping down to pick the ball up and send it on its way with a long, unfettered follow-through. He, too, started off in close with the wrist cocked and the elbow bent, but as he uncorked he let it flow, with the result that his racquet head described a sweeping arc. Sometimes he added a stylish little curlicue at the peak of his windup. Very pretty. I say "caught a glimpse of his swing" because his dorsal region was pretty much obstructing my view. He got down to the ball not by going into a crouch but by tilting forward, with the result that his rear end stuck out in a very confident fashion. Almost as if it were on display, like a duck sticking his tail out in water. Certainly he was very much in his element. And I was in over my head.

A warm-up is supposed to loosen you up, but this one was having the opposite effect on me. I was starting to feel increasingly self-conscious about my stroke, feeling hacky, cramped, and awkward. I was definitely losing the warm-up. But I tried not to let on, and at the end of the warm-up, with great ceremony, I twirled the head of the racquet on the floor. "Round and round she goes, where she stops, nobody . . ." he chooses smooth (who the hell ever chooses smooth?). The racquet drops dead; the tension mounts as we lean over it to see who fate has favored with the serve. An omen, perhaps. Then, "Sorry, I forgot. I don't have rough or smooth."

That was meant as a "psych," for I knew all along that I didn't have a rough or smooth string on my racquet. Someone at school had told me that tampering with this ritual at the start of a match would "disrupt the flow," and that I could score one for me, whoever ended up winning the serve. I didn't go so far as to lick my index finger and draw a stick number one in the air, but I flashed Maurice that kind of a smirk.

I wince as I recall that silly, prep school attempt at one-upmanship, but that was what was in my head at the time. What was lacking in my head was any plan or strategy. Even before the match started I could feel myself sinking, so I clutched at a prank. I was looking for something to give me some confidence, the kind of confidence the top seed displayed the first day of the tournament when he swaggered up to the trophy on a table in the locker room, picked it up, and confidently turned it in his hand until he found his brother's name on it. And then, to the pleasure of his claque from Merion, he read it out loud in a tone of voice that suggested it was very convenient that the engraver already knew how to spell his last name.

To be perfectly truthful, I didn't actually see Maurice do this. But a friend of mine, another prep from New England who had witnessed Maurice's arrival the first day, had me believe that Maurice, with his clubmates in tow, before he checked in even, bags still in hand, had made his way directly to the trophy. Perhaps it didn't happen exactly like that, but we weren't looking to make generous assessments of that Merion gang. Kids, particularly kids that age, tend to think in terms of cliques; and there were definitely two different cliques at this tournament—the Merion group and the preps from New England. We represented the two different centers where junior squash was played seriously, and since we met only once or twice a year for major events, these tournaments were very much "we/they" situations. In retrospect, we were both obnoxious in our own ways. The preps were "sarks," quick and cutting with the comments—cocky-wise-assed. The Merion types, on the other hand, were aloof and stuck on themselves—cocky-smooth.

If that "rough or smooth" psych got to Maurice, he didn't let on. But, who knows, maybe it worked, for I jumped to a lead, 4-zip, 5-1, something like that. It's been a while, seventeen years or half my life ago, so I'm a little hazy on some of the details, but I can still relive the emotions of that match.

Getting off to a good start was all important, for if he got up, it would only confirm what I already more than suspected, that he was much too good. If you think you are outclassed, and your opponent gets off to a good start, you tend to see it not just as a good start, but as final proof that he is unbeatable. The first few points, in particular, you're trying to get a feel for how good he is, what he can do, and you're looking to be impressed, looking for him to do something spectacular. He makes a few lucky shots, and you see them not as lucky shots, but as unbelievable touch or reflexes of the "how can I beat that" order.

But I was ahead, thanks to a few unforced errors. I didn't have a strategy in the sense that one thinks out what one is going to do in advance of the match. My strategy, if that's the word for it, was more a matter of desire than design, i.e., I came out slugging. In my excitement I belted everything I could get my racquet on. No change of pace, no fancy angles, nothing subtle. Every time I got a loose ball, I pasted it down the side wall, with occasional crosscourts to keep him honest. Swore off everything but drives and occasional drop shots, which wasn't hard since I didn't know much else, rather like a teetotaler giving up wine for Lent, it wasn't difficult.

But Maurice had known that headier stuff, and was attempting to make more complete use of the court with a full repertoire of shots.

In terms of squash sophistication, Maurice was age seventeen going on thirty. All the Merion juniors were that way. Every day after school, the squash players from Episcopal Academy and the Haverford School would drift over to the club to practice and take lessons from their two great pros, William F. White and Brendan

McRory. A Princeton coach in the twenties and thirties, "Whitey" came to Merion in the forties and is credited with having developed their early champions. And Brendan McRory helped carry on this tradition when he joined Whitey at Merion.

Since the club is located several hundred yards from the Haverford stop on the "Main Line" commuter run, which cuts through the fashionable suburbs west of Philadelphia, it was quite convenient for many of the men to stop off at the club on their way home from work. This meant, if they stuck around, the youngsters could watch, and sometimes even hit with, the top amateurs of the day, in particular Diehl Mateer, Ben Heckscher, and Sam Howe, who were passing the national title back and forth in those days.

And on the weekends two former national champions, Hunter Lott and Charlie Brinton, conducted clinics for groups of boys. If ever there was a squash mill, the Merion Cricket Club was it. And though some of the names have since changed, the tradition continues at Merion right down to this day.*

The Merion youths didn't always play the advanced shots at the right time, but they knew what they looked like and how to hit them. In particular, they would take their opponents short in the court with side wall/front wall caroms, known as "corner shots." I took stabs at corner shots now and then but didn't really know how to execute them properly, and Bennett, who kept returning us to the basics, didn't encourage experimentation along this line.

But the Merion juniors were full of these shots. They hit both the "roll corner," which is hit to the nearest corner (see Figure 4), and the "reverse corner," which shoots diagonally across the court to the far corner (see Figure 5).

I've since learned how to hit these shots. To hit the roll corner, you set up as if you are going to hit a rail shot, that is, you turn sideways to the front wall and use your normal windup. But instead of hitting the ball directly to the front wall, you angle it into the nearest side wall, 3 or 4 feet from the front wall. You do this not by suddenly changing your stance or radically altering your stroke, but by simply keeping the wrist ahead of the face of the racquet at the moment of impact and following through toward the spot on the side wall where you want the ball to hit. The correct angle and spin is achieved by drawing the racquet face across the

---

*Jim Tully, a two-time U.S. pro champion, who came to Merion in the early sixties, gets much credit for this.

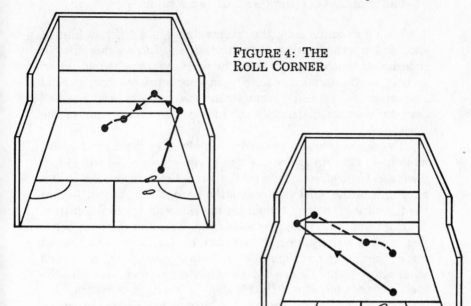

FIGURE 4: THE
ROLL CORNER

FIGURE 5: THE
REVERSE CORNER

inside (side toward you) of the ball and curling under the ball as
you do this.

This shot works best if it is heavily sliced, since the spin will
pull the ball around the corner quickly and make it sit down. If the
ball hangs or comes out off the second side wall, it's easy to catch
up to and this leaves you very exposed. The shot has to be hit
low—a foot, maybe less, above the tin—so that when you are back
of the service line, you tempt the tin with this shot. But if you do
hit it from deep, hit if firmly, as hard as you might hit a medium-
paced drive but more heavily sliced than your normal ground
stroke. If you baby this shot from deep, the chances are you'll
either hit the tin or leave it hanging.

However, when you are short in the court, you want to lay it in
there softly. To do this, you open the face of the racquet more than
usual, cock your wrist back, and then lock it so that the butt of the
racquet leads not only at the moment of impact, but also through
the entire follow-through. On the delicate ones, used when you are
in the front quarter of the court, the feel of this shot is not so much
that of hitting the ball as of carrying it as you push the butt of the
racquet toward the corner.

The other corner shot, the reverse corner, is a different kind of shot. It's punched rather than stroked, and in no other shot in squash is so much scope given to the wrist. As with the roll corner, you set up the usual way and begin your stroke in your normal fashion, so as not to tip your intentions, but you send the ball diagonally across the court to the far corner with a snap of the wrist.

To execute this shot properly, you abruptly check the forward motion of your arm at the moment of contact with the ball (6 to 9 inches in front of your forward foot) and finish the stroke with a hard flick of the wrist that tosses the head of the racquet toward the far corner. The ball should hit the side wall 1½ to 2 feet from the front wall. Spin is not particularly important in this shot. What you want is a sharp, unexpected blow that makes the ball squirt out of the corner and bounce twice before your opponent realizes what's happened. If it doesn't die before the second side wall—the most frequent problem with this shot—it's a cinch to return.

Two other common errors are: 1. turning and facing the corner, thus telegraphing the shot, and 2. pushing the ball into the corner with a stiff arm, in an attempt to carefully guide it in there. The latter makes the ball float too much. This is a shot you can't compromise on. You either hit it low and hard, taking your chances, or you don't hit it at all. Any attempt to push it in there carefully, well above the tin, leaves a setup. And it must be hit low or it will come off the second side wall, a setup. The shot has to be punched with confidence, and if you don't feel like you can make it, don't try it.

Another name for the reverse corner is the "rip corner," I guess because when hit correctly, it rips around the corner. Since the ball rebounds right out into the middle of the court, this shot works only if you catch your opponent with an unexpected angle. When you do, it's one of the most satisfying moments in squash.

Maurice introduced me to the fine points of these shots that first game in the sense that he jerked me around with them. And I was getting the tail end of most of the exchanges that first game, literally. For one thing he did particularly well, better than anyone I'd played up until then, was take me out of the play by "backing me off." Whenever he got a ball that was breaking toward the middle of the court, rather than take it early with a quick jab that might catch me off balance, he would put himself between the approaching ball and me, and then back up, and back up, and back up a little more. It was a perfectly legitimate move. The rules say that the striker can take the ball wherever he wants, and, ostensibly, all he was doing was backing up so that he could take a little more time and room to set up properly for his shot. But if you were in the court with him, you knew that what he was really doing was forcing you to yield ground and obstructing your view. A not incidental effect of this maneuver was that in presenting his hindquarters to me he added insult to injury. I was to learn that this is a classic Merion move.

All the top players use this technique on occasion. But here's the thing: whereas most players move you out of the way with a hip check or a bump of the can that's about as subtle as Bumper Cars, the Merion players back you off with style. Sticking your rear end in somebody's face is not an inherently stylistic maneuver, but somehow the Merion players have managed to convert an essentially silly posture into an art form. Like figure skaters, they tilt their hindquarters gracefully upward as they glide backward. If they bump you, it's, "Sorry, I didn't know you were there."

And that's the essence of the Merion attitude. They're not abrasive. They're not overtly aggressive. Not the pushers and shovers. Not the rock 'em, sock 'em sort. No, they keep their cool; they keep above it all. The very opposite of openly confronting their opponents; they ignore their opponent's presence. Their game is to act as if they are on the court all by themselves. They turn their backs. They take their room. They take their time. As in correct ballroom dancing, they move about gracefully but a little archly, with little pauses for dramatic effect. Just before they serve they strike the Merion pose: they lean forward with the back slightly arched and rear end tilting upward, and then they hold it, not so that their opponents can get ready, but so that they can reaffirm their artistic control over the moment. Or so it seems.

Between points they pad about the court with the quiet confidence that they're playing not a game, but *their* game.*

---

*Squash, which originated in England, was by some accounts first played over here at the St. Paul's School in Concord, New Hampshire. A master, who was introduced to the game during his holidays in England, had a court built at St. Paul's in the late nineteenth century. But squash first caught on over here in the men's clubs in Philadelphia, where the first national championships were played in 1907. Since then the majority of amateur champions have come from Philadelphia, and since the forties, all of the national champions from Philadelphia have been from the Merion Cricket Club.

Until you get used to this routine, the first few times you play them, regardless of the locale, so long as you are in a squash court you feel rather less like a challenger and rather more like an intruder. You feel like your presence is being suffered, if noticed at all. It's as if you haven't been introduced, so they're pretending not to notice you, but isn't that a pair of brown shoes you're wearing to this black tie affair? But they know you're there, or they wouldn't stick their rear ends out so far when they back you off.

Maurice would back me off nicely, clearing me out of the center, but then I'd hear the tin and see him shake his head at the floor, and I'd find myself with another point. Those corners of his were pretty shots, but it was a warm spring day and the courts weren't air-conditioned. This meant the ball, which got heated up more than usual, was flying around like crazy, and to keep his corners from coming off a second side wall, he had to hit too close to the tin for safety. He was outpositioning and outplaying me. But his fancy putaways were getting him in trouble.

That first game was his, except that I won it because he kept tinning out.

The second game was different. Again I got off to a lead, and again he was tipping the tin, but this time it was my drives that were making the difference. That simple shot that I was using down the nearest side wall was now hugging the side wall and bouncing twice before it reached the back wall. There may have been other times, before or since then, when I've hit my rails as well, but I don't remember ever feeling better about them. I was doing what I did best—pasting the ball down the wall—and it was working. I was grooved. I'd found my range. I'm sure I hit other shots. I must have hit a few cross-courts to keep him honest and a few short shots, but as I remember it, every time I got a loose ball, bang, down the wall. And the better I hit, the better I ran, my whole body thumping with a go, go, go pulse. The second game I won, and we both knew it.

Maurice tried to strike up a conversation with me between games, but I gave him a grunt and my back as I turned to continue toweling off. I didn't want to break the mood. Several years later when we were reliving the match, Maurice acknowledged that, seeing I was "unconscious," he hoped to break my concentration with a little chatter. Sort of like waving a hand in front of a person in a trance to try to snap him out of it.

Frequently, when one player gets rolling, there are a lot of missed serve returns. The third game was no exception. Pressing home the attack, I came out hard serving, and I was getting a number of my serves to land in the crease where the back wall meets the floor so that they rolled unplayable. Squash's equivalent of a tennis service ace. Funny, I could never hit that crease in practice, but there I was in a match and winning, and suddenly it was there. And Maurice wasn't. He was never sure whether to volley these hard serves or let them go. The courts were so warm and the ball so lively that it was coming too fast to volley comfortably, but if he let the ball go to take it on the rebound off the back wall, he risked being aced in that crease.

Not only was I hard serving him, but also quick serving him. Taking very little time between points, that is. If you've got a streak going (unless the cornerstone of your strategy is to slow an opponent down) you should rush an opponent as much as you can get away with between points, to get in as many points as possible while things are going your way. That's the principle, but, to tell the truth, I was so excited, gulping down the match, that I was doing this without thinking about it. Eager to keep going, going, going.

Until, all of a sudden Maurice caught one of my fast serves, stopping it dead in midair with his left hand. And he held his hand there for a moment, like a cop halting traffic, to emphasize this stop-the-action gesture.

Christ, what now? Just when I was rolling. Some kind of "psych"? It was a good catch too. Maybe he hasn't lost his grip.

He turned to the ref and complained that I was serving too quickly, not giving him enough time to get ready. Maybe he was right to call me for quick serving him, though I wasn't doing it intentionally. He probably wasn't ready. But beyond that, when your opponent is rolling, you've got to break him up somehow. Check the score, ask for a towel to wipe off a wet spot on the court, retie your shoes, take longer to get ready to return serve. Anything to slow him down. In team sports they call time out to break the other team's momentum, but in squash there are no time-outs, so sometimes you have to improvise, within the rules, of course.

The referee agreed with Maurice. "Frank, you've got to give him a little more time to get ready." I nodded, and Maurice turned to me and, with exaggerated carefulness, he tossed me the ball underhand, as if throwing it to a small child. Very politely. But a lift of his eyebrows and a twist in his smile gave the lie to this seeming courtesy.

I said, "Sorry," and with a mock solicitude strained my neck in his direction to inquire if he was now ready to receive serve. He nodded with a sneer. I continued this routine the next few times before I served. Then I varied it. I grabbed the ball, rushed to the service box, and threw it up as if about to smack a fast serve. Then I caught it, as if suddenly remembering that I was rushing him again. I thrust an inquiring chin in his direction, "Sorry, are you ready," then just as he was nodding, bang, I fired one right at him, catching him off guard. He'd said he was ready, hadn't he?

Again, like that spin of the racquet nonsense, it was an act of bravado. I didn't have a plan or strategy to fall back on in moments of self-doubt, so I resorted to tricks.

I'm not sure that Maurice or anyone else actually picked up these ploys, but they were very much a part of my private world. My interpretation of the match at the time was that I had psyched him, and I boasted of these crowning pieces of one-upmanship when I returned to school. Of course, these stories wouldn't have been told had I not won that match, which I did in three games.

Actually, I was all wet at the time about the reasons for my victory. I had caught him on a bad day and gotten some breaks. But most of all, it was Bennett's basics that made the difference. The old up-and-down game, which I now played without thinking, had provided the foundation for my win. It wasn't very fancy, but on a warm court, the fancy shots are the ones that get you in trouble.

But at the time I thought psyching was what it was all about, and certainly psyching was a big part of the fantasy life of school boy players. The next time I saw Maurice, he was carrying a little red ball around in his pocket, which as a psych he would substitute for the real ball at the start of the warm-up.

Well, we both grew up, somewhat. I'm not such a bad guy on the courts these days,* and Maurice, as an adult, is as fair and courteous a player on the court, and as unassuming, pleasant, and genuine off the court, as anyone I've gotten to know. But in those days we were both full of stuff. I think we've both learned since then that the best psych, the one that really puts your opponent off and gives you the most confidence, is having a good game plan. Sounds simple, but most people don't know how to analyze

---

*I'm a little more subtle now, anyway.

matches so that they can bring out the best in their own games, and the worst in their opponent's.

After beating Maurice, the top seed, I might have had a letdown, but I didn't. I had a confidence in my game I'd never had before, and pasted that ball down the side wall to victory in the semis and finals. So, in three days, I went from number four Exeter player to number one school boy.

My issue of *Sports Illustrated* hit the stands two days after I got back to Exeter from spring vacation. Perfect timing, for when the *Exonian* informed the student body that a snapshot of me was in S.I.'s "Faces in the Crowd" department, celebrating the fact that I had won the interscholastic squash title, I had thoughtfully taken care not to buy up all the copies available in town.

Allison Danzig, the dean of tennis writers, had covered my big moment in *The New York Times,* which was thrill enough, but several days after the tournament, out of the blue, *Sports Illustrated* called me at home with a request for my picture.

Though the "Faces in the Crowd" department offers off-beat fare along the order of 6'2 seventh-grade girl basketball players, ten-year-old skeet-shooting champions, and one-armed kayackers, and though the captions are only a sentence or two of who, what, when, and where's, still it's recognition from *Sports Illustrated.* And for a day or so back at Exeter I received more arm-pumping and back-slapping than any squash player had reason to expect.

A couple of friends took to calling me "Squash Head," a nickname that didn't stick, but should have.

Chapter 3
THE COLLEGE GAME

"My Introduction to the Varsity Game"

When I entered Princeton in the fall of 1961, freshmen were not permitted to play on the varsity squash team. We had our own freshman team and coach. And we practiced among ourselves for the most part, so we didn't get much exposure to the varsity game. By the end of the season I was playing pickup games with some of the fellows on the varsity, but not the first couple of months.

My introduction to the varsity game came late in the fall of my first year at Princeton, but it came, curiously enough, not at Princeton, but at the national juniors. It was my last crack at that eighteen-and-under event, and I figured to be a pretty good bet to make it to the finals, a finals against the defending champ, Billy Morris, who was number one on the Harvard freshman team. At least that's the way I figured it, and as the Princeton sports wagon headed north to the outskirts of Boston, to the Middlesex School, where the event was to be played, Billy was very much on my mind. He had a snazzy Merion game and extraordinary concentration, but he was slow on his feet. If I could keep the ball coming back and move him around a bit, maybe I could get some errors out of him.

But when I checked in for the tournament, my thoughts quickly shifted to someone else. The word was spreading that some kid was entered who was beating Billy in practice at Harvard. He apparently was a young sophomore there who'd only just taken the game up the year before. He'd made it to number two on the freshman team, but now was number one on the varsity ladder. Number one on the number one team. And this after only one season of squash?

"You've got him in the semis," someone told me as they pointed him out, checking in at the other end of the registration desk.

Now to look at him you'd have thought the only way he could get a varsity letter would have been as manager of the team. Very skinny. Big hands. A large head. Huge feet. The rest all arms and legs. He had the makings of a big man, but he was going through that goofy stage where he'd reached his full adult height—6'1 or 2—but his body hadn't grown into it yet. He looked like the kind of opponent you'd like to play in the first round, because you knew he wouldn't be around for the second.

When I saw him, I couldn't believe my eyes. Not because of the novelty of what I was seeing, but because the sight was all too familiar. An eerie jolt of recognition, as if I were coming across someone I'd met in another world, or as if someone had just stepped out of a dream. Both of which were more or less true. Perhaps I should explain.

Standing before me was an adult-sized version of a gangling eleven-year-old kid I'd played tennis against in a tournament in Brooklyn, when I first started playing the ELTA circuit. Since this event occurred toward the beginning of the summer, it fit into my family's schedule. Tennis tournaments were a way of keeping me occupied until we went off to our summer place in Canada. There were also some dreams of glory, since I was a local hot shot on the club's courts.

But these public courts were different. For one thing, the base lines were moved in a little bit so the tennis courts could be fit into the space allotted to them. And directly behind the courts was an apartment building that was festooned with laundry lines and alive with radios blaring and mothers disciplining their children. This tested your powers of concentration. And some of the players took their shirts off.

The gangling eleven-year-old kid fit right in there with what appeared to be a self-taught game. He didn't have a backhand. I mean that literally. Instead, he switched the racquet into the other hand, so he had two one-armed forehands. Most unusual.

The first time I played him, I shook his hand most enthusiastically when we were introduced. That dopey, splay-footed walk of his, his whole body nodding with each step, didn't exude much athleticism. Then I saw his two forehands. The match didn't last long, but I was on the wrong side of the final handshake.

I flung my racquet at the back seat of the car, and flopped

down in the front seat, depressed. But Mother was very excited because of a conversation she'd had with the boy's father. His schedule as a policeman permitted him to see some of this boy's matches. They had shared a bench next to the courts, and while his boy was taking me apart, he observed politely that I had "nice looking strokes." And Mother observed quite accurately, "Yes, but your boy is doing all the winning." He explained that what her boy needed was to learn how to win. "He has to learn how to figure out where his opponent doesn't like the ball and keep giving it to him there. Learn to play strategy. Learn to beat his opponent." This seemed like quite a revelation to her. Mother didn't know anything about tournament tennis other than the times when I was supposed to appear for matches. She kept my pants pressed, got me there on schedule, and was appropriately encouraging before and consoling afterward.

And I didn't know much more than this. The first time I won a prize in any racquet sport it was a lollipop for "good form." That was during my first year of group tennis lessons at the club. The only strategic concept I had more or less mastered was to try to play my opponent's backhand. But that wasn't much help against a kid with two forehands.

Over the next couple of years I'd run into that kid every now and then, but never with any success. For all his apparent awkwardness he seemed to come up with the points when he needed them, and he had the fastest hands up at net I'd ever seen. It was about this time that I was taking up squash, and I remember once wondering to myself what kind of squash player he'd make. Those fast hands would have to be worth something on a squash court. But it was just a daydream. A kid from Brooklyn, the son of a cop, was unlikely to get caught up in the squash world as I knew it. He was the only tennis player I met on the junior circuit about whom I wondered what kind of squash player he'd make.

But now, here he was, the Phenom of Harvard. I reintroduced myself, but there was no great catching up on old times. He just nodded awkwardly with his body a few times and that was about it for conversation.

That may have been his longest conversation that weekend. He was not what you'd call a mixer. He'd appear for his matches then disappear. The Harvard Phantom. He didn't initiate conversations nor did his manner invite them. We'd catch a glimpse of him moving slowly along to or from his assigned court, almost in a trance, his eyes glazed over, face totally expressionless. The calm before the storm.

Watching him play, we couldn't tell for sure whether we were watching a sideshow or the main event. He had the most unusual mannerisms between points. He seemed to be totally in his own little world out there. Sometimes his face was a blank. At other times his eyebrows would flip up and down—in response to some internal conversation? Or he would scratch the side of his head as if anguishing over a problem, his mouth contorted. Was he drawing on some inner source of wisdom, or just sucking on a sore wisdom tooth?

His head would sway, giving it a disconnectedness that suggested his neck was a loose spring. Sometimes side to side; other times rotating as if he were loosening up a crick in his neck, if that's what he was doing. Now and then an arm would lift with a twitch in the shoulder, as if he were doing a modern dance exercise. It was the body language of a retardate. But we knew better. Not only was he a year ahead of himself at Harvard, but the word was that he had taken a graduate level philosophy course his freshman year. But out on the court it was as if, for some yet to be fathomed reason, he had thought it might be amusing to act like a "twitch" or a "spas" between points. Some may have concluded that it was an act especially designed to baffle and bamboozle this prep school crew, but I knew he'd always been out of sync with normal social intercourse.

The thing that was most noticeable about the points was the raw, frenetic energy he poured into them. The scrappiness. There was no ball he'd quit on. If he was nowhere to be found between matches, he was everywhere to be found during them. His presence dominated the court. His stroke was quite similar to mine, a low slice. And he now had a backhand. No more of that two forehand stuff. That much I picked up watching him. But mainly it was the oddball mannerisms that I and everyone else zeroed in on.

Watching him in those early matches, I came up with no plan. I was just going to have to give it the old college try, or new college try, as it were. He lost games in some of these matches, in fact, went five in the quarters, and I had experienced no difficulty in getting to the semis. And he'd only been at it for a year, so he couldn't be that good. That was the line of my pep talk, a line that I didn't completely buy, since if he'd only been at it for a year and was already beating Billy, there were other conclusions that one might draw, like genius. And how about that daydream I'd once had?

The warm-up for our semifinal match was most unsettling. Warming up against Maurice, I had felt outclassed because he was so smooth, looked so right. When Maurice stuck his tail out, he looked as comfortable as a duck in water. But the Phenom was off-putting because nothing seemed quite right. A duck in dry dock.

Which was all right if I didn't feel as awkward as he looked. In the warm-up I never seemed to be taking the ball at quite the right place. The cross-courts were breaking off the wall just where I wished they wouldn't, and he was playing my shots sooner than I expected, sending them back before I was ready—those fast hands.

Once into the match, things didn't get any better for me. I couldn't pick up the rhythm of the play. The Phenom wasn't playing an up-and-down game with corner shot putaways. When I had played Maurice he had controlled the play against me, but I had known what was happening more or less, and had been able to pick up the patterns, leap on the loose balls, and maintain my balance. But the Phenom had me running every which way. Lots of drop shots. He maybe overused that shot, but it was a long hike up to the front, and even if I got there in time, often as not the ball would "nick"—catch the crease where the side wall meets the floor—and instead of bouncing, roll unplayable.

And the Phenom had me twisting, but with less grace than Chubby Checker. In tennis, he'd run me around a lot, from side to side, so that I was increasingly out of position; then maybe he'd come into net and put the ball out of reach. But in squash it was the twisting—twisting to recover from false starts, twisting to get balls that were breaking around me on the side wall, twisting from having to take off in a new direction before I'd recovered from the old direction of the shot before. From above it had looked like he had trouble keeping his balance, but in the court I was the one on my first pair of ice skates.

The Phenom's offense was something new to me, but the most distinctive thing about his game was his retrieving. It was the most remarkable defense I'd ever come up against. The thing about it was that he let you know he was there, not just with the balls he was able to get back, but also with his approach to retrieving.

First, there was no such thing as a ball he wouldn't go for. Almost every player, no matter how willing a retriever he is, will concede that some balls are too far out of reach and not worth running for. Not the Phenom. He wouldn't quit on anything. It's very reinforcing and reassuring when every now and then an opponent stops dead in his tracks and concedes you've outmaneuvered him with a particular shot. The Phenom offered no such encouragement.

No less unnerving were the sound effects. He made a terrible racket going after the ball; with his big feet and clodhoppery way of running, it sounded like he was wearing a pair of motorcycle boots.

Then there were the "LEHHHHHHHTs." If I stood between him and a get, finding himself unable to leapfrog to the ball, he'd climb up on my back, piggyback style, and wail "LEHHHHHHHT" into my ear, in a falsetto of excitement.

These let* situations developed because he seemed to know where my shots were going before I did. He wasn't being unsporting, he just had a very demonstrative way of appealing for lets. Again, he let me know he was there.

So the Phenom was stomping all over me with motorcycle boot gets and piggyback lets. A couple of the gets he made were so good I couldn't think of him in human terms. Nor did his mannerisms between points encourage speculation along this line. His head bobbing. His arm twitching. He was so unreal he might as well have been from another planet. Maybe he was hooked up differently than the rest of us. He was ambidextrous, wasn't he?

Frequently, when you think back on an important match, there is one moment that you remember in particular. A shot, a call, a lead, a comment, something—not necessarily a turning

---

*A "let" is a playing over of a point. As soon as a player hits the ball he must "clear" (get out of the way), and not interfere with his opponent's attempt to play the ball. If a player feels he has been interfered with in his attempt to get to the ball and/or stroke it, he may request a "let." When there is no referee, the point is automatically played over. But, if there is a referee, the referee decides if this is a legitimate request. The referee may decide that the striker was not interfered with or could not have gotten to the ball by following the path he was taking before he was obstructed. In such a case the request is denied and the point is awarded to the other player. If the referee feels the request is legitimate he awards either a let, or a "let point." A let point is the awarding of a point to a player when his opponent unnecessarily or deliberately prevents him from reaching and/or stroking the ball. A let point may also be awarded when the obstruction was unavoidable, but the player interfered with was in a position of real advantage.

point—but just something that happened that sums up the match in your mind. In this case it was a look.

Walking back to the receiver's box at a point when I was feeling the full impact of what was happening, though baffled as to what it was that was happening to me, I caught a glimpse of the most extraordinary looking face staring back at me through the back wall. The little glass window in the door at the back of the court was filled with glasses, beak, and toothy grin. Not really a grin, more a Satanic leer.

After a moment of confusion, I figured out that it was the Harvard coach, Jack Barnaby, his face all contorted because he was straining to follow the action through this little window. Eyes squinting, nose all scrunched up, front teeth bared, the grotesque expression he had on his face at that moment would have spooked a gargoyle. The expression of some evil genius cackling while he rubbed his hands over his invention to destroy the world.

The daydream I'd once had about that gangling eleven-year-old kid's potential as a squash player had turned into a nightmare, complete with a little face that was laughing at me through the back wall.

"Are you doing this to me?" I wondered at that face. All during the weekend, Barnaby had been giving the Phenom a big puff job. "Another victory for Victor, the victorious one" was the phrase he was locked into. He knew he had a winner in Victor Niederhoffer.

But Barnaby was peeking through the window in the door, not only to gloat, but also so that he would be ready with a few words of advice at the break between the third and fourth games. But there was no break.

After beating me in three games, Niederhoffer disposed of Morris in the finals—he seemed to get better as the tournament progressed—and became the first non-Merion player to win the national junior championships. And this only just into his second year of squash.

It was a what-hit-me kind of match. That tournament earned me a number three ranking in the juniors; it also put me on notice that I was going to have to come up with some more advanced concepts than I had learned at Exeter if I was going to move ahead in the college ranks.

I didn't get the advanced course my freshman year at Princeton. Still, my freshman coach, Richard Swinnerton, "Swinnie," was a marvelous old bloke. He didn't teach me a damn thing (about squash), but what an experience it was to have him. We were his last team before retirement. An old Englishman with a varied sporting career, he had come to Princeton in the thirties as a gymnastics coach. Prior to that he'd represented Britain both as a boxer and as a swimmer. His event in the latter was the "trudgen" stroke—a crawl with the upper half of the body, scissors kick with the lower part—which safely placed him in another era. He taught the Kennedys to swim. "Jack was a nice boy, Bobby a brat." He didn't mention Teddy, but if his swimming instructions were anything like his squash coaching, I'm not at all sure about that swim at Chappaquiddick.

But what Swinnie had was enthusiasm. A stumpy little guy with Popeye forearms, he'd throw back his shoulders and strut back and forth above the courts as best he could, alternately swearing at his bad leg and pausing to stick his jaw into the practice sessions below. I'd hit the ball too low and he'd boom down into the court, "Hit the ball higher, Frankie." I'd hit the ceiling, and "Hit the ball lower, Frankie."

I could grasp those principles more readily than the ones he tried to explain to me with diagrams. He had some theory about the angles that I could never quite grasp. He'd say, "Come on Frankie, let me show you something. You don't understand the angles yet." Then he'd grab a piece of paper and start scratching away. Soon he'd be so deep into his explanations that I was too embarrassed to ask which line represented the front wall. I tried to demonstrate interest without getting too close, because when he got worked up, he'd start spitting his words.

One reason I had trouble understanding his angle theory was because his diagrams were always hopelessly out of perspective—in large part due, no doubt, to his glass eye, which I think had something to do with his boxing career. But glass eye or no, up till our year when his leg stiffened up too much, he used to go out on the court and grapple with members of the frosh team. His former charges told me that his racquet absorbed a good bit of the blame for mishit balls. He did explode at the slightest provocation. Heaven help anyone who cut practice. And he was forever making little asides about those politicians up above in the athletic department. How he would have been up there at the top himself, if he hadn't been inclined to speak his mind. I was glad he was still in the front lines, where he swore like a platoon sergeant, though I believe it was in the Royal Navy that he served His Majesty for a number of years.

That salty tongue was the glory of our road trips as he would regale us by the hour with tales and jokes, which I won't retell here. We coaxed him into telling those stories to take our minds off his driving. That glass eye was a bit of a problem there. I don't know if it was legal for a person with a glass eye to be at the helm, I know it shouldn't have been, for that's where Swinnie insisted upon sitting when the van was headed for an away match. He blew up at the way Americans were forever blowing their horns; none of us dared tell him the reason why they did so. (Not even a few light jokes about how "the right side is preferred over here, Swinnie.")

And he refused to fool with any maps, because he already knew how to get there: "been doing it for years." When it turned out that that road had been moved, he'd go through his "Pardon me, Gov'nuh" routine to get directions from whatever pedestrians were still upright.

But we got to all our matches on the day they were to be played and had a pretty good team, undefeated save for Harvard.

Swinnie would blow up at something and we'd have to tiptoe around him for a while, taking care to keep on his blind side while we were still on his bad side. He was a character; the mention of his name would set heads shaking and smiling, but we all respected and loved him. Because he was real. And because he cared. He gave me a big lift once by taking me aside, when I was wising off about something, and told me to cut the funny business, that he saw something special in me, that I should believe in myself and develop my talent for the game to the fullest. Maybe he told that to everyone, but it meant a lot to me.

The next year Swinnie retired and soon after had an operation for cancer. We worked it out so that each of the members of his former teams would visit him on a different afternoon at home, where he was recovering. Bluff and hearty as always, he insisted that I look at his long purple scar that went halfway around the globe. "They can't destroy me," he boasted, and we marveled at how quickly he was back on his feet.

But he knew. And when he died several months later, I knew I'd lost a friend.

That first year I traded off at the number one spot with Peter Svastich, who had played at Andover and was much improved.

The manager of the varsity team used to say that since cockfighting had been made illegal in New Jersey, the Svastich/Satterthwaite challenge matches were the best show in town. We never got that violent, but we were both full of stuff and still going through that stage when we thought "psyching" was what it was all about.

The thing about Pete was that sometimes he'd give up. But if things were going his way, or looked like they might, he'd fight like hell. So the trick was to put him off.

In one of my more adolescent moments, I evolved the following ploy for a particular challenge match. Every time there was a critical point and I was serving, I'd make him guess as to whether or not I was going to deliberately fault the first serve by lofting it into the ceiling. I can't remember whether or not this tweaking resulted in a victory in that match, but I do recall that the next time we played, when he was serving on a big point, he sought to get me back by deliberately faulting the first serve. However, he had not yet fully mastered this ploy, for he got careless on the second serve and double-faulted. That match I won.

Pete and I became very close friends, but not that year.

Purposely faulting your first serve is a pretty bush thing to do. (Unless, of course, you're bushed, in which case make sure you knock it out of court and behind a radiator.) I think I happened upon that ploy because the ceilings were so low in the Princeton courts that any time you tried a high lob serve, there was a good chance you'd tip the ceiling. My next year, the varsity coach showed me two serves that are very useful in low-ceilinged courts, the slice serve and the criss-cross serve.

The Slice Serve.

This service is a cross-court that clears the service line on the front wall by just a shade and lands about a foot beyond the service line on the floor. Ideally, it would hit the crack where the side wall meets the floor and roll unplayable (see Figure 6).

You can't bank on it nicking, but so long as it comes in low, it's very difficult, if not impossible, to volley, and so is a great serve to use against a good volleyer. And if your opponent starts moving forward so that he can cut it off early in the air, you can catch him "cheating" by throwing in a high serve that will go over him. So the slice serve nicely complements the lob serve, because with the lob you go over your opponent's guard, forcing him to take it deep, while with the slice you slip it under his defense so that he has to twist and take it low. In both cases you must take care that the serve is not hit so hard that your opponent can just let it go and

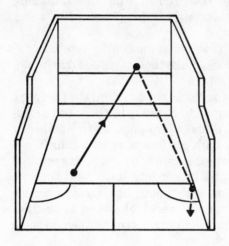

FIGURE 6: THE
SLICE SERVE

play it easily off the back wall. Still, to be effective, the slice service must be hit crisply. If you float it, your opponent can either take it early or play it off a lollipop bounce.

You want to give the ball plenty of backspin so that it can be hit firmly yet come in low. The way to do this is to hit the ball at about shoulder height with a sidearm slicing action.

You should take care not to telegraph which serve you are going to hit by the way you prepare to hit it. If you decide you just want to go with the slice serve in a particular match because your opponent is eating up all your lob serves, you can keep him guessing by varying, just a little bit, the angle at which the slice serve comes in. But keep in mind that a bungled slice serve—one that doesn't catch the side wall pretty close to the service line on the floor—will likely be a setup.

The Criss-Cross.

This is a fast overhand serve that is angled so sharply that it hits the side wall immediately after hitting the front wall, about 2 feet back of it, and cuts diagonally in front of the receiver. Again, it has to be hit just a shade over the front wall service line or it will land in the wrong service area (see Figure 7).

This serve is very difficult to volley because it is breaking across the receiver's body, but if the receiver lets it bounce on the floor, he'll have to move very fast to keep up with it.

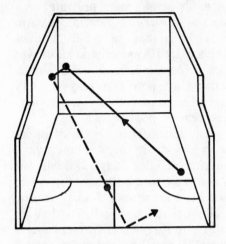

FIGURE 7: THE
CRISS-CROSS SERVE

It's a difficult serve to get in because if the angle is a little too sharp or if it's hit a little too high, it will fly foul. Therefore, nobody uses it as a second serve. But sometimes the receiver will volley the questionable criss-cross serves for fear that if he lets them go and they land in, he'll not be able to catch up with them. Particularly if on a previous point he let one go that turned out to be good. The ones that are questionable are also the ones that are the toughest to volley. If my opponent lets one of my criss-crosses go, only to have it fall in, the next time I use that serve I angle it even a little further over, so it's even tougher to volley. If he lets it go, it will probably go out, but he'll probably try to volley it anyway, because he got burned the last time.

With those two new serves in my repertoire, I had some pretty advanced concepts on how to start the point, but, unfortunately, I didn't pick up any varsity concepts from the Princeton coaching staff on what to do next.

Our varsity coach, John Conroy ("Silky John") in his tweeds and silver gray hair to match, was a strikingly handsome man in his mid-fifties. There was some debate as to whether he looked more like the chairman of the board or the Arrow shirt man. Certainly he was a smooth and able organizer, very good with the clipboard.

In addition to coaching the varsity squash and tennis teams, Conroy had one of the top administrative posts in the athletic department. And in his spare time he did a fantastic job organizing the Princeton Township junior tennis development program.

He viewed his coaching duties as primarily organizational. Application form in hand, he walked his share of tennis families around the campus. However, this extra organizational effort was not necessary for squash. Since Princeton is near Philadelphia, family and regional ties guaranteed a few Merion players every year, usually from the Haverford school. It was these Merion players who gave Princeton its reputation for good squash.

Jim Zug, a senior from Merion and a former national junior champion, played number one on the varsity my freshman year. We played every now and then after practice. Maybe I'd win one game during these sessions as the tall blond outmaneuvered and outshot me. He had a very good head for squash. And, of course, being from Merion, he had excellent tailwork as well. Zug had inherited the number one spot from three-time intercollegiate champ, Steve Vehslage, also from Merion, and also a former national junior champion.

Along with the Philadelphians, a few good New England prep school players would always wend their way down to southern New Jersey. I like to think of myself and Pete Svastich as the outstanding examples in our class at Princeton.

In addition, several tennis players would take up the game their freshman year, one or two of whom might make the varsity the next year. The tennis players who took up squash at Princeton and other squash-playing colleges most likely were from the Northeast and had squash courts available to them in their hometowns, but had gone to schools that didn't happen to have squash teams. With one or two exceptions, they were "preppies."

An example would be Keith Jennings, who was a year behind me. He came from New Canaan, Connecticut, where squash was played, but he had gone to Lawrenceville, which didn't happen to have a squash team then. He had been the top junior tennis player on the New England summer circuit, and with blazing "dogs" and lightning hands he was readily adaptable to squash. All that talent made me nervous. I and some of the more experienced players gave him a few pointers now and then. I guess I should have told him that top spin doesn't work so well in squash, but I didn't want to overcoach him, and he seemed to be doing pretty well as it was. In fact, his senior year he was one of the top intercollegiate players.

Anyway, after college he defected to platform tennis, a silly thing to do even though he did win a national championship in it. So I don't feel so bad about having not done everything in my power to hasten his development.

There were a number of excellent, nonsquash-playing tennis players kicking around the Princeton campus with nothing to do during the winter because there were no indoor tennis facilities at the time. Many of them would have made useful squash players, since they were already racquet athletes.

Not all good tennis players make good squash players. Because the walls give points second and third lives, retrieving plays a more important role in squash than in tennis, so tennis players who are not good at scrambling and running their way back into points are not likely to make first-rate squash players. But playing squash will improve their ability to cover a tennis court.

However, many of the tennis players, particularly the southern boys who formed the nucleus of Princeton's formidable tennis team, were suspicious of squash. They were afraid that squash might ruin their tennis strokes, so they lay fallow over the winter, which was too bad. Too bad for the squash team; too bad for them.

That squash is bad for your tennis is a fallacy. All the famous Aussie tennis players, Newcombe, Laver, Rosewall, Hoad, Emerson, Roche, play squash as well. Not as well, really, but as a diversion and as a way of improving their fitness. When not on tour, Rosewall has been known upon occasion to fill in for his Sydney club in a squash league match, as an amateur. (Imagine showing up for a league match and being introduced to some guy called Ken who looks remarkably like Ken Rosewall, and turns out to have a super backhand.) Even when on tour, the Aussies sometimes dip into a squash court between tournaments.

I once, in connection with an article I was writing, asked Harry Hopman, the famous Australian Davis Cup coach, what effect he thought playing squash had on tennis. He said he thought squash was good for tennis, that it was particularly good for developing stamina and speed of footwork, but advised against mixing the two sports in the same week because squash is so "flicky." He then went on to tell me that in his day he used to play a lot of squash. In fact, he'd play a tennis match in the afternoon, a squash match that evening, and then go back to tennis the next afternoon. The way he managed this was right after squash, if he knew he had a tennis game coming up, he'd swing a tennis racquet to get the feel of the different racquet weight and stroke; and immediately after his tennis game, he'd swing a squash racquet, if squash was next. And when not overseas playing Davis Cup, Hopman won several national squash titles back home.

The best squash player among his tennis protégés was Frank Sedgman, who mixed in a lot of squash during the forties when he was learning tennis. After winning Wimbledon and Forest Hills, Sedgman turned pro not only in tennis but in squash as well, and became the top pro in Australia in both sports.

Another former Wimbledon and Forest Hills champ who is an excellent squash player is Vic Sexias. One year he was ranked in the top ten in the U.S. in both squash and tennis. And Roger Taylor, the British tennis ace, claimed in the *British Squash Player* that playing squash has helped his tennis.

Squash is likely to improve your tennis because it makes you a better racquet athlete. It tunes up your reflexes, improves your agility and flexibility, and does great things for your stamina. Since a squash match usually doesn't take as much time as a tennis match, and because the distances are shorter in a squash court, a lot of nonsquash players have the impression that squash isn't as taxing on legs and lungs as tennis. What they don't realize is that squash requires more quick changes of direction than tennis, and that it's the stopping and starting, twisting and turning, leaping and lunging that really takes it out of you. Let me put it this way. To prevent blisters, in addition to wearing two pairs of socks, I use a pair of Dr. Scholl's footpads. After one tough squash match, they are so shredded I have to replace them. If not, I know I haven't been putting out. But in tennis, I can go several weeks with the same footpads, and I end up on the running end of a lot of points.

Along with your legs and lungs, squash will improve your eye. After a winter, or whatever, of keeping up with a speeding squash ball, you'll find you hit more balls in the center of your tennis racquet because of your improved eye, agility, and racquet face control. But I warn you, the first couple of times you switch back to tennis, you may think your tennis racquet has become warped because its oblong head doesn't look right after you've grown accustomed to the circular head on a squash racquet. But both racquets are 27 inches long, and the center of a tennis racquet is not far off that of a squash racquet. The tennis racquet and balls will feel heavy, which should remind you to steady your wrist and use a full-armed backswing.

The big difference in the strokes is that in tennis you frequently come up and over on the ball to get some top spin, whereas in squash you don't, or at least you shouldn't.

The tennis court will seem ridiculously big, particularly since there are no walls to give you an assist in case you don't get to the ball directly. And the long, high bounding bounce of the tennis ball will put you off. The first time back nothing seems right. But before long, everything will fit into place, and once you get your tennis timing and mental set back, you'll reap the benefits of your improved racquet athleticism. And if you go back and forth between the two games frequently, you'll get to the point where you can adjust to the differences almost immediately, without thinking about them.

I will concede that if you want to have classic strokes in both sports, it's better to get your tennis strokes grooved and then take up squash. While squash is not as wristy a game as many people think—not as wristy as, say, badminton—still there is more flicking and snapping of the wrist than there is in tennis. For some reason it's easier to learn to put your wrist into a stroke than to learn to hold it steady. Maybe, because throwing your wrist into a stroke is more fun. If all you know is the quick, explosive, choppy tempo of squash, it is difficult to get the feel of the smoother, longer, more controlled rhythms of tennis. But a "grooved" tennis player won't lose his feel for tennis if he plays squash.

A not-so-grooved beginning or intermediate tennis player will, alas, still be in need of tennis lessons, but in the meantime squash will have improved the hand-eye coordination and racquet face control aspects of his stroke. And the nonracquet elements of proper stroking—the footwork, the body work (getting the hips and shoulders into the ball), and the eyework—are the same in both sports. If you've improved in these areas in squash, the improvement will carry over into tennis.

If you are seven years old and want to develop championship form, then learn tennis first. Otherwise, play the sports you want to play, when you want to play them, and you'll find they reinforce one another.

I'm afraid these words will be lost on today's intercollegiate tennis players. Most of the squash-playing colleges in the Northeast now have access to indoor tennis courts, so there is less incentive for the first-rate tennis players to take up squash in the winter.

And, with the introduction of the soft, English ball and the seventy-plus American ball, which can be used in hotter climes, and with the installation of air conditioning in many squash courts, squash is no longer just a winter sport. The result is that the top squash players will have less of a tennis background than those of the past. So at the top, the sports are growing apart, and there will probably be fewer college players on both the squash and tennis teams than there were in my day.

Conroy was, I think, very fair in that he started me off number one on the varsity ladder my sophomore year. Like I said, he got us well organized. He started me off at the top because the year before in the university tournament I had been runner-up to Zug, who had since graduated.

Being number one meant I was assigned to practice in the number one man's court, its principal distinguishing feature being that it was the number one man's court. All the courts were the same, except that the court for the top player was the first one you saw after climbing the stairs to the walk which looked down on the twelve or so courts. (This was before the days of the Jadwyn gymn and its two exhibition courts, that can accommodate three hundred plus spectators per match.) Makeshift stands with three or four rows of seats were sometimes assembled for team matches.

Though all courts were alike, to play in the number one man's court each day was, nevertheless, a very satisfying thing to do. Being number one also meant I got the best competition in team matches.

We played as a nine-man team against ten other colleges. Cornell, Dartmouth, and MIT were automatic nine-zippers, although there'd always be one donkey on our team who out of carelessness would manage to be down 1-2 at the break before coming to. These schools didn't inherit good players, nor did they have strong systems for developing them.

Amherst and Williams usually picked up one or two pretty good players and might win an individual match or two against us near the top of their lineup, but most of their players were on loan from their tennis teams.

Tom Poor, who had played number two at Deerfield,* came into his own his sophomore year at Amherst. I had not expected much of a match, but he got rolling in an up-and-down game, and I found myself down love-2 in our first meeting, sophomore year. I

*Deerfield Academy, a prep school in New England.

broke his rhythm up by opening the third game with a number of wacky shots. I hit the ball high and hard into the side walls, a little "planned randomness," so that neither of us knew exactly how the ball would come out. I had to take care that I didn't hit myself with my own shots.

It was a desperate, down 2-love move on my part, but on that day it worked. Tom was a fairly mechanical player and this threw a monkey wrench into the works. He looked at me as if I had taken leave of my senses. But with the ball coming at him fast and at funny angles, he fudged a few shots. I was smart enough on that day to play the wild man shots just enough to get him out of the groove, but not so much that he got used to them. Indeed, if I'd kept it up, he would have caught on that they were all coming out in the middle, easy prey so long as he didn't get frenetic. But the wacky angles threw him for a moment. The funny stuff got me back in the match, which I went on to win 18-17 in the fifth.

I really owed that victory to Dad, who as I noted earlier, taught me the value of "junk." How unfair to him that on the same day that I edged out Tom, he lost to Tom's father in a New Jersey C league match. Naturally, by one point in the fifth.

The above schools were like the weaker prep school teams I'd played at Exeter; the service academies—Annapolis and West Point—were like nothing I'd seen before. Their freshman teams were never much because their players were still playing tennis in the squash court. The academies never attracted the club and prep school types who had played squash before college. The event for us the first year was not the squash but the ambience, beginning with the snappy salute at the entrance to their compounds. The uniforms and marching. The erect postures at "chow." The "sir" that punctuated all communications to us from the undergraduate host who sat with us during chow. All this occasioned much eye rolling, rib elbowing, and repetition of the words "Mickey Mouse."

The court ambience was, shall we say, gung ho. Their galleries were packed with undergraduates who were required to be there. With no cool or respect for the polite, handclapping traditions of squash, they earned their "cheering credits" by urging their man on with "C'mon Pete"*s* and "Let's go baby"*s*. Sometimes they didn't even wait for the point to end to share their thoughts. Hadn't they ever seen a proper match before? Maybe the wrong platoon had been marched to the courts and the designated squash rooters were demurely attending a wrestling match.

It was kind of fun the freshman year because we had enough

experience on our opponents to dazzle 'em with our fancy shot work. The only real hazard the first year was the wild follow-through of their tennisy strokes. A few whiffs by your ear and you learned to keep your distance, to hit cross-courts to get them on the other side of the court from you, and to hold your racquet high to protect your face.

They hit the ball cross-court, cross-court, cross-court, as if rallying to warm up the ball. Any shot that used an extra wall—say, a reverse corner or a three-wall nick—would confuse them.

But they improved. After a year or so of intercollegiate competition they got so they knew where these extra wall shots were going. They were never stylists, and they always did more running than their opponents, but they were fit and could run themselves out of a lot of trouble. The PT (physical training) emphasis at the academies dominated their approach to squash.

They learned to keep the ball well above the tin so that while they didn't make many putaways, they also didn't make many errors. The Army coach used to put a piece of tape across the front wall several feet above the tin and have his boys play games above that line. It's not a bad exercise, I suppose, except that it puts too much emphasis on defense if used too often. To attack effectively you sometimes have to hit the ball as low as 6 inches above the tin, but not much lower.

I remember being somewhat confused when I saw one of the players from Navy every now and then, before returning serve, walk to the back wall and push it carefully with his index finger. It turned out that somewhere on his person or racquet he carried little strips of adhesive tape, which he would stick to the back wall every time he made an error. A routine originally intended to help him concentrate on keeping down the errors, it had become, I guess, a superstition with him, a ritual he had to perform whenever he played. Once I discovered this, I ached to play him; there were so many ways of monkeying with his little routine. It's just as well I didn't, for my attention would have been focused on the wrong wall. But the routine and gung ho ambience of the academies made me want to play tricks.

The shot that gave me the most pleasure during my whole undergraduate career was a wall trick that I played on Richie Oehrlein, the number one man for Army. They called him the "Rubberman" because he was so hyper he was forever bouncing and stretching. He was, naturally, in superb shape and giving me some trouble because he was retrieving so well. Finally, I brought him to match point in the fourth game. It was one of those situations where if he could pull out the game, given his superior fitness I might be in some trouble. After a number of careful exchanges along the wall, he mishit a ball that came out short and in the middle. Without thinking I tried a "Philadelphia shot" by slamming a forehand high into the front wall at such an angle that it immediately ricocheted off the left side wall and then came diagonally across the court to hit deep on the right side wall.

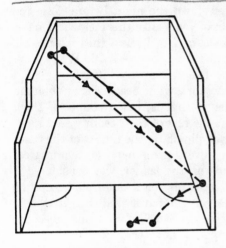

FIGURE 8: THE
PHILADELPHIA SHOT

The thing about this shot is that it picks up a reverse spin when it hits the first side wall so that when it hits the second one, rather than coming out at the expected angle and rebounding off the back wall, it comes out straight, parallel to the back wall. Sometimes so close to the back wall you can't take a swing at it. Something you would only know if you had seen it before. Richie hadn't and he made the fatal mistake of not volleying the ball before it reached the second side wall. This one came out so tight to the back wall that the Rubberman could do nothing other than bounce in place with a look of puzzlement on his face, which I could see from the forecourt and added to my sense of triumph. So much for the PT approach, thought I.

The shot was even written up in the *Daily Princetonian*. I bring it up to counterbalance the surprise that Richie's younger brother, Walter, had for all of us the next year, which I will describe later in the chapter.

The academies pushed the PT approach about as far as it would go. The thing you wanted to avoid was getting into a long match with service academy players. The thing you hoped to avoid was hot courts, since the higher the temperature in the courts the more the ball heats up and the livelier the bounce. The livelier the bounce, the harder it is to put the ball away, and thus the greater the emphasis on PT over squash IQ.

Yale accused Navy of pushing the home court advantage too far by actually turning up the thermostat in the courts. I think Navy claimed that if it seemed a bit stuffy in the courts, it was because the blowers had broken down the night before. Yale refused to play Navy for a number of years after this incident. I have no opinion on the merits of this case. But I guess these things all even out. Army canceled Princeton from its pre–World War I football schedule on the charge that the Tigers were biting.

Harvard refused to play Navy for a while because they thought Navy had "stacked" their lineup—that is, put a couple of their lesser players at the top so that the rest of their team would have easier matches. Again, I have no opinion on the merits of the case. But as I understand it, at Navy every game between teammates, whatever their relative positions on the ladder, was considered a challenge match, which could account for sudden shake-ups in their lineups. I think making every match a challenge match is silly because, while it does encourage extra effort, it also discourages players from experimenting with new techniques.

At Navy during the warm-up your opponent would sometimes let out a Kung Fu grunt when he went to hit the ball. I later learned that their coach told them to do this to unnerve us. There was some speculation that the Navy coach also encouraged his boys to take big follow-throughs to intimidate their opponents. I don't believe this. I think there were a few unreconstructed tennis players in their midst, but they weren't unsporting. In fact, the boys at Navy and Army were some of the best mannered on the court. Why, if things got a little tense, under pressure they'd lapsed into calling you "sir."

We tended to look down our noses at the academies' approach to squash, but they came up with very strong teams, which is remarkable when you consider that none of their players had ever held a squash racquet before.

As with Navy, you never knew what Penn's lineup would turn out to be, but for a different reason. Penn scooped up all the good squash players who didn't get into Harvard, Yale, or Princeton, which worked out pretty well, except that they always had two or three aces who were playing academic probation.

If Penn had ever been able to field their complete lineup, they would have been invincible. They didn't need a squash coach as much as a tutor; but they had a very fine squash coach in Al Molloy. I think he was the best intercollegiate coach for stroking. He taught his boys to take their racquets back high so that even in cramped conditions they could swing with a long arc and hence get plenty of power. As in the Bennett stroke, the wrist is cocked so that the racquet is at right angles to the forearm,* and the forearm is rotated to open the face of the racquet. And as in the Bennett stroke, the racquet is taken back with the arm in close to the body and the elbow bent at right angles. But instead of taking the racquet back horizontally, the racquet head is lifted and pointed toward the ceiling so that at the peak of the backswing, the racquet is held vertically with the racquet head about even with the ear. Cocking the wrist and turning the torso is what takes the racquet back. The forward swing is begun with an uncoiling of the body, and the racquet head is then dropped by lowering the arm so that as in the Bennett stroke, the racquet is brought through a horizontal hitting zone, with the butt of the racquet leading into the stroke, and the racquet face kept open throughout. Molloy, quite properly, is a stickler for keeping the racquet face open so that the proper slice can be imparted.

He had his boys drill every now and then with a half-backswing, to make sure they were putting the racquet on the ball the right way at the moment of impact, getting the correct spin. A drill he advised them to use whenever they seemed not to be making good contact with the ball. Also a swing to be used when hurried.

The high backswing requires more precise timing than the low one. The bigger windup means you have to be ready sooner, and because the swing comes down as well as through, if you don't catch the ball just right, you might hammer it into the floor. So it makes sense to first learn a shorter, lower backswing and then build up to a bigger windup. Also, squash being an active sport, you

---

*The wrist should be cocked the same way for both sides. The right wrist should be bent to the right for the backhand as well as the forehand. The idea on the backhand is not to put the wrist into the stroke, but to keep it steady and strong, as in a karate chop. If the right wrist is hinged back to the left, there's not nearly as much strength in this position as when it's bent the other way.

are frequently rushed and the half-backswing is necessary for rapid swordplay. The ability to clip the ball cleanly with a quick punch is invaluable on these occasions. Also, when you are near the front of the court, you can't hit a drop shot off of a full windup, so to disguise your intentions you should take a short backswing off which you can hit either a drop or a drive. So Molloy's idea about practicing the short as well as the full backswing makes a lot of sense. But when you have the time and are deeper in the court, that high backswing enables you to get the power you can never get with the lower swing.

Molloy was an ex-Marine. A little guy, he had that proud yet chip-on-the-shoulder look of the tough little drill sergeant—lean, short red hair, stubborn lower lip. Indeed, in his coaching he was bent upon toughening up his country club recruits, most of whom were from Merion. "You guys look pretty, but can you fight?" He once lined his team up in the gallery and took one of his best boys out on the court and beat him by just lobbing—like the sergeant who lines up the recruits the first day and kicks the shit out of the one with the biggest muscles—just to get their attention. His point was that the country club types had fancy offenses, but they played too many nonpercentage shots. He wanted them to cut back on the showy shots, that under pressure end up in the tin. "It's the errors that will kill you, so keep the ball out of the tin, and get it into your head that a good defense is every bit as important as a good offense." He was right.

But the concept of tough points really came through in his "leatherneck" dedication to holding the "T." He taught that squash was a heated contest for possession and control of the T. The T is the spot where the service lines on the floor intersect (see Figure 9).

It's a good central position from which to operate. You can retrieve almost anything starting from there, and working out of the T you can get to balls early—"cut them off"—and keep your man behind you so that he is doing most of the running, and any attempt at a winner by him would be foolhardy. You, on the other hand, are close enough to the front wall to aim as low as 6 inches above the tin so that you can mix in some short stuff along with the drives that pin your outpositioned opponent to the back wall. Everything works better from the T; all coaches and instructional books agree on that.

But Molloy was particularly adamant on the point that who

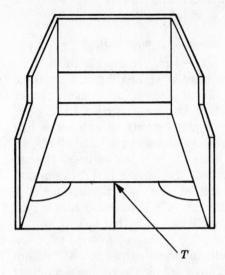

FIGURE 9: THE "T"

T

would control the T would control the match. He psyched his boys up to get that T. "If rushed, use a short backswing rather than let the ball go to the back wall. Get out front, hold that ground, and don't give 'em an inch."

The problem, speaking as an opponent, was that some of his boys learned that lesson too well in that they crossed in front of you and parked themselves on the T even when they hit lousy shots and didn't deserve that position. They were in your way all the time, which meant you had to stand up to them by calling a lot of lets. Otherwise, they'd bluff you and bully you into taking the ball behind them when you had every right to take it in front of them. Learning to stand up to your opponent is an important part of the jockeying for position. "Don't forget to call your lets" is a helpful reminder you frequently hear when you have to do battle against a player who has a reputation for getting in the way. You have the right to take a straight path to the ball.

The exhibition court at Penn was second only to Harvard's in seating capacity. It is a pit that can be viewed from all sides. A pit was appropriate for some of the heated contests for the T that transpired there.

Don't misunderstand me. My characterization of Al Molloy as the proponent of leatherneck squash is a caricature that's fun to play with. He's also a gentleman, very knowledgeable on the fine points of the game, and has given me a number of useful pointers over the years. (Also, not all the Penn players were on academic probation; and not all of them got in the way.)

At Yale the boys were taught volley, volley, volley. That's the formula that had worked for their coach, Johnny Skillman. Jobs were hard to find during the Depression, and Skillman, a graduate of a local community college, found himself doing maintenance work around the Princeton gym in the early thirties. In the odd moment he'd venture into the squash courts to knock the ball around with the kids. He had the eye of a semipro baseball player, and demonstrated enough aptitude to catch the notice of the national amateur champion, who was then living in Princeton and looking for games. The champ started working with Skillman on a regular basis and, as Johnny remembers it, kept telling him to quit trying to volley everything, to let the ball go so that he could set up on it as it came off the back wall, and back his opponent off, Merion style. But Johnny respectfully followed his instincts and within a year he was most disrespectfully beating the national amateur champion. So he entered the U.S. professional championships and won. Next he was made Princeton's squash and tennis coach. Several years later he was earning good money as the pro at a club in Greenwich, Connecticut, but he gave it up to return to college coaching, this time at Yale, from which he retired in 1975 after nearly forty years of service. He parlayed that volleying attack of his into an education for his son that included prep school, an exchange year in an English boarding school, and Yale, both college and graduate school. His son is now the headmaster of a distinguished secondary school. One can forgive Skillman if he was a bit of a Johnny-one-note when it came to volleying.

There's a lot to be said for volleying. A so-so volley from midcourt may be better than a good ground stroke from deep, if the volley is done so quickly that it prevents your opponent from getting back into position and if it helps you stay out in front of him. But if you have to stretch too much to volley a ball, the shot you come up with won't be worth it. You should try to catch your opponent, not yourself, off balance.

A squash volley should be hit with a short backswing—that's all you have time for—and a longish follow-through so you can guide the ball. Aim the ball with your arm, not with your wrist. A common mistake is to flap the wrist as if fly-swattering the ball.

Unlike tennis, in squash you shouldn't try to put the ball away with your volleys. Taking a ball out of the air and aiming it close to the tin is too risky. And sharply angled volleys that would be putaways in tennis simply rebound to the center of the court in squash.

A very few players can consistently hit corners and drops for winners off of their volleys. I say that because I have a devastating backhand-cross-court-drop-into-the-nick volley. Sometimes it's even devastating to my opponent. The trouble begins when I make one of these shots, for it means I'm going to miss three more trying to recapture that magic moment.

The smart squash volley is a simple cross-court or rail shot, hit several feet above the tin if you must hit it low, but in most cases you'd do well to hit it about the same height that it came to you. Volley to hold your position out front in the court. Volley to rush your opponent. Picking up the tempo or pace of play doesn't necessarily mean hitting the ball hard but hitting it soon. And when you rush your opponent this draws errors because he can't execute properly. The cumulative effect is to make him tired and discouraged. A tired and discouraged opponent, pinned deep in the court, will try a lot of dumb shots. (If he makes one of them, express great admiration, as this will encourage him in his folly.)

In tennis you break your wrist on overheads and high volleys to smack the ball. But in squash it's not power, it's control that makes the difference in the volley. A high ball that's hit super hard will only come off the back wall. And if you try to correct this by hitting low, you'll end up in the tin. If you've got a good shot at the ball it's fine to snap your wrist to accelerate a forehand volley, but don't try to hit the ball low by breaking the wrist. To aim the ball lower than it is at the moment of impact, slice the ball by leading with the wrist throughout the entire stroke. You should, in fact, slice all volleys for control. A final point: if you have to reach so high that your arm is fully extended, let the ball go. It's either heading out of court or you'll get a good shot at it off the back wall. And you can't control a volley—or any other shot for that matter—if the elbow isn't at least a little bent at the moment of impact.

So there is a lot to be said for (and about) volleying, but the problem with Skillman's volley, volley, volley approach was there was no allowance for individual differences. Volleying had worked for him, he wanted all of his pupils to do the same. But he had had remarkably quick hands. Faster than most of his pupils. And with his extraordinary eye and feel he could consistently volley into the corners for winners. The beauty of the game of squash is that there is more than one way to come out a winner. But rare is the coach who will take five different people and show them five different ways to win, based on their individual assets and liabilities. Each individual has to learn to lead from strength and to protect his weaknesses.

Skillman's famous words of advice to each of his boys before they stepped into the court for a match were: "Farmer (for some reason he called all of his boys, and everyone else, for that matter, Farmer), go out there and get on top of him. I mean that, Farmer, you stay on top of him."

A George Gobel look-alike with a teddy bear personality, Johnny was such a good guy I think his players would have played well for him no matter what he told them. I got to know the Old Farmer really well when I was a graduate student at Yale. He made me his freshman tennis coach (I declined the freshman squash job because I was too busy with the circuit) and he, of course, made me volley more. A real Yale institution, he had friends everywhere on campus, and he was the person I went to for help in getting a freshman counselorship. He was the kind of guy who was always looking to help you and always fun to talk to. Maybe he called everyone Farmer because of all the "BSing" that went on around his office. He was one of the finest men I've ever met, and I was very sad when he died several years ago.

Yale, Penn, the service academies—they were all good, but Harvard was the best, even better than Princeton. What squash I learned during my undergraduate career at Princeton, I learned from Jack Barnaby, the Harvard coach. Sometimes indirectly through his players, but as often as possible right from the coach's mouth. Whenever I saw Barnaby I'd try to get within earshot of him, which, given the volume of his voice, wasn't hard to do. He always had three or four people around him, and he was always talking squash. So full of squash it was just bubbling out of him. Ask him a question—anything except how to beat one of his boys—and he'd open his right hand so that his palm was now the face of a racquet. As he talked he would take imaginary strokes for emphasis. Before long he'd be down in a crouch, acting out an exchange between two famous players (at least one of them from Harvard) to illustrate his point. All hunched over in a player's crouch, he'd stick his head out like a turtle and, with that plastic comedian's face of his, would burlesque the sequence of looks on the players' faces as the point developed. All the while keeping the commentary going out of the side of his mouth, punctuating it with imaginary blows brought to life with sound effects. If a squash game could be broadcast over radio, Barnaby would be the man who could do it; but it would be a shame to miss all those facial expressions.

Barnaby had great lines for everything. If someone hit beautiful shots that too often ended up in his opponent's lap, he'd say, "That guy is playing the court instead of his opponent. That's what you do in golf, play the course. He'd make a good golfer."

He'd talk and talk and talk, and I'd listen and listen and listen. And as I got to know him, which wasn't hard, I'd quiz him with a checklist of questions I'd saved up for him since the last time I'd seen him. I spent so much time around him, you'd have thought I was his number one protégé, not the number one man on his principal rival's team. But squash was his craft; it was his life. He loved to coach, and I was an enthusiastic pupil, albeit from the other team.

I was always happy to see him, except on those occasions when all I could see was his face leering at me through the little window in the door of the court. Because that meant at the break he'd be telling his boy something that was not wholly in my own best interests.

Barnaby was a great psychologist. Just after a match, he'd criticize his winners, never his losers, because the winners were in a more receptive frame of mind to take the criticism. He'd wait until the next day, when the loser had cooled off and wanted to know what hit him, to point out where he had gone wrong.

Which is not to say that he dwelled on his player's shortcomings. He was always talking up his boys. The great thing about him was that he boasted about the boys way down on his ladder as well as the hot shots up at the top. Each of his players had a distinctive and special talent as far as he was concerned, regardless of relative ranking on the ladder. Sure, he had Niederhoffer at number one, but he also had Johnny Thorndike down at five or six—"my hustler" who is always working in the court and "brings home the bacon for us," i.e., is undefeated. He knew that a win at number nine was as good as a win at number one. He was forever telling anyone who'd listen about "my clutch player," John Francis, down at number eight or nine, who staved off match points against Princeton in the deciding match.

That was the price you had to pay for an interview. You had to listen to his retelling of great Harvard victories. He wasn't boasting really, it was just that he had a very un-Harvard boyish enthusiasm. Each time his team won a big match or one of his players won a title, it was like his first big victory. Which couldn't have been further from the truth. By the time I got to know Barnaby he was well into his fifties, and had compiled far and away the best intercollegiate record in the—I want to say "in the history of the game," but Barnaby would dispute that. He would insist that his predecessor at Harvard, Harry Cowles, was the coach of coaches.

To hear Barnaby tell it, you would think Cowles invented the game of squash. Barnaby would often begin his explanations with: "Remember what a great player and coach I told you Cowles was, well, he used to say . . ."

Cowles was brought in as coach after World War I, when Harvard built its first squash courts. By the mid-twenties Harvard had thirty courts and the most concentrated play anywhere in the country. There were no pro championships then, but Cowles was generally regarded as the best player in the game. By Barnaby, anyway. Also the best coach, for the national amateur champion from the mid-twenties to the early thirties, when Cowles retired, was either a Harvard undergraduate or recent graduate.

Yale, Princeton, and Penn, in that order, built courts in the mid-twenties, but formal intercollegiate competition didn't begin until the early thirties. Prior to that, these schools played in inter-club leagues and state and national amateur team championships. Cowles's teams were "undefeated in officially scheduled intercollegiate matches." That's what it says under his picture at the Harvard courts. I don't know what happened in *un*officially scheduled intercollegiate matches, but I do know he won at least half a dozen national amateur team championships.

Barnaby once explained to me that the Cowles squash stroke was an adaptation of his court tennis stroke. Before coming to Harvard, Cowles had apprenticed as an assistant pro in court tennis at the Newport Casino in Rhode Island and then in Boston. Court tennis is the original game of tennis, played in an enclosed area that replicates the early courtyards where tennis was first played. The rules are too complicated to go into here, except to say that a premium is placed on making the ball die as close to the walls as possible. Therefore, slice is very desirable, and, in fact, the racquet, which looks like a warped tennis racquet, has a lopsided head that enhances the ability to slice the ball. Apparently the court tennis stroke that was in favor in Boston when Cowles was learning the game was executed with the racquet head held low, which is what the Harvard squash stroke is. I dug that little tidbit out of Allison Danzig's *The Racquet Game*, long out of print, but well worth tracking down because it is an excellent history of the early days of squash and several other racquet sports in the U.S.

I take particular interest in the origin of the Cowles stroke because Bennett told me that when he started coaching squash at Exeter, he traveled down to his alma mater to take lessons from Cowles. So the Bennett stroke that I learned at Exeter was the Cowles stroke. So goes my racquet genealogy. And the Cowles connection also explains why in those days I stroked the ball like the Harvard players. Interesting to me, anyway.

Barnaby was Cowles's most devoted disciple. Not his best player. I don't think he ever got above four or five on Cowles's lineup, but after graduating from Harvard, in 1932, with jobs hard to find during the Depression, he became Cowles's assistant on a "temporary basis." Cowles retired several years later, and Barnaby stayed on for forty years after that, retiring in 1976. During his apprenticeship under Cowles, Barnaby developed into an excellent player, able to give Cowles's number one men a go, but Barnaby's real forte was as a coach.

On the average, Harvard didn't get any better material than Princeton, Penn, or Yale, but Harvard got more out of its material. The thing about the Harvard players is they always seemed to do better than expected, and they were expected to do pretty well. But even when they didn't have much on paper, with no outstanding athletes, or having lost two-thirds of their team to graduation, they'd somehow come up with a good team. And they never seemed to have "bad losses" (losses to obviously inferior opponents), the lapses that are so characteristic of youth. Why was it that they always outperformed themselves?

They had good competition on their ladders and entered two teams in the Boston A league, which provided better competition than most of their intercollegiate opponents. So competition was certainly an ingredient in their success.

But the biggest factor, I believe, is that they had the concepts. Their freshman coach, Corrie Wynn, drilled his boys on the stroke and game that I had learned at Exeter. (Some considered Corrie the second best intercollegiate coach; that was certainly the thinking at Harvard.)

So they learned the concept of backspin, the low, open-faced stroke, the rail shots, and the cross-court. But with the cross-court the Harvards started moving into some advanced concepts. At Exeter, as I mentioned before, we were taught the perils of having our shots hit the side walls, because this would give our opponents a chance at the ball on the rebound. We were weaned from the side wall, so to speak. But at Harvard they got the advanced course and learned how to use the side wall to improve their shots. Not only on the cross-court, but also on the drop shot and the three-wall nick. But first, the cross-court.

The Wide-Angled Cross-Court

The key to this shot is to break the ball around your opponent. Many times a cross-court that is hit so that it won't hit the side wall passes right by your opponent, easy for him to reach. But if you hit it so that it breaks on the side wall a foot or so behind him, he will have more difficulty in reaching the ball because of the wider angle. If it breaks in front of him, he will have an easy time getting it on the rebound, so the art is to be able to hit it so that it will break around and away from him.

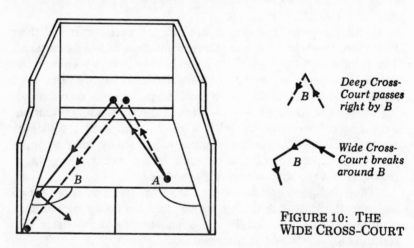

Deep Cross-Court passes right by B

Wide Cross-Court breaks around B

FIGURE 10: THE WIDE CROSS-COURT

I had always thought that the ball was not supposed to hit the side wall on the drives, which is true if you can get the ball by your opponent without doing so. But frequently the only way to get the ball by your man is by breaking it around him. It's a good way of driving him off the T. Another nice thing about the cross-court that breaks on the side wall is that sometimes you catch the nick.

That's nice, but the key concept is to vary the angle of your cross-courts according to where your opponent is in the court, so when the ball hits the side wall it breaks around and away from him rather than toward him. A real twister, as Mr. Niederhoffer demonstrated to me in our first match.

The Harvard players used this wide-angled cross-court more and hit it better than the other college players. First, because they understood the concept (most college players didn't), and second, because they practiced it all the time. The aim point, when practicing this shot alone or with a partner, is the nick a foot behind the service line on the floor, on the assumption that your opponent will usually be pretty close to the service line, so a shot that lands a little behind the service line will break around him.

The Drop Shot

The cross-court along with the rail will drive your opponent off the T, pin him deep in the court, and establish you out front. What next? You can keep hitting the ball cross-court and down the line, hoping that one of these shots will die before it reaches the back wall or maybe catch a nick. And in the meantime, you can run your opponent side to side. That's what most players do; to the extent that they run their opponents, they run them side to side. But at Harvard they were taught that it's much tougher on your opponent if you run him up and back than if you make him go side to side. The court is longer than it's wide, and it's tougher to turn around and tougher to run backward than it is to shuffle side to side. Now you don't have to go to Harvard to learn that a few sprints up and back are much tougher than a long point side to side. Most players know this in their gut, if not in their head. The problem is how to move your opponent up once you've got him back.

The Barnaby solution was the drop shot. Most players think of the drop shot as a delicate little floater, hit so soft and low that it hardly comes out at all. And they execute it with a flick of the wrist that, whether they realize it or not, puts some top spin on the ball, and this top spin works contrary to their objectives. A drop shot hit this way is known as a "feather drop." If it's hit with feathery touch, the ball is actually descending as it kisses the front wall. Too hard or high and it comes out too far. Too soft or low and it's into the tin. So you have to hit it just right. And this shot is immeasurably improved if you happen to have been born with extraordinary touch.

But the Harvards went about the drop shot differently. The distinctive thing about the Harvard drop shot is that it is angled so that the side wall operates as a brake. Ideally, the ball catches the nick, but even if it doesn't, so long as it is not hit too hard, the worthy opponent will have to contend with the side wall and not get a clean hit at the ball. It looks like this:

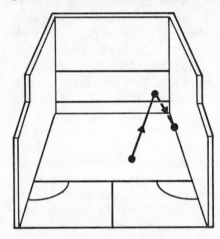

FIGURE 11: THE
DROP SHOT INTO
THE NICK

A couple of things about this drop shot. It's hit with a firm wrist. The wrist leads throughout the stroke and the racquet is made to curl under the ball to give it extra backspin. The Harvard players used backspin and the side wall to deaden the bounce, which meant they could give themselves a safe margin above the tin and so didn't have to rely on touch, luck, and inner grace.

Most collegians, to the extent that they had a short game, would use corner shots—the "roll corner," which is hit into the near side wall, and the "reverse corner," which goes to the opposite side wall (see Figures 4 and 5 in chapter 2).

The Harvard players would hit occasional roll corners in situations where you'd expect a drop shot or rail shot. What made this shot work was the fact that you'd be zigging to cover a drop or rail, only to discover that the ball was zagging around the corner. They'd hit it well above the tin, relying on a heavy slice to get it to sit down.

But except for this combination, the Harvard players had nothing but disdain for the corner shot. Barnaby argued that whereas the drop shots keep the ball safely along the walls, the corner shots bring the ball out in the middle. If they hang, they're setups. So, unless you've outfoxed your opponent, a corner shot has to be hit super low to be effective. Too low to be a percentage shot. That's what my former Exeter teammates up at Harvard had to say about my reverse corner shots. My answer now is that a number of champions have been corner shot specialists. One nice thing about the reverse corner is that you don't have to slow the ball down, which means it is easier to execute at times than the drop shot. For a while, under the Harvard influence, I stopped using the reverse corner. But I've since put it back in my repertoire. It's such a natural shot for me, I'd be a fool not to use it. For me, the percentages are pretty good with that shot. There's no such thing as "the best shot." Each player has to determine what shots work best for him. Barnaby would certainly agree with that.

The Three-Wall Nick

The third distinctive shot in the Harvard repertoire was the three-wall nick. This one goes side wall, front wall, and then into the nick on the other side wall, you hope. If it doesn't nick and your opponent anticipates it, you're in trouble.

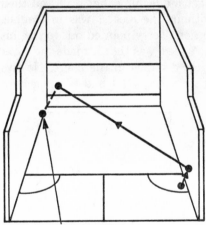

Catches the crease
and rolls unplayable, you hope.

FIGURE 12: THE
THREE-WALL NICK

This is a very advanced shot but I learned it in a very basic way—namely, I got beat with it. In our first meeting since Exeter Terry Robinson, now a sophomore at Harvard, carved me up with it in an invitational tournament. I went into the court very pleased with myself, having that morning finally cracked through against Billy Morris. By then I knew his moves, and I moved faster on the court. I would do the same against Terry, who I'd dominated at Exeter our senior year. But Terry didn't play like he'd played at

Exeter. He was still a big tiptoeing bear, and he was still trying to work me over with the angles, but this time it wasn't with gimmicky serves, but with—well, I wasn't sure exactly what it was, but I could never get comfortable in the court and he seemed to be making a lot of lucky shots, particularly with that three-wall number. I suggested as much after the match with a, "Gee, you really couldn't miss, *today*." (In other words, "you lucky bastard.")

Terry caught my drift and responded, "Barnaby teaches us to be lucky." He explained that Barnaby taught them to go for nicks with their drops, cross-courts, and three-wallers. They weren't going to get a nick every time, but at least by going for it they increased the likelihood of getting it. Most players don't make nicks because they don't go for them.

But more important, Barnaby taught his boys how to use these potential nick shots so that they were effective even without the nick. The key, Terry explained, was to hit combinations. For example, the rail shot set up the three-wall nick. So Terry would hit several times down the rail to get me leaning that way and then pop a three-waller. With or without the nick, I was in trouble.

The beauty of that combination, Terry pointed out to me, his eyes filled with a mathematician's glee, was that it made me cover the diagonal, which is the longest distance in the court. No two shots could have ended up further apart, yet I had to cover both options.

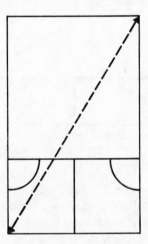

FIGURE 13: THE
DIAGONAL

"Barnaby teaches us to hit every shot with a purpose," Terry explained. "He is the best teacher I've ever had in anything," he added.

I could see what he meant. That was a tournament over Christmas vacation my second year at Princeton, and from then on, I hung around Barnaby like a necklace.

Part of the genius of Barnaby was that though he had a system and decided views on shots, he didn't try to make everyone play the same way. Like a good director or editor, he exploited the distinctive talents of each individual. If you were a good volleyer, he'd show you how to make that the cornerstone of your attack. If you were by nature a slugger, he'd show you what you could do with that approach. Barnaby didn't do what most coaches and teaching pros try to do: he didn't try to remake his pupils into his own image. Instead, he custom made them.

His prize player, Vic Niederhoffer, was certainly no assembly line product. Barnaby is reluctant to give an all-time ranking of his top players—as reluctant as a devoted mother would be to name which of her children she loves the most—but he will allow that Vic was the best pupil he ever had. "You only had to tell him once, just once."

Barnaby recalls that the first time he met Vic, he said to him, "Hey, I hear you're a darn good tennis player." To which Vic replied, "I'm OK at tennis, but that wall game, I'm going to be terrific at that." (Of this straightforward approach, Barnaby says, "He's like Wagner was, he knows what he is good at and doesn't bore you with all that false modesty.")

The next time Barnaby saw him, Niederhoffer was alone on a squash court with a racquet, a ball, and a British book on squash that he'd found in the library. (The British game, as noted earlier, is different from the American.)

One of the first things Barnaby got him to do was to stop switching hands. The story goes that Vic would be playing along with one hand, and then as a "psych" would announce to his opponent, "Now I'm going to play you with the other hand." Barnaby encouraged him to specialize.

Another of Vic's early psychs was to wear into the court a winter cap with a visor and ear flaps. A thinking cap? Barnaby got that hat off him and set to work on his head.

So the stories go. I can't vouch for their accuracy, but I can vouch for the fact that there were lots of Niederhoffer stories floating around.

Vic was different, all right. But there are lots of three dollar bills in circulation around any campus. Take away his squash prowess, and nobody would have paid much attention to Vic around Harvard's Hemenway gym. But since he was reputed to be a squash phenom, people wanted to know more about him. The first question was always, "Are you sure this guy is that squash ace?" (The answer to that question was never really believed until he was seen in action against a more promising-looking athlete. And even then, it was seeing that he was winning the points, rather than the performance itself, that dispelled any lingering doubts.) Once it was determined that this, indeed, was that squash ace, the quips and quirks of Vic's rather unusual behavior were scrutinized for clues to his genius.

The question in most squash player's minds was how good would he get? At the time he won the juniors he seemed to me virtually unstoppable. Yet Jim Zug, number one on the Princeton varsity, beat him in their team match, as did Ralph Howe of Yale, who won the intercollegiates that year.

The next year, Howe, then a senior at Yale, was the only collegian who could beat Vic. I remember very well my own intercollegiate match with Ralph Howe. He aced me the first three serves, and those were slow serves, hit underhand. I was a sophomore and this was the big Princeton/Yale match at Yale. The gallery was packed, and I was nervous. This was the reigning national intercollegiate singles champion I was going into the court with. Ralph worked me over with a Merion warm-up, which is to say, the only time he looked at me was to give me an isn't-that-a-pair-of-brown-shoelaces-you're-wearing? kind of inspection.

He won the toss, and the first three serves he hit I didn't make contact on, not even a foul tip. Unlike the Princeton courts, the Yale courts had very high ceilings, which meant he could get his lob serves way up there. Before serving, he would pause for the longest time, staring at the front wall, which didn't help my nerves any. But what I guess he was doing was squash's equivalent of spot bowling: picking out a spot on the front wall to aim for. I don't know for sure if that's what he was doing, but I have since learned that you can get good results on a slow serve if you pick some spots, real or imaginary, to aim for on the front wall. I don't aim for spots on any other shots, there isn't enough time. In the heat of play, you're doing well if you can keep your eye on the ball. But when you serve, you make your own time, so there's no excuse for not taking care with it. That's what Ralph told me ten years later, when I got him to show me how he hit his slow serve.

The precise location of the spots you aim for depends upon the height of the ceiling, the resiliency of the front wall, the heat of the ball, what kind of spin you put on the ball, where you stand in the service box, and so on and so forth. In other words, the spots may change with courts and even in the course of a match. With the motion I use, I find that the spots that I should aim for are a little to the right of center on the front wall, whether I am serving to the backhand or forehand. But the motion for the slow serve permits a lot of personal variation, like putting in golf, and there is no real orthodoxy except that the stroke is underhand with a short backswing and a long, smooth, upward follow-through. The racquet face starts off open (tilted backward). Some players slice this shot so they can aim high without hitting the ceiling; others aim lower, but put a little top spin on the ball so that it rises more off the front wall. Either way, the goal is to get as high an arc on the ball as possible.

What you're trying to do is to get the ball to "creep around the walls," as Barnaby puts it. When it's in the air your opponent never gets a good clean hit at it because it is out of reach or too close to the side wall, but if he lets it go, it will drop so close to the back wall, he can't take a proper backswing. The lob serve should be so high it can't be reached until it hits the side wall, and so soft, it only just grazes the side wall and drops almost vertically.

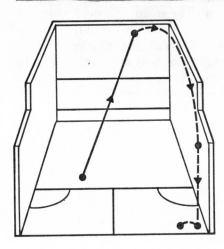

FIGURE 14: THE
LOB SERVE

As the receiver, unless you see that the ball is going to come well out off the back wall so that you can back your opponent off, you want to return it as soon as possible, to catch your opponent before he gets set up on the T and so you don't get pinned deep in the court. The usual response is to volley the ball after it hits the side wall, before it hits the floor, letting it drop to head height, because if your arm is fully extended, you can't get off a decent volley. But sometimes you can't get at it in the air, and have to take it on the bounce off the floor. If the serve is a good one and drops right next to the back wall, so that no backswing is possible, you still have a chance to get it if you face the back wall, choke up on the racquet so that you are holding it half way up the shaft, and flick a lob over your shoulder. In fact, once you get the hang of it, you can lob the ball tight along the wall, and put your opponent in the same predicament you were just in.

That's how I handle the slow serve these days. But Ralph had a dastardly one and I didn't have all this accumulated wisdom at the time. So I got aced the first three slow serves. They were good serves, but he also had me so tight I felt like I had a pin in my elbow and in my shoulder. It wasn't until the third game that I had an exchange with him that lasted more than three or four strokes. Years later, Ralph observed quite innocently, "We never played in college, did we?" I had to agree.

The big showdowns that year were between Niederhoffer and Howe in their team match and in the finals of the intercollegiates. Ralph of Merion, sleek, immaculately groomed, would pause during the warm-up to pick a piece of lint off his freshly laundered white sweatpants. Vic, of Brighton Beach, hair tousled, shirt half tucked in, would show up looking like he'd overslept and hadn't had time to get himself together before going out on the court.

Ralph was the master of the reverse corner; Vic, the drop-shot specialist. Both had incredible speed, but a different kind of speed. Ralph, like a cat, would tread softly, then pounce. Vic, like a howling hound held back on a leash, would be falling all over himself, dying to be let loose on that cat.

And cat-and-dog fights were what they had. The court was just too small for two such huge squash egos. Each player was absolutely convinced that he was the best, and the other was trying to take advantage of him. Theirs was the only intercollegiate team match for which a referee was provided. And they needed one, for they got into some terrible squabbles. The Yalies claimed that Vic was the perpetrator with his ridiculous calls for lets and prolonged, unsolicited explanations to the referee. But the Harvard view was that Ralph was slow to get out of the way, and that he egged Vic on with subtle hip checks.

Vic was demonstrative in his appeals; Ralph would speak softly and slowly, just barely able to hold his temper. Vic was continually letting it out, Ralph holding it in, but it was the same stuff, rage at the thought of losing. Both had the killer instinct.

The more experienced Ralph won both their team match and their finals in the intercollegiate singles, both in four games. Having won all my matches at number one, except against Ralph and Vic, I was seeded fourth in the intercollegiates that year, behind Ralph, Vic, and Bob Hetherington. Hetherington, a Yale senior who'd been a standout at Deerfield Academy, though only a number two man on his college team, was seeded ahead of me because the year before he'd made it to the finals of this event by beating Zug in the semis.

I was pleased to be seeded fourth, but less pleased when I lost in the second round to George West, also a senior at Yale, who played number three on their team. Until they got to Yale, West had been Ralph's nemesis at Merion. West rode my draw to the semis. It was a disappointing loss for me, but still it was a good first year in the varsity ranks, one full of promise.

The next year, Ralph had graduated and Vic had the intercollegiate field to himself. Vic, incidentally, was elected captain of his Harvard team. He wasn't "one of the boys," but his teammates seemed to like him and he certainly had their respect. Vic was also a much improved player and now a serious contender for the national men's title. As it turned out, he helped his old college rival, Ralph Howe, win that event by extending four-time national champion Henri Salaun to five games in the semis. It was a grueling match and after squeaking it out, the aging Salaun had nothing left for Howe in the finals.

Vic was so superior to the college crew that at the time of the intercollegiates he was pulling all-nighters to work on what was to be his summa cum laude senior thesis on the stockmarket. My game, however, was not progressing. Though I had played number one all sophomore year, Peter Svastich and I were now trading off at number one. A goalie on the soccer team, Pete had good reflexes and could stretch nicely for the ball. He had a lot of natural ability, but, like me, had no plan to his attack. Our challenge matches were now a little more civilized, and we called one another "'Tich'" and "'Thwaite," but we didn't become really good friends until we got out of school and were no longer so directly in competition.

After a so-so season, which got me only a number seven seeding in the intercollegiates, I came alive in that event and made it to the semis, where I lost to Vic, who went on to beat Tom Poor in the finals. It had been an up-and-down season, but on the strength of my showing in that tournament, I came out of that season ranked third in the college ranks and with high hopes for the coming season, which would be sans Niederhoffer.

My senior year looked like a Princeton year. The year before, Harvard had lucked out against us. Down 10–14 in the fifth game of the deciding match, somehow their number eight man had pulled that one out to win the match and another Harvard team title. But this time it looked like we couldn't lose to them. They had lost six of their top nine to graduation, and we only two. When the big match came around, I remember going into the court with Princeton leading Harvard 4 matches to nothing. But I also remember, when I came out, we'd lost the match 5–4, and they'd won another intercollegiate team title.

This year proved an even more up-and-down season for me than my junior year. Though I finished the season at number one, I played as low as number three in one match, behind a teammate I should have been able to beat with my left hand. Still, a Niederhoffer-less intercollegiate singles was a wide open event, and I brought enough clean shirts to last me through the finals. Brand new shirts, sporting a Princeton tiger leaping over crossed racquets. But one shirt was all I needed. I got upset by the number three man on the Harvard ladder in the first round.

The big surprise, though, was Walter Oehrlein of Army, who became the first person from a service academy to win the intercollegiate singles title. The possibility of his winning this tournament had never crossed my mind, but looking back on it, though he only took the game up his freshman year, he was a very strong tennis player and so knew something about handling a racquet. And the courts at Penn, where this event was played that year, were pretty hot, particularly in March, so that they rewarded the fitness and error-free consistency that his coach demanded of him. I would gladly have traded the Philadelphia shot that I had tricked his older brother with, and the several team match wins that I had had over him, for his intercollegiate title.

Why didn't I deliver on the promise of my sophomore year? I had all the enthusiasm and, as future matches would prove, the ability, to be the best among these players, but instead of improving, I seemed to get a little worse each year in college.

What went wrong? Was I psyched out? That's what most of us

used to give as an excuse when we lost to someone we thought we might have beaten: "I got psyched out." Meaning that somehow, mysteriously, I tensed up and couldn't function properly.

Well, Barnaby didn't believe in all this business about people losing matches because they'd gotten themselves psyched out. Matches, he once told me, were lost not by people being psyched out, but by poor stroking and strategy. Getting psyched out is a result of not knowing what you should be doing. Barnaby was a great believer in having a game plan. He would send his boys into the court with a plan of attack for each opponent. The plan would psych them *up*, give them something positive to think about, instead of worrying about all the things that could go wrong. I wondered what sort of plans he gave his boys for me.

Barnaby also had an overall plan for his players' development. Years later he told me that in bringing his boys along he'd show them advanced shots early on, to keep squash interesting and fun and to show them where they were headed. But the first couple of years he spent most of the time drilling them on the basics—rails, cross-courts, and strokes.

Once they seemed to have a pretty good grip on the fundamentals, Barnaby would encourage them to go "shot crazy," as he called it. He felt that to learn how to hit the more advanced shots, you had to both practice them with drills and go through a period of overusing them when you played. The latter is the only way you can develop the ability to hit them in the heat of a match. He didn't mind if for a while his players used drops and three-wall nicks at the wrong time, but once a player seemed to have developed a feel for how to hit these shots, he'd get him to cut back on them. He'd work on teaching him when to use these shots. Encourage him to use combinations. Bring him back to the real world of percentages and of setting short shots up by creating openings with good length. Barnaby would fit the plan to the man, but his general thinking was: basics the first two years; shot crazy, junior year; and put it all together, senior year.

Looking back on my college career from this perspective, I see that there was no plan for my development. I arrived very strong in the basics, with a good up-and-down game, thanks to Mr. Bennett. I could beat a lot of people with it, but to improve I knew I needed a more sophisticated game. Yet I had no firm idea of what this game might look like and how to go about acquiring it.

Any system of coaching is better than none. A strong coach,

even if he is wrong most of the time, can probably get more out of his material than a coach who doesn't coach. Unfortunately, at Princeton, unlike at Harvard, Penn, the service academies, and Merion, there was no system or distinctive style of play. And though today I know the systems of these other places, at the time all I knew was bits and pieces of them.

I picked up ideas here and there, particularly from Barnaby. But Barnaby wasn't my coach. He was great for ideas, and a good sounding board, but I'd see him infrequently, and he wasn't in charge of my development. The result was I spent four years trying this and trying that, but never settling on anything. I'd see someone use a shot and then go crazy with that shot for a while. But with no direction, I'd swing back and forth. I'd get it into my head that volleying was what it was all about and volley everything for several weeks. Then I'd play someone who'd back me off with great success, and I'd knock off the volleying and start waiting, waiting, waiting for the ball. One week I was holding the racquet way down at the end to get extra leverage for power; the next, I was choked up on the handle, almost on the shaft, thinking to improve my touch.

For a while I went crazy with corners, popping reverses and rolls anytime, anywhere. Then I talked to someone from Harvard and became determined to replace all my corner shots with drop shots. Some weeks it was shoot, shoot, shoot; others, get, get, get. Some matches I was a shot maker; others, a slugger. I was mindlessly copying the styles of other players. And like a parrot, I soon knew a lot of phrases, but I couldn't make any intelligent statements.

Looking back on it all, I had a pretty good record, and many good times, but it would have been more fun if I could have seen myself improve a little each year. And I was frustrated by the feeling that I was not coming close to achieving my potential.

A great thing about squash, though, is it's not just a school sport, and so you don't have to give it all up when you get out of school.

And, in my case, I had all those brand new squash shirts, still in their cellophane bags, left over from the intercollegiates of my senior year. How could I quit with all those shirts left over, each representing a victory that might have been?

Chapter 4
THE AMATEUR'S GAME

General Rule. *An amateur squash racquets player is a person who plays or teaches the game solely for pleasure, recreation, or honor . . .*

(Rules of Eligibility, United States Squash Racquets Association)

Charlie Ufford is someone we all look up to. The fact that he is 6′5 (possibly 6′6) has something to do with it. But it could be fairly said that he is the height of the amateur game for other reasons as well.

For one thing, he has won every major amateur tournament, except the nationals. And perhaps because he never won the big one, he has kept coming back year after year so that he has had one of the longest careers on the amateur circuit. I started competing against him when he was in his mid-to-late thirties, no longer a good bet to win the nationals, but keen as ever. He set his ambitions to suit his age, and he got a big kick out of introducing fresh-faced kids to the subtleties of the classic game.

That was another thing about him, he played the classic game, tight rails and a variety of corners and drops. More on this in a moment. The point here is that he is a gentle giant. True, he was an all-American fullback, but that was in soccer. I don't recall ever seeing him fast serve the ball. And what a fast serve he would have had, if it had been in his nature. He had the leverage for it, and though not muscular, he was solidly built. But for him squash was a game of subtle maneuvers, and he wanted to win with guile. No towering inferno, he was that infernal tower, nevertheless. With a step he could reach either side, and with a couple of giant steps (normal steps for him) he could touch the front wall with his nose.

When it was his turn to hit, there was no getting around his size. Which is not to say that he was in the way when it was your turn to hit. Considering his size, it was remarkable how few let situations he caused. The only time I can recall him swearing was at himself, on those rare occasions when he caused a let situation. Rare because he controlled play so well. Rare also because Charlie was a great sportsman, and avoided all but the unavoidable "unavoidable obstructions."

Squash for Charlie was an exercise in self-control, and at the top of his list was sportsmanship. For a referee to call a double bounce on him would be like accusing the pope of skipping church on Sundays. Sometimes he'd mystify referee and opponent alike by stopping play to call a "double hit" on himself—that is, he would claim that his racquet had hit the ball twice. (Who the hell calls a double hit on himself? I do, now that I've seen Charlie do it.)

There's a lot of self-congratulatory nonsense that is said about sportsmanship. At practically every amateur function, someone, usually not an active player, but an elder, starts popping off about the wonderful sportsmanship that we have in our game and only hopes that such standards can be maintained. At first I was greatly impressed by all this, but I grew to understand that "sportsmanship" is sometimes a code word for: "We're all splendid fellows from the same schools and clubs, gentlemen one and all. It's a little frightening to think what might happen to our game if it opens up." But apart from this nonsense, sportsmanship *is* a part of the game. Without some self-policing and self-restraint, at that speed, in that small space, the game gets ridiculous.

I said squash for Charlie was an exercise in self-control. Now to be perfectly honest, Charlie is no saint. On several occasions he has shown his displeasure at a referee's call by tilting his head and popping his eyes in disbelief, but those are the only excesses of emotion that he gives expression to on the court, other than to congratulate an opponent on a good shot. For the most part it was the agony of contemplation and, as the years went by, of impending exhaustion that showed on his face. But at the end of the match his face would break out with a great big winner's smile—if he lost. However, if he won, he would leave the court shaking his head in modest disbelief. The way players at the top of the game behave has a real influence on everyone else, and I tried to win, and lose, like Charlie.

Charlie was a symbol, to me and many other players, of what the game could be. The first time I saw him play was in an exhibition match during that Racquet and Tennis Club interscholastic event at which I played Maurice. Charlie was the first top men's player I'd ever seen play. The thing that really impressed me and everyone else was the supple subtleness of his wrist. Well, maybe it was subtle suppleness. Either way, you couldn't tell which shot he was going to hit until he hit it.

Charlie is a master at what's called "holding his shots." Now in theory, the best way to throw an opponent off is to rush him by taking every ball as soon as possible. But what Charlie does is draw his racquet back early and then hold it there for a moment. I said a moment, but it seems like forever as you worry about all the shots he might hit, then again might not. This little pause throws your rhythm off.

Like a good quarterback, he varies the count. Sometimes he takes the snap early and leaves you standing there. Other times he goes for a long count and draws you off side as you commit too soon. The point is, with that little hitch he disrupts your flow and disturbs your balance, mental as well as physical.

He holds you with that pause because he holds several different options on his racquet. You can't tell what he's up to until he's done it. There's no way to anticipate his shots. There's no way you can tell from the position of his feet or the way he dips his shoulder or the cant of his racquet what he has in mind. Each time he hits, he turns sideways to the front wall, gets down to the ball, and takes his usual windup. It's at the moment of impact that he directs the ball with subtle adjustments of his wrist. When he goes for a reverse corner, he flicks his wrist at the last moment, and you ask, "Where did that come from?" But if it's a drop shot, instead of throwing his wrist, he'll firm it up and curl under the ball as he strokes it, to lay it down with a little extra underspin, at least I think that's what he does.

I admit, he's no different from everybody else, he hits only one shot at a time. But every time he plays the ball, he works you over not only with the shot he hits, but also with the three or four shots he doesn't hit, because when he sets up, he's got you worrying about them too. And that's very draining.

Few of us are endowed with such a snaky wrist or capable of such sneaky timing, but there's a lesson here for all of us just the same. Most inexperienced players try to fake out an opponent with false advertising. They look to the left, then mishit to the right or take a huge windup as if about to blast the ball; then all of a sudden they drop the head of the racquet and give the ball a little tap for a drop shot . . . into the tin. Very tricky.

Squash is just too fast moving for all this excess motion. These superfakes are as easily missed as made, and the worst time to make an error is when you are in a position to put the ball away. You can make these shots when you're not under pressure, but when the heat's on, "hot dogs" get roasted.

Deception in squash should come, not from the swing, but from what's come before. So long as you don't telegraph what you're going to hit, the only basis your opponent has to go on is what you've done in the past in that situation. What you should do is create an expectation from your previous shot choices, then fool him by doing something different. But this only works if you can keep your shot a secret. And the way to do this is to be like a baseball pitcher: don't try to fool them with your windup, just concentrate on not giving your pitch away. Set up the same way for each shot. The only adjustment you should make in your wind-up is, the further forward you are in the court, the shorter the backswing you want to take, because if you take a big backswing when up front, there's no way to coordinate a consistently effective drop shot. And, anyway, the closer you are to the front wall, the less backswing you need to hit the ball firmly to the backcourt. So when short in a court, take the racquet a half to a third of the way back. When you do this, you threaten the drop shot, but there's still enough of a backswing there to permit you to hit a crisp drive as well.

When Charlie's out front, he continually catches his opponents leaning the wrong way, and frequently "wrong foots" them (that is, gets them to take off in the wrong direction). Sworn testimony to the contrary, he doesn't have eyes in the back of his head; it's just that the eyes in front of his opponent's head can't read his stroke, nor his mind.

Watching Ufford, and playing against him, I learned the importance of disguising my shots. That was the positive effect. The negative thing was that all I saw were his finishing shots, his putaways. Like most spectators, I failed to appreciate the way he earned the right to attempt a putaway. Since he put the ball away more and better than his opponents, I concluded that the way to be a good player is to hit lots of shots. Particularly when playing against Charlie, since if I didn't get in there quickly with a shot, he would. When I played him I tried to outshoot him. Against a good shooter there's a temptation to shoot a lot because he puts you in the mood: "If he's doing it, why can't I?" Also, when you think you're outclassed, conventional wisdom has it that the only way you can keep in the game is to take a lot of chances. That's the conventional wisdom, but I can't think how many matches I lost, or at least lost worse than I might have, when I was breaking into the men's circuit because I tried a lot of silly shots, thinking this was the only way that I could keep up. What I ended up doing was making a lot of errors, and an attempted putaway that isn't a putaway, if it doesn't at least stretch your opponent, is a setup. But the better players, sad to say, are not easily stretched. They are all quick to the front wall, one way or another. Which meant my short shots were like the cat's cream they got lapped up so quickly. Still, when I started playing the men's circuit, I figured the way to win was to play like Charlie—or what I thought was like him.

I started playing the amateur circuit after I got out of college. After a year "off," teaching in Brazil, I returned to Yale graduate school. New Haven also became my base of operations for an assault on the squash circuit.

Until quite recently all the major tournaments on the "national" circuit were played in the Northeast. Weekend invitational tournaments were the blocks of a season that would build to the nationals, which were held over a long weekend in mid-February.

The typical invitational tournament would have a sixteen-man knockout draw, with two rounds on Saturday and two on Sunday. (In some cases a doubles tournament would be held at the same time for aging and/or out-of-shape singles players.)

Tournaments held in cities were played at men's clubs, either in college clubs or in "racquet and tennis" clubs. ("Racquet" for "hard" racquets, the precursor of squash racquets, and "tennis," not for the modern game of tennis, but for "court" tennis, the original game of tennis as played by Henry VIII and from which lawn tennis evolved.) Tournaments held in the suburbs, more often than not, were put on by country clubs known as "Cricket," "Hunt," or "Field" clubs.

Squash tournaments were social events as well as athletic contests, and players were invited to bring wives or dates to watch them play and to join them at various cocktail parties and at the *de rigueur* Saturday night dinner dance.

The players were all amateurs as defined by the amateur eligibility clause, the latest wording of which was drafted for the national association by a task force, headed by trusts and estates lawyer Charlie Ufford. Though on the circuit there were some students, a couple of doctors, a few teachers, and even a painter once, by and large the players were lawyers, brokers, and securities analysts, all of whose work lives seemed to focus on the conservation of wealth, their clients' and their own.

As an undergraduate I had played in a few invitational men's events on the weekends we didn't have team matches, but it wasn't until I got out that I really started to work at becoming a men's player. The men's game was different from the college game. If you took away the side walls, most college players wouldn't notice. But the men would. They used more of the court. They had more variety. They were trickier.

As noted above, Charlie was a standout in these men's events. He typified the amateur game at its best, and so I tried to ape his style, albeit imperfectly.

My matches became cat-and-mouse exchanges. Which was fine, except that more often than not it was my opponent, not I, who ended up with mouse on his breath. But, as they say, "You can't lose them all." There was no denying that I was very good at covering court, and sometimes I got hot, so I had my moments—small ones—a few semisignificant wins over players ranked in the teens, and I even won a few minor tournaments. And after a couple of years of this, the national ranking committee conceded me the number fifteen slot (out of fifteen) for the 1967-68 season.

A national men's ranking was nice—very nice. There's a big difference between being a "damn good squash player" and a "nationally ranked one," and those first couple of years all I wanted to do was to get a national ranking. "Please, just give me a national ranking, and all my squash ambitions will be satisfied." That's the way I saw it until I got ranked. Then all I wanted to do was move up.

The next year, 1969, I finally got to the semis of a major tournament, the Cowles. The Cowles is put on by the Harvard Club of New York, and it is named for the famous Harvard squash coach. Held a week or two before the nationals, the draw usually includes a good percentage of the top amateurs from the U.S. and one or two top Canadians as well. To tell the truth, I entered the semis through the back door, for I got there by beating someone who had upset a seeded player in the first round. But no matter, it was the Cowles and I was in the semis, and that's moving up.

One of the great things about making it to the semis of a tournament is that you're "still in" Saturday night. That means you've got a whole evening to feel good about having won your Saturday matches and to look forward to more squash on Sunday. A whole evening of thinking up modest replies to compliments on your play. A whole evening of getting up for tomorrow's match.

In this case I had a lot to get up for. My reward for getting to the semis was a match against the top seed, Charlie Ufford, who I had never beaten. The last time we had played had been a year earlier in the first round of the nationals. Three close games. That was the third or fourth time I had played him. Each time I'd put on a good show, stiff resistance for a game or two, but that was about it. At the end of that match in the nationals, he had shaken my hand, and then shaking his head at the gallery had announced, "He's tough."

I cherished those words of praise from the great master. But by the time the Cowles rolled around a year later, the prospect of once again looking good in a losing effort had lost its appeal. I had yet to beat a major player and was wondering if I ever would. But before Sunday morning comes Saturday night.

As with most of the invitational tournaments of this era, there was a black tie dinner on Saturday night. But unlike the others, instead of a dinner dance, the Cowles is a stag evening. The amateur players and officialdom are joined by the local club pros, who are invited to attend the dinner to join in the toasts and merriment, but not to play.

Cocktail hour begins at seven, and well I remember promptly bellying up to the bar at the '69 Cowles to order a beer (the drink of all "still in" squash players), and to position myself at the side of Jack Barnaby.

Barnaby arranged his intercollegiate schedule so as to never miss a Cowles dinner. He was there to tell us about Cowles. But I wanted to know about Ufford, and so I (skillfully) steered the conversation around to his two-time intercollegiate champ of the early fifties.

"How come you let Charlie graduate from Harvard hitting all those reverse corners? I thought you were only allowed to hit drop shots at Harvard?" queried I of the old master.

"Sure, but isn't that a great shot the way he hits it. When I saw he had a shot like that, I told him to use it. It reminds me of Cowles. He never thought much of the three-wall nick. He thought it was too risky. If you didn't catch the nick, it left you in a bad position. Except one afternoon I was standing next to him in the gallery during a match, and he started to cheer every time Germain Glidden tried a three-wall. Glidden was popping those three-walls and Cowles was punching his palm and yelling 'That's it. That's it.' I couldn't believe it. I asked him, 'You told me the three-wall nick was no good, how come you're cheering?' He told me, 'I never said it was no good for Glidden. When you're that fast you can cover your mistakes. Then it's a great shot, for Glidden.' Cowles set rules but wasn't afraid to break them for his great players. When you've got a corner shot like Charlie's, you've got to use it," Barnaby added.

"Well how do you play him?" I asked. Then I went one step further. "How should I play him? I've got to play him tomorrow." Barnaby was being so honest I felt I had to come clean about what I was trying to get out of him in this conversation. I knew the one thing he didn't do during our college years was tell you how to beat his players just before a match, and I didn't feel right tricking him into it, even if it was a postgrad session.

He paused. "Well, he did go to Harvard." Another pause, and then a twinkle, "But I like to help young players along.

"Here's the thing. You're not going to beat him playing his game. Don't try to play all these delicate little shots against him. That's his game. You do that and he'll spin you around like a fruit in a one-armed bandit and you'll need a compass to figure out where the front wall is. No. What you've gotta do is keep hammering him. Forget about all that finesse. Dempsey wasn't the most skillful fighter but he was the champ, and he took care of a lot of Fancy Dans because he kept on coming at 'em, took everything they had, and kept socking 'em in the arms until the pretty fighters couldn't hold their arms up anymore. And then Dempsey'd move in and put 'em away. So you've got to absorb all the fancy shots. Don't let them bother you. But keep coming at him. Look at it this way. Charlie's the big bear and you're a swarm of bees pestering him. One bee never bothered a bear. He can swat it away. [Barnaby casually waves away a bee with the back of his left hand.] But a swarm of them? [Barnaby is now worried and starts spastically swatting with the palms of both hands like a baby rejecting a spoon.] And sooner or later they're gonna get through to him. [Barnaby is now writhing, his head buried in his arms.]

"So what you've got to do is keep peppering him. Fast serve him. Don't let him get set. Hit hard. Get everything back. Keep coming at him. He can't hit those fancy shots all the time if he's not ready. And here's another thing, he's so big it's tough for him to turn, so break the ball around him. Make him turn hard. Figure he's still gonna make some great shots. But you're not going to get discouraged. Keep after him. Dig for everything. You're that swarm of bees. And sooner or later you're going to get to him."

What Barnaby in effect told me in those five minutes was that Charlie, who had been my role model, who I'd tried to emulate, was not really the person after whom I should be patterning my game. I wasn't going to beat him at his own game. Charlie Ufford was better at playing like Charlie Ufford than I would ever be. Face it. We had different builds, personalities, and styles. But take heart. There were things I could do that he couldn't do, and there's a way for me to put him off and that's what I should concentrate on.

Dinner at the Cowles is announced by the piping of a gentleman dressed in full Scottish Highlands regalia, who weaves through the cocktail party skirling his invitation to dinner. Why this "pie-eyed" piper is a tradition I have no idea. We all order one last drink, for soon the bar will return to a cash basis.

We repair to the adjoining high-ceilinged, darkly paneled banquet room, where the proceedings are sternly overseen by bewhiskered elders of Harvard past, looking down on us from their portraits with dyspeptic smiles on their lips. Grim countenances. No need to be so reproachful. Though the chairman will make the obligatory somewhat off-color joke in his introductory remarks (even Charlie once told a naughty one), the humor at the Cowles dinner is not particularly racy for a stag dinner.

What goes on behind those closed doors? At the head of the head table sits the honorary chairman of the tournament joined by the real chairman, who presides over the event, and representatives of the various associations—the Met., the U.S., the Canadian, and if we're lucky, the Bermudian as well. Various other worthies are there too, but I can't remember who they are or their reason for being there. But each is acknowledged by the real chairman and each says a few words, hopefully a few words. Then a paean to the honorary chairman, someone over fifty who may or may not have been a titled player in his day, but has certainly made a "great contribution to the game" over the years, and, of course, is "a great sportsman." Ah, sportsmanship . . . There are some stirring words on that topic, reinforcing our shared "we-ness." All of us in black ties, none of us with clip-ons. (Just as the worst scoundrels of politicians become "elder statesmen" once they retire, the most vicious of players become "great sportsmen" if they hang around these events in their declining years.)

The pros in attendance are acknowledged ("We sometimes forget what an important contribution they make to the game.") and each is asked to stand up and take a bow. The fact that W. Stewart Brauns has provided the wine is "hear, hear!"*ed.* (Mr. Brauns is reputed to have the most extensive and active collection of squash-related cufflinks in the world.)

It's a long yawn until Barnaby gets the floor. Lest we forget in whose memory this tournament is held, Barnaby is there to tell us a Cowles story. Tonight he tells the one about Cowles and Beekie Pool. (Beekman H. Pool.) Pool was born to hit. He could hit the living bejesus out of the ball, which he did at every opportunity and which was fine except that his best drives would come out off the back wall, thus spoiling his attack. Cowles tried everything to get him to slow down, but nothing seemed to work. Man must hit ball. There was no way to get into Pool's head the concept of easing up. Most coaches would have given up at this point. Not Cowles. He just concluded he was working on the wrong head. So he got hold of Pool's racquet and went to work on that head. He restrung it as loose as a snowshoe and sent Pool back in the court, this time with instructions to hit as hard as he could. Sure enough, the ball stopped coming off the back wall, and with that butterfly net of a racquet, Pool snatched the national men's championship while still an undergraduate.

Dessert completed, cigars are passed around. Props for what happens next, the Calcutta Pool. The orderly seating around the tables breaks up. The huddling begins. Not everyone will bid, but everyone feels something of a tingle as "Who do you like?" becomes the topic of the moment.

Men who spend their weekdays placing bets on the Big Board appraise the eight names scrawled in chalk on a blackboard in the corner of the room. These are the four semifinalists from the Cowles and the four from "The Jacobs." The Jacobs, named after recently retired Harvard Club pro John Jacobs, is a second-flight tournament held concurrently with the Cowles. A far grimmer event since unlike the Cowles, where everyone pretty much knows where he stands, virtually everyone in the Jacobs figures he should be in the Cowles and is better than everyone else in this lesser event. It's bad loss-ville, and the matches sound like feeding time at the zoo, but the winner of the Jacobs is automatically invited to play in the Cowles the next year, and the betting's fun on Saturday night. Still, players who just miss out on being invited to the Cowles often as not duck the Jacobs.

The Calcutta Pool is always exciting, but it is at this moment that Niederhoffer's "retirement" from squash is most felt. His second year out of Harvard, while a graduate student out in Chicago, with absolutely no one to practice against, Vic had finally won the nationals. The next year the nationals were played in Chicago, but Vic refused to defend. He had been refused membership in the club where the event was to be played. The club was willing to have him practice there, but not as a member. Why should he put on a show for them if they wouldn't have him as a member?

He alleged they were discriminating against him because he was Jewish; they alleged it was Niederhoffer they weren't high on. The next year he was out on the West Coast teaching in the business school at Berkeley, and "retired?" from squash.

Whenever the Chicago incident would come up in conversation, I would argue the Niederhoffer side of the case. I did so with very little real knowledge of what had happened. I doubt, in fact, that either side did themselves proud. The club probably would have taken an extrapresentable Jew, but why should a Jew have to be extrapresentable? Vic probably went out of his way in dress and manner to be less than presentable. Why make a bad situation worse? Still, I didn't like the smell of the Chicago side of the argument.

Mind you, the topic didn't come up very often. The truth is that nonactive players, no matter how completely they once dominated the game, and no matter how often they think about their glory days, are not missed or even remembered nearly as much as they think they are. As soon as a player drops off the circuit, he's almost immediately and completely forgotten. He's no longer a factor. He may think, "Well, they all know that if I were still active, I'd still be beating them." But if he's not in the tournaments, they don't think about him. And when they do, they're likely as not to say to themselves, "Well, the game's changed [whatever that may mean], and I'm not so sure he'd have been able to adapt."

When you come down to it, except for the person who did win, nobody much cares who won two weeks ago. It's who's going to win this event that excites interest. But at the Calcutta Pool, the Nieder was missed.

He had won this tournament several times, but it was his Saturday night performances that were most memorable. This scholarship kid from Harvard, in his first year in the tournament, bought *himself* in the bidding. He had already won a major invitational tournament that year, so the bidding for the right to choose him must have been in excess of $1,000. Those who knew him at Harvard might not have been so surprised. A legendary poker player, he may have paid for his racquets with his poker winnings. And as a freshman he had chaired a weekly discussion in his dormitory on the stock market. He liked to figure the odds and then play them. But he wouldn't stop with just buying himself. This future broker of businesses would then start exchanging a piece of himself for positions in other players, laying off in case of injury, but always in the process of bartering improving the expected return on his investment. And maybe getting in on some of the action in the other tournament. He'd make the bold bid, then cover quietly, all the while improving his position. That's the way I understand it. No one ever knew for sure exactly what he was up to. I could guarantee only one thing, that he'd structure it so that he'd make more money if he won than if he lost. He liked the pressure.

In the seven or eight Cowles that I've been to, I don't remember seeing anyone else buy himself outright. The understanding was that the syndicate that bought the player must offer that player a chance to buy in at up to 25 percent.

There was something very bold, boastful, and very direct about standing up and betting a not piddling sum of money on yourself. A direct violation of the upper-class reserve custom of understatement that traditionally governed the amateur squash world. The other players did on occasion place bets on themselves, but they did it quietly. Vic, on the other hand, would lay off his bet quietly.

For a while, it seemed to me that there was a certain irony and even hypocrisy in the fact that a Calcutta Pool, which encouraged people to bet and hence make money off of squash, should be at the heart of this citadel of the invitational amateur tournaments. Was not the understanding that a player had a right to buy up to 25 percent of himself a direct violation of the letter of the amateur eligibility clause? Well, perhaps of the letter, but not of the spirit of the gentleman sportsman, of men of means wagering on horses from their stables. The scene summoned to mind old prints of cock fights, with gentlemen in tall, cylindrical hats leaning over the pit to witness the outcome of their wagers.

W. Stewart Brauns, who spends his weekdays creating markets

on the floor of the stock exchange, is the auctioneer. His mission is to get the bidding up, since the tournament committee skims 10 percent off the total bids to put toward the expense of running the tournament, namely the expense of the cocktail hour and the Saturday night dinner. The bidding is for the right to choose one of the eight semifinalists. After the club takes its 10 percent, what's left in the pot goes to the syndicates that own the winners and runners-up of the two tournaments.

The players hope to go for a lot, as proof of the esteem in which they are held by the squash community. But the consolation of going cheap is you're offered better odds.

I go for $300 in an eight-man pool that totals $4,200. Charlie goes for $800. My plan notwithstanding, I decline to buy a piece of myself.

Sunday morning. A warm-up against Charlie is always a bit of a shock. Looking down from the gallery, you don't really appreciate the relative size of the players, at least not the way you do in the court. I'd forget how big Charlie was until I was standing next to him in shorts in the court; and then I would remember my Short Hills Country Day basketball career and those funny match-ups in elementary school when everyone was required to go out for the same sport. Every now and then after an inconclusive struggle for the ball, I'd end up jumping for it against someone a foot taller— the most dramatic demonstration to a young lad that size helps in sport. Unless you aspire to be a flyweight wrestler or a jockey, or are resigned to being a coxswain, being small when you're growing up seems a handicap in sport. The whole point behind growing up is to get bigger. Bigger is better. Size is strength. Athletes are big and strong. Nobody talks about the advantages or desirability of being small. Nobody says, "Hey young fellow, I bet you're going to be real small someday."

So in the warm-up I couldn't help feeling a little "undertall" and couldn't help wondering if I were up to the job. Nor did the referee help matters when in making the introductions, just prior to play, he reminded us that Mr. Ufford was not only the top seed but also a two-time winner of this event and a two-time finalist in the national singles.

It was at this point that the number fifteen-ranked Mr. Satterthwaite, a former first-round loser in this event, again reminded himself that he had "a plan."

Indeed, I did have a plan. The first game I was all over him.

Everything went my way. I won the serve, which meant I could let him know with a fast one right at him that I was coming after him, right from the first stroke. He slipped in a few corners and drops that game, but he never got started; I never let him get started.

I never let him get set up. He needed time to hold his shots with that little pause at the top of his swing and I wasn't giving him time. I was juiced up. Taking the ball early. Sometimes catching it on the rise, even.

The swarm of bees was all over the big fellow. Particularly effective were cross-courts that broke around him, that is, that hit the side wall just behind him and forced him to turn. The hot pursuit was the key. I kept trying to get my racquet on one more ball than he wanted me to. Poor Charlie, it must be tough to be so big. To have to bend down so much to get to the ball. To have to lug all that apparatus around the court. To get those long arms and legs all twisted up when balls break into him. I felt big for being small, for I could scramble and recover from sticky situations in a way that he could not. I'd trade that for reach. Ah, squash, the small man's revenge!

So I won the first game 15–7 or 8. Nothing like a plan. Too bad I didn't learn how to play him before now. I wondered how the other semi would turn out.

Yes, it's so easy when you're winning. And when you're winning big you feel like you could never lose again. The only question in your mind is how you ever lost a match.

Game two, however, went a little differently. I continued to fast serve him and to get on top of the ball early. But I was feeling so good I started going for more and more shots. Feeling like I couldn't lose, I got a little too expansive and started showing off my repertoire, which included drops into the tin and corners that came out in the middle.

In that second game, I reverted to the old me. I once again tried to outshoot the shooter. But the thing was that whereas I was just willy-nilly popping sometime shots, he was maneuvering me out of position before attempting winners. And he was really rolling, sometimes wrong footing me with where-did-that-come-from? reverse corners, other times laying down drop shots that were snug along the wall.

People would say what a great shot maker. What a wrist. And that's what I would say, except when I was down in the court with him, where he would demonstrate to me that the point was usually pretty much over before he hit his finishing shot. He'd maneuver me out of position, drive me deep with cross-courts and rails, and then, and only then, would he hit his shot. He'd have me so out of it that he didn't have to cut it fine, just hit it firmly. Of course, every now and then he'd shoot from behind me, when I wasn't expecting it, and he'd counterpunch off my attempted winners if I left the ball hanging. That was the problem (for me) in the second game. Too often I was trying to win points with fancy shots, not with position. It was like I was out there practicing exhibition trick shots. I was playing the court, not my opponent. And my opponent was meanwhile outplaying me. He was also outbreathing me, but I had misjudged his conditioning and, if anything, he was getting to the ball more easily that second game. That's the thing about older players, carrying all those extra years, you'd expect them to get slower and slower, but sometimes it takes them a game or so to loosen up, particularly if it's the third or fourth match of the weekend. Charlie now appeared to be well warmed up, for he won the second game as decisively as I had won the first, and I was now less concerned with who might win the other semi.

Charlie's first concern during the two-minute break was to get his breathing back under control. Hyperventilating (or, if you like, panting) doesn't do any good. Those short, shallow breaths don't get any air into the system. That's what I'm told, and somebody must have told this to Charlie, too, for he would take a deep breath, hold it in for a while, then let it out slowly through lips that were pursed to regulate the flow of air. All the while, pacing the length of the court, very methodically, hands on hips.

As he got into a rhythm of long, deep breaths, with those lips puckered and eyes popping, he looked like he was trying to blow smoke rings, an art he was unlikely to have mastered. For like most (though not all) of the top squash players, he abstained from smoking. And that was pretty much the extent of the Ufford conditioning program.

Typical of the top amateurs of that era, he wasn't one for training. "I tried working out once, calisthenics and running laps, but it was so boring, I quit," he once told me. Since he didn't take pain in workouts, he took a lot of pain on the court, particularly as he got older. He would play himself into shape, or as good shape as he was going to get into. He once told me that every year toward the end of the summer, remembering all the fun of the game, the stroking, the strategy, the excitement of the points, he just can't wait to get back into the old squash court. It's not until he gets back into the court that he remembers all the pain and exhaustion that must be fought back in the course of a match. Over the summer he forgets about all that agony, but back in the pit, he wonders why he looked forward to the season with such sweet anticipation.

Unlike most players, Charlie would never leave the court between games. His theory, I believe, is if you leave the court your eyes will lose their adjustment to the bright light of the court, and this may hurt you in the first couple of points of the next game. There may be something to that, but I like the break of leaving the court, particularly if I've just lost a game.

But Charlie never varied his between games routine. Long after he'd gotten control of his breathing, he would continue to pace the court, hands still on hips, head tilted forward, lips still pursed. Those drawn lips suggested deep strategic contemplation, particularly since his eyes had a glazed over abstractedness, as if he were contemplating his next move on an imaginary chessboard beneath his nose.

That chess analogy is used often to explain squash and Charlie's game in particular. When not comparing the caroms off the walls to billiards, people are continually telling us that squash is really just like chess, because like chess, squash is an intricate game of position and maneuver in which both players attempt to gain control of the same space. And like chess, squash is a game for thinkers. "Physical chess" is the term that every journalist who does a feature on squash invents anew. And people are always saying that the savvy players, like Charlie, plan four or five moves ahead.

Well, it's true that Charlie did play a game of chess the night of the Calcutta Pool. And it's true he takes the cerebral approach to squash. But the chess analogy, in my opinion, doesn't really tell us much about the role of thought and strategy in squash.

For one thing, in squash, whether you realize it or not, you have to deal with the element of chance. In this regard it's like a game of skill that involves a roll of the dice or a deal of the cards. The point is that you can make any shot on the squash court, but some shots you're going to make with more regularity than others, just as you can roll any number from two to twelve, but a seven is more likely than a two or a twelve. In squash, as in gambling, anyone can have a hot streak, but only a skilled player can win consistently. The problem is that most people don't really understand that squash is a game of probabilities and percentages. When you roll dice and come up with "boxcars" or "snake eyes," you know damn well you had a one in a thirty-six chance of making it; you can look at the dice and see that each die has six sides, and each side has only one number on it. Unless you've loaded the dice or are a candidate for Gamblers Anonymous, when you get a favorable but unlikely roll you don't say to yourself, "how skillful of me." But in squash, when you get away with a drop shot hit half an inch above the tin, there's a natural tendency to congratulate yourself on your skill. And if it was a big point, everyone will be telling you what a great shot you hit, and you'll find yourself easily persuaded.

The smart players in squash know there's an element of luck involved, but they give luck a chance by playing the percentages. That's what Charlie would do; he was a marvelous gambler. They say that though chess requires more cerebration than backgammon, chess players sometimes make lousy backgammon players because they get flustered by not being able to control the dice. They come undone when they play it just right and then get beaten by a lucky roll. In squash you can play the point or even an entire game just right, and yet lose it because your opponent's dice are hot. Yet over the long run, it's better to know and play the percentages than to trust in lucky dice.

It's not that players like Charlie don't take chances. They do, but they take "calculated risks." They know that there's no such thing as a sure winner or a sure loser. Perhaps most importantly, they know when they've gotten away with a low percentage shot, and so they don't go to the well too often. If a lesser player gets away with one lucky shot, he often as not pays the price by missing six more.

Charlie also knows when he's tried the good percentage shot but happened to miss it. And so he has the courage to try it again, when the opportunity arises. Since he knows the percentages, he doesn't get sucked into "If he can make it, I can make it" dumb duels. He knows when his opponent is getting away with shots he won't get away with over the long run. To play squash, you have to learn to contend with the element of chance, and so, you have to learn to be an intelligent gambler. Because it's a game of chance and probabilities as well as position, I think squash is more like backgammon than chess.

The chess analogy also breaks down when you consider the

time factor. Or the lack of time. In chess you make your move and then punch a clock, and your opponent has x minutes to think. Not so in squash, which requires an almost instantaneous response. Much of the time in squash you're playing from habit and reflex. The thought that's involved goes not so much into the play as into developing the right habits and responses in practice. You can't think about hitting a reverse corner or a three-wall nick when the opening presents itself. You have to instantly see the opportunity and pop it so that it will be gone before your opponent (and even you) realizes what hit him. No time to consider all the options. If you think too much you'll fudge the shot from indecision or take too much time to let your opponent get back into position.

The essence of a putaway is that it's hit before your opponent can even consider its possibility. You can't stroke your chin while you consider various possibilities, you must stroke the ball.

This is why the notion that a great player "plans eight strokes ahead of his opponent" is nonsense. It doesn't work that way. What happens is you probe for openings, hitting the ball deep and mixing it up. You try to smoke your opponent out by putting pressure on him with your drives. It's like a base line exchange in tennis in which you move your opponent about, keeping him deep until he coughs up a short ball, which gives you an opportunity to follow it into the net. You can't tell when the opening is going to present itself, and when it does, you don't go through a complicated eight-shot sequence in putting the ball away. In squash, when you get the opportunity, you simply pop a short shot and cover the response. And if your opponent makes a good response, putting the ball safely back into play, the mature player will say, "OK, we start the point over." The immature player will figure that since he almost put the ball away he really deserves the point, and will try to put his opponent's response away whether or not there's an opening. The key is to recognize not only the openings, but also what's not an opening. Restraint. This you learn in practice and through coaching. By hitting the tin and asking yourself did I really have a good chance of making that shot.

Through trial and error you develop a feel for openings and percentages, just as you develop a feel for the racquet, the ball, and the play off the walls. The strategic thought in a match is not in pausing to consider each move, but in developing a simple overall plan, and in monitoring what's going on during the game in relation to that plan. You can decide how you're going to probe. (Against Charlie I was determined, as much as possible, to keep breaking the ball around him.) And you can resolve to look for opportunities to try a particular shot. But you can't know in advance when the opportunities will present themselves, and so you have to be alert to what's happening, rather than what you hope will happen if all goes according to plan. You plan several moves ahead only to the extent that you set patterns and then break them. You mesmerize your opponent by hitting three balls down the wall, then you fool him by slipping in a three-wall nick.

If you know who your opponent is in advance, you can practice a particular strategy and develop habits for that match, hitting more of one shot and less of another. But in the heat of play you have very limited control over your responses, and you are doing very well indeed, if you can keep one simple thought in mind. Under pressure squash is a game of reflex and habit, and you play pretty much the way you practice. During the play itself, squash is not a deliberative or contemplative game. A smart player is one who has thought things through at his leisure, and has, through work and practice, developed "smart habits," which he can trust in the heat of play. I don't know if it's true, but I once heard that Harry Hopman used to send his Australian Davis Cuppers into matches with instructions not to think. That's how well he prepared them in practice. Anyway, if you think too hard during a point, you'll fail to act on opportunities and will cripple your game.

Only between points in games does the deliberative chesslike thinking go on; and to the extent that thought plays a role, Charlie was thinking as he paced between games. I don't know what he was thinking, but he sure looked like he was thinking up something good.

Under Charlie's influence during those formative years, I became quite expert at looking like I was thinking hard between points and games. I developed mannerisms suggestive of deep strategic contemplation: much squinting of eyes and puffing of cheeks. And if I lost a game particularly badly, I'd make it a point while pacing during the breaks to cock my head suddenly, as if something brilliant had just occurred to me. (And sometimes something would occur to me, like the sudden realization that my opponent was left-handed.) My mannerisms may have been more effective than my actual thoughts, but this thinking that I was thinking helped me, for it gave me heart. More important than the strategy itself, perhaps, is the fact that you *have* a strategy, for that gives you hope. You fight harder when you have a plan.

And in this case, as much as anything, my plan was to keep

fighting. I resolved to quit trying to outshoot him and to get back to being that swarm of bees. That's all. And that heavy breathing of his was fanning my competitive fires. (In other words, I sensed he was tiring, and that's how I could get him.)

Indeed, he was tiring, and in the next game I could see him swatting away at those bees with more and more annoyance. But the thing I really liked about the start of this game was I'd finally calibrated my putaways against him so that they were not only safely out of his reach, but also safely above the tin. I wasn't cutting them any closer to the tin than I had to. The principle here is that you never want to hit a "better" shot than you have to. If you've got a setup on an overhead in tennis, the object is not to see how close you can put it to the tape, but to see how far in you can hit it and still put it comfortably out of reach. You're looking for the safest shot that gets the job done. Back to those percentages again; you don't want to assume any more risk than you have to. And part of taking the measure of your opponent is developing a feel for how far you have to have him out of position to try a short shot, and how high you can hit your corners and drops above the tin and still be able to put the ball away.

The past game, I had taken some dumb chances, but this game I was in the groove, hitting shots that were no better than they had to be. The best shot is the safest one that will get the job done.

But what I hadn't figured on was that Charlie could get taller on the big points. I got up 10–6ish, but once I hit double figures he made a couple of gets that I hadn't planned on, and left me standing there. The difficulty of playing an older player is that it's hard to tell just what he can or can't do. A young pup runs for everything, and you learn pretty early on in the match what he can get and what he can't, so you can adjust your margin above the tin accordingly. But the older players (and the out-of-shape younger ones) can surprise you. They save something for the big points. Early in the game you hit a couple of routine drop shots and they're nowhere near them. A big point comes along, you hit the same drop shot, and they not only get to it but counterpunch a winner off it. If you had known they could be that fast, you would have held off attempting a drop shot until you had them further out of position.

All top players get faster toward the end of the game, it's like the finishing short strokes in crew or the kick at the end of a foot race. But the older players who are still competitive tend to speed up the most, relatively speaking, because they've been saving it up. The well-conditioned player keeps the pressure on by putting out on every point, trying to make every point a challenge for his opponent, conceding him nothing—and that's squash at its best. But the older players can't put out all the time. They take breathers. They refuse to run for some drop shots. You're looking for them to run out of gas, and when they don't run for a few shots, you think they're gone. But they're not. You get lulled into a false sense of security.

The thing about older players covering the court is that it's not that they don't make sensational gets, they just don't make as many of them as they used to. But the ones they do make tend to come at the wrong time, like when you're playing for the game.

I had thought Charlie was gone, but he wasn't. Sure, he was tired, but he still had a few gets left in him. And he wanted this third game. Seeing him convert two points off a couple of short balls that I had thought were put away, I panicked. I could feel him coming, and I lost my head for a moment. Instead of settling down to play tough end-of-the-game squash, I went for a couple of cheap winners that ticked the top of the tin.

He caught me at 11 all and now, though the score was dead even, the momentum he had developed was the cue for the underdog to lay down and play dead. We all knew he was supposed to win, and now it looked like the number one seed had decided to take control of the match. That's how I felt, but again, I reminded myself of the plan, and decided if I was going to go down, I was going to go down the right way. I blocked out everything else and became that swarm of bees again: thwap, thwap, thwap. Break it around him, make those gets. A cross-court nicks, and I've got the point. He tips the tin on a drop shot he wasn't set up for, and I have another point. A fast serve catches the crease and rolls unplayable 14-11. I hit a screamer down the rail and the third game is mine.

To be honest, maybe those weren't the exact shots, but it was something like that. I regained the momentum, not by pulling a "psych," as I had against Maurice, but by remembering the plan, which is the way mature players do it. (Anyway, can you imagine anyone having the gall to try gamesmanship on Charlie Ufford?)

Winning that third game gave me confidence, not just because it put me up 2-1, but also because I had stood off Charlie's challenge. He wanted that game, but I got it.

"Many is the expatriate, walking the streets of London barefoot, who had Charlie Ufford down 2-1 and lost." That's what someone had once told me about Ufford's capacity to come back. He's basically a slow starter and not infrequently he'd seemingly get himself in a little trouble for the pleasure of getting out of it.

It was tough to keep this warning in mind, for having won that third game, I felt like I'd won the match. Charlie stayed in the court, for some more pacing and puffing. I left for a sip of water, and, more importantly, to catch my breath out of his hearing. I'd gotten winded, too, at the end of that game, but I didn't want him to know this. I wanted him to think of me as brimming over with energy.

I saw Barnaby in the locker room, and for once he was a welcome sight at the 2-1 break. So often before, he had been waiting to drape a coach's arm over my opponent's shoulder. I asked him what now; he said the key was to get a fast start, to beat him to 5, and make him work very hard in the early points so he'd feel it was an awfully long way home.

The start of the fourth game I was a veritable hornet's nest. I beat him 5-1 or 2, on earned points—tough rallies where I was on him the whole time, working us both very hard. Then I got into one of those moods where I couldn't miss. I say I couldn't miss, but I had nothing to do with it. It was my racquet that couldn't miss and I just happened to be holding it. Like a divining rod, my racquet had a will of its own and insisted on pulling me along. Why fight it? It was taking me to the gold.

When you get hot like this, you don't think, you don't direct or control. You don't ask questions. If you do, you'll snap out of it. You just let your racquet take you where it's going to take you. The worst thing you can do when you've got a streak going is to think about keeping it going. You have to just let it happen.

Nor can you plan a hot streak in advance. You can't go in the court resolved to play "out of your mind." No, you start off very much within your mind. You develop a plan. And you work at putting it into effect. If it does work, sometimes you find that everything else starts working, and you could be out there hitting the ball blindfolded with a Coke bottle and still be putting it away.

I got myself up and Charlie down with that swarm of bees routine. The hot streak at the end was a celebration. So it looked like I'd be wearing shoes stateside, for the time being, anyway, for this time Ufford did not come back, and the last game was a rout.

Ever the gentleman, though tired and not pleased with himself, he gave me that Big Smile and what seemed to be an extra congratulations, as if taking a little personal pleasure in the fact that after all these tries, the kid was finally able to break through. That's what he communicated in the handshake, though there had been no evidence that he was pulling for me until after the last point, and for that matter, I don't recall him whistling in the locker room afterward either.

That afternoon, I played for the title against Ralph Howe. Correction, he played for the title—it was the only major one he hadn't won—and I was just happy to be out there in the finals of a major tournament, playing against Ralph Howe. Ralph was not seeded first only because the year before he hadn't played enough tournaments to qualify for a ranking.

I had no plan for Ralph. No plans in this tournament beyond Ufford. Beating Ralph, who had always cleaned me in the past, seemed out of the question. I just hoped to avoid embarrassment, particularly when I found the gallery was as packed as any I'd ever seen—seen from the court, that is.

I had never really gotten my act together against Ralph. The first time I played him, you may recall, was that intercollegiate match in which, as a young sophomore, I whiffed his first three serves, and they were slow ones at that. The several times we had played since then, I was yet to get a game.

But this time there was improvement. He won the first game, but I got the second. And the third game came down to 1 point. Then I regressed. I got so excited on game point that I fanned a routine cross-court. What happened was I let it get by me, and by the time I got a swing off, it was no longer there. What happened was I choked. I couldn't believe I could go ahead against Ralph Howe. (And he didn't believe it either, for earlier in that same point he had stretched out to make a sensational get off a drop shot I'd hit to get the damn point over with, one way or another.)

But I resumed putting on a good show by winning the next game to tie it up. Not bad, thought I, getting into a fifth game against Ralph Howe. And not bad, thought he, winning that game to finally capture the one major championship that had eluded him.

After the match, there was a small reception for a presentation of trophies. Barnaby gave me mine, and in addressing the group he said that beating Ufford and getting into the finals of this event meant I had now entered the ranks of the big boys, and he welcomed me into the "Hall of Fame." The "Hall of Fame" is a heading on the back page of the Cowles program under which is listed, each year, the previous finalists in this event.

And when the champagne started to flow (out of the silver chalice, the permanent trophy that was filled to the brim and passed around communion style so we could all dip our noses in what I guessed was the blood of Harry Cowles), Germain Glidden, a Cowles disciple of the thirties, who won his first of three national men's titles while still an undergraduate and later founded this event in Cowles's memory, told the congregation he thought I had the makings of a national champion. I took that with a squeeze of grape.

Glidden had pulled me aside earlier, right after the match, and given me a little pep talk, that I appreciated but didn't really understand at the time. He said I had all the equipment, I could run, I could hit, I'd proved that, but I lacked one thing. I lacked belief in myself. Against Ralph, I had backed off in the big points. If I was going to be a champion, I'd have to believe I was the best.

Champion? I was thrilled to be functioning at this new level. Thrilled to have been in the finals. To have had people bidding for the right to choose me in the Calcutta Pool. To know that from now on, every year, my name would be printed up on the back of that program, a reminder that I'd once been in the finals of a major championship.

I was no longer a dangler on the circuit but a serious entry. I didn't know if I could be a major player, but I now knew that at least I could beat one.

Chapter 5
THE NEW YORK GAME

"Niederhoffer Out to Make a Comeback"

My New York friends on the circuit talked about how New York really toughens you up. Not only because there are a lot of good players, but also because it's a tough league.

I became a believer my first match. My opponent's name wasn't Hyde, but Mr. Hyde readily identifies him. To set the scene, it was a Tuesday night, the night for A league matches, and I was representing the Princeton Club in my first A league match. I was curious, but not really super up for this match. I was still getting over the weekend before. I had had a double match point on Sam Howe (older brother of Ralph and two-time national champion) at the White.* Sam went on to win the tournament and I went on to a certain celebrity because *The New York Times* used my near miss as the headline for their coverage of the event.

By Tuesday I had gotten over the disappointment of having lost and was enjoying the fact that I had come so close against such a highly regarded player. (No real competitor would enjoy a loss that much, so that was a clue to my frame of mind as a competitor at the time.)

I felt like the press had paved the way for my grand entrance into the New York league and wondered if my opponent had read that piece on my "impressive loss." If he had, he didn't let on when we introduced ourselves. We had never seen each other, but I was

---

*The William F. White Memorial, a major invitational tournament, held at the Merion Cricket Club in memory of Whitey.

sure he must at least know who I was from my number seven national ranking, and his reputation had certainly preceded him.

Mr. Hyde was a notoriously bad actor on the court. He set the standard, so to speak, for bad acting. People who had never seen him play would snort at the mention of his name and judge poor performances on their level of Hydeness. Everyone agreed his behavior was terrible, bad for the game. And everyone wanted to know when he had a tough match coming up. As one New York wag once explained it to me, going to see a Hyde match was like going to the Indianapolis 500 to see a car crash. There was that sort of excitement in the air. His matches, alas, were all too few, because over the years he had been banned from practically every tournament. Banned from the circuit, perhaps, but not from the New York league.

Upon learning who my first opponent in the New York league would be, I had given Jay Nelson a call for a briefing. Jay was a friend from the circuit who played for the Harvard Club. With his wry sense of humor I knew he would enjoy hearing I was about to have "baptism by Hyde," as I put it.

Jay agreed that it was a very appropriate introduction to the tough New York league. I asked him just what to expect and how I should play Hyde. (Camaraderie on the circuit transcends interclub team rivalries.)

He pointed out that actually Hyde is a good guy, he just gets freaky on the court, that's all. The bird gets out of the cage now and then. But he said that since I was a much stronger player than Hyde, his antics shouldn't get to me. In fact, I would probably enjoy the match because he's such a character. That's the best way to approach it, just stay above it all and enjoy him as a character. Jay didn't want to spoil it for me by telling me some of the stunts Hyde pulls, but wanted me to let him know how it went.

This was a big moment for me. Over the years, the pro at the Princeton Club and various team members had been asking me when I was going to move to New York and come play for them. Now, finally, I had finished my residency requirement and course work for a doctorate at Yale, and was free to live in New York while I worked on my thesis.

I indicated my availability and was given the number one spot on the Princeton Club team without a challenge. I felt like a big deal until I showed up for the match. It was an away match, but it wasn't like showing up at a host club for a weekend tournament. There, a succession of people greet and look after you, you are their special guest for a special weekend. But here, it was 5:30 Tuesday night and everyone was rushing about looking after himself and nobody was particularly interested in my arrival, except as it represented a threat to his court. Since the courts for team matches were blocked off, not assigned, it was first come, first served.

To be fair, when I found Hyde, he was most genial. In fact, all this affability was hard to square with the legend, though Jay had said he's a nice guy, off the court. But once the little door was closed behind us, the four white walls started to have their effect. You could see it in his face. He started to get twitchy, with a Tony Perkins/Bruce Dern nervous, psychotic look.

Nevertheless, at the conclusion of the warm-up, I was still able to get through to him. I inquired whether he wanted to play it as a point or a let if he hit me with a ball that was going directly to the front wall.

"Let," he grunted. Not an eloquent response, but reassuring, nevertheless, for it suggested he at least wouldn't be looking to hit me with the ball.

And so the match began. Presumably it was the calm before the storm, for nothing much happened. I was feeling my way through, keeping my distance physically, and psychologically. He wasn't much for clearing—that is, getting out of the way—when it was my turn to hit, but I was a much better player and I wasn't going to let his crowding bother me. What concerned me more than the closeness of my opponent was the closeness of the court. It was like a sweatbox in there. Unlike suburban courts, these were on an upper story, and heat rises. Furthermore, the courts were enclosed in the building, and the ventilation was not good. This meant that points wouldn't be won by Fancy Dannery but by toughing them out. It wasn't the kind of court I was at home in, but then again if it was a matter of toughness, he was no Jack LaLanne. He had two builds, really. The top half was middle-aged, out of shape. Narrow shoulders, a nothing chest, and a potbelly. All of which went well with his pasty face and suggested nicotine stains on his fingers, though I didn't see any. You wouldn't give him much of a chance if it weren't for two very long and strong quartermiler's legs that made up the other half, or I should say three-quarters, of his body. Anyway, midway through the first game he was already puffing. Well, what else to expect from someone in his late thirties?

I, meanwhile, was tiptoeing around, watching him more than the match. He was a little ahead in the score, but so long as I didn't let him get too far ahead I figured I could turn it on toward the end of the game. But about two-thirds through the game, he missed a setup and #%&! (He said a very naughty word.) It wasn't the word itself that jolted me, though I was accustomed to playing in the presence of women, where such language was less in use. No, what threw me for a second was the sight and sound of it. His body convulsed as if he were sneezing but what came out was a very loud, adenoidal groan, suggesting a speech impediment, though he had no problem suggesting what was on his mind.

OK, so that's it. He has a foul mouth and a temper. Fine. I can handle that. In fact, I like that. I take it as a cue to really turn the pressure on. So I stepped up the pace and in the process leaned into a three-wall shot that didn't nick, it rolled.

The shot left Hyde at the back of the court. But not at a loss for words. For he turned to me and emoted, "Are you going to do that (expletive deleted) shot all day?" And lest there be any doubt as to what (expletive deleted) shot he was referring to, he threw his racquet to the exact spot where the ball had caught the crack, albeit three-quarters of the court away. Now a less accomplished racquet thrower might have missed his mark and most likely would have busted the head of his racquet in the process, but Hyde, despite the violence of his windup, let the racquet go with a deft underhand shuffleboard motion so that it slid safely to its target.

I, as you may have surmised, was not ready with an answer to his question. But he indicated that his query was merely rhetorical in intent by turning his back on me and, hands on hips, wandering to the front of the court to retrieve his racquet. When he finally returned, he won the last 5 points of the first game.

Round two went better for me. Hyde was now fully warmed up, alternately swearing at himself and swearing at my shots, but I was used to that by now, and, as Jay had said, I was a better player, and so I took this game fairly easily.

The third game was a battle. It shouldn't have been, but figuring I had the match under control, instead of pressing home the attack, I let up a bit at the start and let myself fall behind a bit in the score.

Remembering that I didn't want to be down 2-1 at the break, I dug in at 3-8 or thereabouts. It was about this time I realized that Hyde didn't have such a bad game. He was not fluid, but he cut a lot of balls off with leggy lunges. And he had a major league reverse corner that he could get to sit down even on this court.

He had the right squash instincts in his play, he was also a magna cum grad of the Hit 'n Stand School. If he hit a bad shot, he'd cover it by not moving out of the way, forcing you to call a let or hit him with the ball. Let points are not awarded in unrefereed matches, and a ball that hit him on the way to the front, was, as we had agreed before, a let.

I couldn't bring myself to exercise a little frontier justice—that is, really nail him with the ball once—but I did give him a few "love pats" with the ball, which he took in stride and rather seemed to expect. He apparently preferred taking the pain to losing the point. (I later learned that in most league matches, you win the point if you hit someone with the ball that was headed directly for the front wall. Hyde hadn't told me this.)

I caught him at 12 all. The next point, he hit a corner that was gone, but not quite. Somehow I got my racquet on it and flipped it to the front wall, a save that left him standing there.

"What about that get?" he yelled.

And that's where I made my mistake. I was sure I'd gotten it, but instead of answering, "Yes, which side an I serving on?" thereby changing the topic and thus closing the debate, I said, "I thought it was up, but do you want to play it over?"

Not knowing how else to handle this character, I had locked myself into my mechanical gentleman mode—the mode one uses with assigned roommates one can't stand, as a way of avoiding the unpleasantness of a confrontation. And Jay had suggested I keep my distance.

Hyde seemed surprised at my offer, but he didn't turn it down either. I later learned from other Hyde victims that when he asks, "What about that shot?" he isn't so much questioning that get as trying to come to terms with the fact that you made it. A compliment, really. We played it over. He won the replayed point and the next 2 points for the game.

He was gone in the fourth game. The ten minutes he took at the five-minute break were not enough to revive him, and after contesting the first few points, he permitted me to serve out the game. Which brought us to the fifth.

The one thing harder than coming back from a game you've lost 15-2 is keeping the momentum going after you've won a game 15-2, particularly in situations where your opponent has simply let the game go. You quickly forget what it takes to earn a point. You get accustomed to no resistance, but you can bet your opponent will try to get something going at the start of the next game, and when he gets back up on his feet and starts swinging again, it always comes as something of a shock and may take a few precious points to get readjusted to it.

Hyde picked up a lead and held on to it for a while. The match was getting a little messy. More shots out in the middle, more lets. And the floor was covered with "sweat spots"—little puddles of sweat that looked like mini-mirages but were very real when you slipped on one of them. Ordinarily I would have pressed for a time out with towels to mop the floor, but I could see he was getting punchy from the exertion, so I wanted to keep things moving.

I caught him at 10 all and got him into a long point, which he lost and acknowledged by throwing down his racquet, walking up to the front, and sitting down with his back propped up against the front wall and his legs spread-eagled. He then started mumbling somewhat incoherently about what a tough point that was, and punctuated his discourse by blowing his nose on the front of his shirt.

I meanwhile was standing at the service box, impatiently bouncing the ball on the floor. I was trying to let him know that "Play shall be continuous," but I wasn't really getting through to him.

I later learned from other Hyde fans that a better way to drive the point home in this situation is to start banging the ball against the front wall, each time hitting the ball a little harder and a little closer to him so that you end up etching his figure like the dagger thrower in a circus would. A minority opinion is that he likes to play chicken with you when you do this, and this only delays him.

I have no idea what made him finally get up and resume play, but I assure you he did; otherwise I wouldn't have lost the next few points and the match.

He opened the door to the court and gallantly insisted that I leave first. He plied me with drinks, and with a wink and a nudge he confided, "Gee, I really enjoyed that match," as he dashed off to make the 7:17.

I waited around afterward for a while, but there was no voice from the wall telling me to "Smile, you're on 'Candid Camera.'"

Hyde proved to be atypical, but only in his excesses, for New York squash is "hot court squash." And I don't mean that just in the sense of the courts being hot, though certainly on the average they

are ten to twenty degrees hotter than most suburban courts. Whatever the reason or reasons, New York matches have a tendency to
heat up. The ball heats up like a mad bee and so do the players.
And it starts getting a little crazy. You can't put the ball away. A
corner shot is a joke, a drop shot hangs, and everything else comes
off the back wall or breaks into the middle. And when the play gets
sloppy, every fifth hit is a let; you may not think it's a let, but
when there's no referee, if your opponent asks for a let, you're
supposed to give him a let, not lip. Supposed to, but sometimes
these matches get a little out of control. New York squash is *mano
a mano*. You may not be facing each other and circling, but you're
wrestling for the T nevertheless.

It's a head-to-head confrontation. Whereas the Merion players
make a game of ignoring their opponent's presence, the New York-
ers don't. In the New York game there's no pretense of trying to do
anything but beat your opponent.

If the courts are like pressure cookers, so is New York in general. New York is rush, rush, compete, compete. And, as any visitor
to New York can tell you, you have to look out for yourself just to
get around, much less to get ahead. There's the jostling for space in
subways, particularly during "crush" hour. The traffic lights are set
faster than any other place I know of, which means you don't
really have time to look for little old ladies to help across the street.
Take a ride in a cab and you feel like you're a passenger in a
demolition derby. The density and intensity of the place are not
conducive to a leisurely game of squash. Court bookings are for
thirty minutes rather than the forty or forty-five minutes you'll
find most everywhere else. And the second that time's up, the frenetic tapping of racquet heads on court doors is enough to make a
woodpecker reach for an aspirin.

Opponents arrive seconds before they're due on court and leave
still toweling off from their shower, to return to their office or make
their commuter train or catch a curtain call or whatever it is
they're rushing off to.

But it's not just that the courts are hot and everyone's on edge,
it's also the kind of person that New York attracts that makes New
York's "hot court squash" hot. New York attracts people who are
aggressive, who like to compete and like to win. One top New York
player, who took the game up in his late twenties, explained it to
me this way, "I knew how to win in other games before I took up
squash, so for me learning squash was mostly a matter of learning
how to apply that skill to this game."

There's no one style in New York in terms of strokes and strategy. There's a diversity of players. In the A league you come up against hotshot graduates of just about every college team, and the rest have worked their way up through the D, C, and B leagues. Each club pro has his own system. The need to compete is the common denominator.

And more competition was what I wanted. Before moving to New York in '72, I had been moving back and forth between New Haven and Washington, alternately slugging my way through a PhD program in organizational behavior at Yale's Department of Administrative Sciences (now called the School of Organization and Management) and taking on various jobs with the Federal government, including a two-year stint with the National Institute of Mental Health and several consulting assignments with the Cost of Living Council.

In New Haven and in Washington there was no one who could really push me, so when I practiced I had to "invent competition." I played players back-to-back to get tougher workouts. The best back-to-back competition around was provided by the Sadler brothers, Fred and Blair, who were identical twins. They weren't joined at the back, mind you, but they were so identical I'm convinced they got up in the morning and shaved looking at each other. The great thing about practicing against them was that they never seemed to get tired. That was because they could sub for one another and you wouldn't know it. A possibility, incidentally, that cast a double shadow of suspicion over their tournament victories.

Doctor Fred and lawyer Blair, who off the court teamed up to work on health policy issues, happened to be in Washington and New Haven the same times I was, and so they were my sparring mates for a number of years. They were excellent players, both on the fringe of a national ranking, but I had a little more oomph. While at Yale, I also worked out with the team, but again I had the edge, and it's no good always practicing against people you know you can beat if you turn it on. What you end up doing is sinking to their level and beating them by 2 points in the fifth.

In both Washington and New Haven there were also some excellent veterans and some not bad A players. Sometimes I would try to make matches more exciting by spotting my opponents points. This makes for a more exciting workout. But unlike handicapping in golf, handicapping in squash never really works. You can make it a close match in terms of the scores, but you can't improve the points. You can't improve the quality of the play. Points in squash are too interactive; you play off each other's shots. If you're a better player, you overwhelm your opponent and he sends back feeble responses. A vet or a lesser player can't make you play a series of long tough points. They don't give you the feedback you need to calibrate your game, so in these workouts you have to keep asking yourself, "Was that putaway really a putaway or just a putaway against this fellow?" It's hard to pretend that your opponent is tougher than you know he is. If you try to prolong points by not putting the ball away, all you end up doing is practicing sloppy shots.

I didn't become a "contender" until I moved to New York. Prior to that I had sort of leveled off as a second-echelon player. I was consistently in the top ten in the national rankings, but always in the second five. I was what the British would call a "useful" player. I was also frustrated. I had my moments—good showings against top fivers, flashes of potential, and occasional spectacular victories. But no less occasional were my "bad losses"—losses to clearly inferior players.

I needed toughening up. I was known for terrible lapses of concentration and had difficulty playing three hard games in succession. Though I played on the circuit, I wasn't really "match tough." New York remedied that.

Over the years New York's contribution to championship squash has been to toughen people up. With no strong squash at local colleges and, until recently, no junior development programs in the area, New York has never had a homegrown champion. But there have been a number of national champions and contenders who didn't fulfill their promise until after a couple of seasons in New York. The majority of New York's great squash players have been graduates of the "Harvard University School of Squash," beginning with W. Palmer Dixon, who won the national title playing out of New York in 1926. He, in fact, had won his first national title the year before while a senior at Harvard. He led a parade of Cowles's alumni who, upon graduating from Harvard's championship teams, decided to take up residence in New York and thereafter seemed to trade the national title back and forth throughout most of the thirties. Previous to this influx of Cowles's players to New York, Philadelphia had pretty much had a lock on the national title. But the construction of a number of courts in the men's clubs of New York in the mid-twenties,* followed by the accomplishments of Cowles's graduates, established New York as a serious squash (racquets) town.

Since then, New York, Philadelphia, and Boston have vied for top honors, with the squash fortunes of each city periodically rising and falling. Philadelphia reasserted itself in the forties and fifties, mainly because of the strong junior development program established by Whitey at Merion. Boston, always strong because of the number of Harvard graduates who live there, would now and then be heard from when a Harvard student or recent grad would get hot and be in contention for the national title. But New York, which I would guess has always had the toughest league play because of the nature of the place and the people it attracts, has had to depend upon its job market for its top squash. Sometimes several top players happen to be in New York because their work careers have taken them there,† and at these times New York has been overwhelming on the national scene.

One of these times was '72. That year New York swept the nationals, taking the singles, team, veteran, and senior titles. New York was the place to be for a squash player; it had become the capital of U.S. squash.

In New York I found I no longer had to "invent competition." There were a dozen or so good practice opponents around. They weren't all potential national champions, but the variety of styles, temperaments, and courts kept you alert. And for the first time in my squash career I had the opportunity to play practice games against the very best players. This meant that now, when I played these men for real, I felt at home with them in the court and didn't have to waste points in matches adjusting to the tempo of top play.

---

*Although a squash racquets court was built in the 1890s in the old clubhouse of the Racquet and Tennis Club, for some reason squash tennis caught on before squash racquets did at the clubs in and around New York. It was solidly entrenched until the mid-twenties, when several prominent squash tennis players became convinced that squash racquets was the better of the two games and persuaded their clubs to install the two-foot wider squash racquets court. There's no one quite as zealous as a convert, and Arthur Lockett, who was a leader of this movement, not only got his University Club switched over to squash racquets, but in 1925 he also donated a trophy bearing his name, for intercity team matches with Philadelphia and Boston.
† And sometimes they happen to find careers in New York because of squash connections there.

And in New York—what with city and state championships,
Lockett Cup tri-city team matches, and league play—there's ample
opportunity to play the top players for real. But one should not
conclude from this account that the squash competition occurs
only on the court. Indeed, a good deal of maneuvering for position,
I learned, occurs off the court.

Before league play can happen, players have to get themselves
sorted out—into the various clubs and onto the appropriate ladders. The most likely starting point in the precommercial club era
was the college club. The Harvard Club, the Princeton Club, the
Yale Club, the Columbia Club, the Dartmouth Club—they all have
squash programs. Players who lack the necessary college affiliation
might start off at the Seventh Regiment Armory, which has a couple of courts and has teams entered in all the leagues. A squash
record, not a military one, is what gets you in there. In addition to
these, there are a number of more exclusive clubs that offer squash
programs. Clubs that ascend into higher Waspdom, a pecking order
of Jewish clubs, and an Irish club that calls itself an athletic club.
These clubs have waiting lists.

In finding the right first club, and in later deciding whether or
not to "trade up," a number of factors are considered: the location
of the club, physical and social; the size of the initiation fee; the
dues for your age bracket; the court fees. Do you like the way the
courts play? Are the courts overloaded? How good is the pro, as a
player and as a teacher? And how good are the other players there
to practice with? Also to be considered is the not incidental question of whether or not you can get into the club in the first place,
and if so, how long it will take. Good squash players are frequently
jumped to the top of waiting lists, and, if they're interested in such
things, as a rule, they can get into one better club than they might
ordinarily be able to, if they were not good players.

The serious players look at all the above factors, but quietly
and to themselves they ask the real question: can they get a good
position on the club's team. In my case, along with six or seven of
the other top players in the city, it was imperative to be number
one on an A team. A season at number two would be a season of
second-best competition. Not everyone is looking to be number
one, but everyone who is interested in league play is looking at the
probable lineups at the different clubs to see where he might fit in.

So, finding the right club involves a lot of jockeying for position. But the really fancy footwork, I must say, is displayed in

"playing the ladder." The amount of sea-lawyering that goes on concerning ladders for league play never ceases to amuse me. (It probably would have ceased to amuse me long ago if I hadn't had a safe number one spot on the Princeton Club ladder.)

As a rule, people seem more interested in challenging up than in accepting a challenge from below. A friend of mine insists that one of his teammates likes to use the following ploy to avoid challenges from below. When a person who is below him on the ladder calls him at his office to request a challenge, he has his secretary put the man on hold, and he immediately gives the person above him a call to offer a challenge. He then takes the call from the person below him and says he's awfully sorry, but he has already scheduled a challenge with the man above him, so he can't accept the challenge below him. The counterploy is to offer this man a challenge in the presence of the man above him so he can't fudge. Which sometimes means finding out when they are playing a challenge match and waiting outside the door to the court, like someone trying to serve a subpoena.

The key to a well-run ladder is to have simple rules that are well posted and well enforced by the team captain or the club pro. The Exeter ladder was the best one I've ever seen. If you won your challenge match, you automatically challenged up the next time. If you lost, you had to accept a challenge from below, and there was no possibility of talking your way out of it. Ladders that permit you to challenge two spots ahead, and which don't force you to play down if you lose, give a lot of scope to the fast talker. Another nice thing about the Exeter ladder was that challenge matches were scheduled by Bennett twice a week, which meant there was a lot of action, and there was no quibbling over the date. Obviously, in New York people are too busy to play challenge matches twice a week, and business trips and responsibilities make it impractical to set a rigid schedule for challenge matches. But it's not unreasonable to make it a rule that if you lose a challenge match, you must accept a challenge from below and win it before you can challenge up again. A rule like that would reward fancy footwork on the court rather than off.

When you don't have simple rules that are well posted and well enforced, people are permitted to entertain very peculiar notions about how a ladder works. I recently heard about a person who accepted a challenge match over the phone, showed up at the agreed-upon time, played the match and lost the match, but then refused to swap places on the ladder because the challenger had neglected to say the magic words "I challenge you" just before the beginning of the match. An argument apparently ensued.

The big challenge for me was the league. After that less than promising start against Hyde, I was determined that I would suffer no more "bad losses." As it turned out, I did better than that, for I went undefeated at number one for the next year and a half, and I didn't skip any matches, which meant I had a couple of good wins in there as well. At the end of the 1972-73 season I won the cup for the best individual record in the A league, an accomplishment I was particularly proud of because it meant I had finally licked my concentration problem. Training myself to concentrate on my match midst all the Tuesday night distractions—the competition to get a court, the differences of opinion that must be resolved without a referee, and so on—made it that much easier for me to keep my mind on the business at hand when playing in weekend tournaments, and it's no coincidence that from here on out I never again lost to anyone below the top three or four amateurs in the game.

I had learned to always win the matches I should always win. The problem, of course, with matches you figure are no problem is that it's tough to get "up" for them. There's the temptation to show up at the club just before you're due on the court with other things on your mind; this can cost you the first game, no matter who you're playing. Or worse, you hang around the courts watching everyone else's match, which tires your eyes and can drain you emotionally, so much so that by the time you take to the court you feel like you've just played a couple of matches.

You can't get "psyched up" for every match, but you can force yourself to go through your prematch preparations before every outing. There's no one best way to get ready for a match, everyone has to find what works best for him. But the two things you want to happen are that physically, you are well on your way to being warmed up before you begin the official warm-up with your opponent, and, mentally, you are focused on the business at hand.

With respect to the physical, you obviously don't want to start your match already tired because of too much warming up, but players tend to err on the side of too little warming up. I know I did. Thinking I was saving myself, I would try to conserve energy during the warm-up with the result that I would get a slow start, and then end up having to work twice as hard to catch up. But then a squash-playing doctor, who seemed to know what he was talking about, told me that an energetic warm-up is important because your muscles don't perform efficiently until your body heats up a couple of degrees. So now, before I go on the court, I not only do some leg stretches (to prevent injury) but also some light calisthenics and a little running and/or hopping about to get my body going. I also like to hit by myself for five or ten minutes, about fifteen minutes before I'm due to start my match; this is something that most of the tournament players do.

You can't always get a free court to warm up in, particularly when you're playing a league match, but when you play a match without a referee you can take as much time as you want to warm up.* And you should. It's particularly important to take plenty of time warming up for a league match, because the chances are you had to rush to get to the courts and had a lot of other things on your mind when you got there. So you need a little extra time to focus in on the match.

A game of squash, no doubt, can be a cathartic release for job and city tensions, and as one squash widow once told me, she doesn't resent the time her husband spends away from the family to play squash because "Man who beats little rubber ball is kind to wife and children."† But to compete effectively, you must be composed.

On the other hand, there is such a thing as being too composed. Jim Fuchs, a former world record holder in the shot put, who plays squash for the Yale Club, once took a couple of pills for a headache before one of his matches. The headache cleared up all right, but he felt strangely sluggish throughout the match and very slow off the mark, which was unusual for a former fullback who could run a 9.6 100-yard dash. After this less than successful match, he took a more careful look at the label to see what was in these pills and discovered that he'd taken a couple of sleeping pills by mistake. It's one thing to be composed, quite another to be "COMPOZed."

The way to make easy matches easy is to get off to a good start. If you break your opponent early, then everything else fits into place and the match becomes a playful romp—for you, that is.

---

* Referees, on the other hand, usually hold you to the official five minutes.
† That was before the courts opened up to women in New York. These days she's got her husband saying, "Woman who beats little rubber ball . . ."

Consider the alternative. You take it easy at the beginning of the match, figuring you can always catch up if you fall behind. But when you do fall behind, you begin worrying about losing more points, and "bad loss psychology" starts taking over. Instead of playing to win, you are playing not to lose. Whereas you should be on the offensive, running your opponent all over the court, you're now afraid to try any shots. You start slugging or go into a defensive shell; either way you limit the effectiveness of your game. Meanwhile, your opponent, who originally was just hoping not to be embarrassed, smells an upset and is playing the match of his life. He starts making shots he doesn't ordinarily make, you stop making the shots you ordinarily make, and the whole thing gets worse and worse, from your point of view.

The key is to take charge right from the start. I don't have a game plan for every match. Against opponents I figure I should beat pretty handily, unless they have an outstanding strength or weakness, I don't try to play them any special way to put them off. Instead, I try to impose my game, on the assumption I can overwhelm them with my normal game as long as I keep the pressure on. The way I keep the pressure on is to keep reminding myself, "Position, Patterns, Pace."

Position. Am I out front, controlling the T?

Patterns. Am I moving my opponent around, making him "cover the diagonal" with rails and three-walls, drops and drives? Sometimes when I lose my bearings in a rally or a game, I start chanting to myself, "Length, length, length," to try to regain control and set up my short game.

Pace. Am I taking the ball early, cutting down my opponent's reaction time? Always pressing forward, leaning into my shots?

In a game of quick reactions, which is what squash is, I've learned you just can't loaf, even against clearly inferior players. If you let up just a little bit, say 5 percent, it can make a 50 percent difference in the score. That little extra time that you give your opponent is all he needs to look like a squash player. If you're not quick to the ball, you're quick to the showers.

These are the things I try to think about when I'm playing what's meant to be an easy match. It also helps to remember that the more trivial the match seems to me, the bigger the event it is for my opponent. And the better you get, the bigger the prize you become. A few years back, when Charlie Ufford was still at the height of his game, a worthy but routine A player caught him napping in a league match and toppled the gentle giant. Charlie was soon back on his feet, and I daresay had forgotten the match by the time he reached home that evening. This, after all, was only a league match. But his victor was so pleased with himself he went out and bought himself a trophy and had it engraved to mark the occasion. Which just goes to show that anyone who is willing to pay the price can get a trophy.

Clubs, ladders, leagues, tournaments—with all this competition, the New York squash scene wouldn't be complete without the return of Mr. Competition himself, Mr. Victor Niederhoffer.

Vic obliged in the fall of '71, when he took a term off from teaching at the business school at Berkeley so that he could put more time into the New York office of a financial consulting business he'd started several years back.

He joined the Harvard Club of New York, and the word passed that Niederhoffer was out to make a comeback. What made his comeback attempt so interesting was that the squash world already had a champion. Just as Vic had put the whammy on the competition during his championship season in 1967, Anil Nayar, also of Harvard, though by way of India, had totally dominated the field the past few years. Based in Boston, Anil had had to sit out most of the previous season because he had wrenched his knee skiing over Christmas, but the two years before that he had won everything, and had reduced the competition to measuring itself in terms of how close it could come to him before losing. Now, in the fall of 1971, he was reported to be fully recovered from that skiing mishap.

The "Bombay Bomber" could crack the ball so hard his drives sounded like cherry bombs. Yet he was just a little fellow. 5'8; 140-ish with arms the diameter of a garden hose. He used a very un-Harvard high windup to hit the usual Harvard three-walls and drops into the nick. But he also had his own specialty, "the short kill," a forehand cross-court driven into the nick about 6 feet from the front wall. It was so fast and unexpected, and such a complete winner when it rolled out of the nick, it made everyone smile when he did it, everyone except his opponent.

To say, as many people did, he was fast on his feet was to miss the point, for what he had was the ability to get to most balls without running. The way most people get to balls easily is by controlling the T, but Anil never contested the T and seemed perfectly content to hang back in the court a bit. He seemed to watch his opponent very carefully and never commit himself until he knew exactly where the ball was going. Then he would take big, big steps, and if pressed, he would stretch out into a full split, the grace of which would be enough to make Nureyev hang up his tights.

The only time he breathed heavily was at the conclusion of each match . . . with a very polite sigh of relief.

So how could you beat that? You couldn't. Not only did Anil win the intercollegiates three times, but in 1969, his senior year at Harvard, he won the national men's title. The last undergraduate to do that was Charlie Brinton of Princeton in 1942. Anil was meant to return home the next year to help run some of his family's businesses, but he devised excuses for hanging around over here, and, not incidentally, prolonging his North American squash career. He set up a little import business that he seemingly ran from the trunk of his car, which was filled with exotic clothing and trinkets from the East, not to mention a line of squash racquets, clothes, and sneakers that he also carried. He spent a year at the Harvard Business School. He courted his wife-to-be, Linda. And he won squash tournaments.

The feeling was that he had not even been tested by the present competition, and that there was no telling how good he could get, if challenged.

Maybe Vic would provide that challenge. Maybe he would bring out the best in Anil's game. Then again, maybe he would bring out the worst—Anil did live dangerously close to the tin. For a national champion he made a surprising number of unforced errors. The one thing I've found that all ex-national champions boast of is that in their day they made precious few unforced errors. Anil couldn't say that and keep a straight face; in his case, it was his "uncalled for" gets and winners that kept him ahead of the game.

I felt that somehow Vic would find a way to win. Winning seemed more important to him than it did to Anil, who at times seemed almost embarrassed by his successes.

Vic liked to put things on the line. It was the challenge of Anil's dominance as much as the change in residence, I assumed, that had brought him out of retirement. But I'd have felt better about his chances if he were not putting so much of himself on the line. Indeed, that line was sagging so much it threatened to snap. What I'm getting around to are the water wings that were around his

waist, the chipmunk cheeks, and the stovepipe legs. He was carrying an extra 25 pounds, at least, and appeared twice the player I'd
remembered.

But if I was having trouble remembering that gangly, skinny
kid, the semis of the first tournament of the season, the Lordi, held
at the New York Athletic Club, refreshed my memory. Those
damn cross-courts and drops of his had me back on my first pair of
ice skates again. And that hard "criss-cross serve" that breaks
across the body, that was another reminder of Niederhoffer past.

I'd forgotten about that serve of his. He didn't invent it. In
fact, as you may recall, I first learned it from Conroy at Princeton
(see Figure 7 in Chapter 3).

We all used this serve every now and then, but we used it as a
gimmick, the way you might throw in an occasional underhand
serve in tennis. But Vic used the criss-cross a lot. He didn't win
many points outright with it, but it was an irritant. For one thing,
because it was hard to know whether to play it or let it go. To play
it you had to volley it or it would get away from you. But if you let
it go, it might land out of court and be a fault. So on the close ones,
you sometimes would end up swinging at a "sucker pitch." And,
because a criss-cross is breaking into and across you, it's an uncomfortable, cramped volley. And the timing of this volley is particularly tough because whereas the ball is coming at you from the
side, your swing is toward the front. You want to return this serve
either cross-court or down the wall, anything else will come out in
the middle, but getting the correct angle on the return takes some
doing. As a general rule, the closer the path of your stroke is to the
path of the approaching ball, the easier the shot. In other words,
it's easier to hit a ball back where it came from than to try to
change its direction. But so often in squash, to be effective, you
have to change the ball's angle. It's the challenge of having to field
the ball from a variety of different angles and then creating new
angles off of these that keeps the game interesting. Certainly, Vic
kept things interesting with that criss-cross serve. He opened most
games with it and used it on all the pressure points. Vic was the
only player who worked you over with that serve. I'd get used to it
as the match wore on, but then on a key point, he'd throw me off
by changing the angle a little. And as I started to tire, and cheat on
footwork, I would make bad errors returning that serve.

Each time I played Vic in college, he'd remind me with that
serve that I should do something about improving my return of it.

But the only way to practice the return is to have someone hit it at you, and nobody hit it as well as he did. And, anyway, I'd forget about that serve from match to match.

Since Vic was getting good mileage out of that serve, you might wonder why the rest of us didn't practice returning it, and why we didn't develop it into a weapon of our own. In retrospect, I wish I had, and today I do use it quite often. But at that time it was just one of a number of things that were going on in the court when you played Vic, and since it wasn't a finishing shot (like a three-wall nick), it wasn't a big shot that made you sit up and take notice.

It wasn't as if he'd invented a fast serve that nobody could touch. It wasn't anything like that. It was just that he saw something in a serve that nobody else paid much attention to. He saw by using it and varying it, he could put a little extra pressure on his opponent. Right from the start of the point he'd get you a little off balance with it. And keeping you off balance, preventing you from ever getting comfortable in the points, seemed to be pretty much what his game was all about.

That criss-cross serve that I hadn't had to contend with for six or seven years was another little reminder that Vic was back on the circuit. And once again he had me thinking, I've got to do something about improving my return of that serve.

And once again I gave it the old college try. And, if I say so myself, I put on a good show—for one game. He had me off balance much of the time, but I hung in there and showed him a few shots of my own and won it 15-11.

I hadn't figured on winning the first game. My plan had been to try to extend the rallies by digging out all his shots. If I could make the fat boy run, maybe he'd poop out by the second or third game. But the problem was his game just naturally jerked you around, and to work him, you had to work yourself a lot harder. After the first game, I needed a rest and let up to the tune of 8 and 6 the next two games. He wasn't in top shape maybe, but he was getting around the court all right, and controlling play as always. But, refreshed after the five-minute break, I roared to 10-5 in the fourth. I couldn't believe the lead. Nor could Vic, for he won 10 of the next 12 points to take it 15-12. Apparently, he didn't want the bother of a fifth game, and who was I to come between a Nieder/Nayar showdown?

The thing that surprised me about their match that afternoon was Vic's strategy. I had expected a little "envelopment action," but Vic opened up with very straightforward hard hitting and hard running. He apparently was bent on toughing it out against Anil. I had expected something cute, like crazy angle junk shots or, maybe, alternate lobbing and driving to throw off his rhythm. Certainly, there would be lots of change-ups and attempts to cross him up. I remembered someone asking Ralph Howe several years back how he thought Vic would do against Anil if they ever played, and Ralph said Vic would win because "he's too smart for Anil." So where was the big play? And wasn't this a little stupid? Everyone knew you weren't supposed to take Anil on directly. Didn't Vic know that Anil was a physical wonder? And certainly his own conditioning was suspect, especially in a fourth match of the weekend. It just didn't add up. Vic should be pacing himself, and finding ways to slow Anil down, yet he came out fast serving and blasting.

But apparently Vic knew best, for he won the first game 15-10. It wasn't fantastic squash. Anil seemed distracted. I remember he looked at Vic funnily a couple of times, as if he couldn't quite believe all this was for real. Vic does take some getting used to in the court. Not just the criss-cross serves, the cross-courts, and the combinations, but also the sound of his running and the sight of his between point mannerisms. And the overall impression Vic gives off of raw determination and desire, that, too, can put you off.

Anil, as always, made a few brilliant moves, but in general he seemed tentative and unsure of himself. Did Vic have him psyched out? There had been quite a build up to this match. Anil was making even more than his share of unforced errors. Certainly this wasn't Anil at his best.

In the second game there was no let up in the frenetic pace, but Anil seemed to have settled down a bit. I won't say he was now comfortable in the court with Vic, but he seemed much more focused in on the play, and picked up the game 15-10. At the end of this game, Vic motioned to his wife for something and she produced from her purse two packets of granulated sugar of the table variety. Have you ever tasted it straight? That's some price to pay for instant energy.* But Vic, who would eat sugar to win, did build up a nice little lead at the start of the third game, only to have Anil catch up and then beat him to 13. Vic, in no condition to go five games, put everything he had into catching Anil at 13. I say every-

---

*And I'm not so sure that sugar taken in this form does provide instant energy.

thing he had, for Anil set 5 and then won 5 to take the third game 18-13.

The fourth game was a formality. Anil took it 15-8, finishing it (and Vic) off with a dazzling display of three-walls and short kills. Everyone was mightily impressed, except Vic, who after shaking hands with Anil, as he followed him out the little door, paused and took a look back over his shoulder. He shook his head at the court and with both hands waved it away with disgust, as if to say, "Forget about this one, I wasn't playing well."

Those who had expected tantrums on the court from Vic were sadly disappointed. He did, index finger raised, volunteer a few lawyerly explanations for why he thought he should be given a let. But the only let-related histrionics he indulged in were the looks of injured innocence that accompanied his appeals of referee's decisions that went against him. If this was bad acting, it was bad only in the sense that it wouldn't make it in a grade B movie rendition of a martyr feeling his feet begin to toast at the stake.

Incidentally, the "nonverbal cues" that accompany the appeal process are an area of the dramatic arts that has sadly been neglected by the academy.

The rules do not permit you to express an opinion unless asked, nor to conduct an informal referee's clinic from the court, but where does it say you can't give it a little Marcel Marceau? If your opponent asks for what you consider an unreasonable let, spin around and look at the referee with total disbelief, like you just noticed he has two noses; or shake your head and start laughing; or grab the ball, go over to the service box, get into a crouch as if about to serve, and then look back over your shoulder at the referee as if to say, "Are we ready? Has this nonsense been taken care of yet?"

The possibilities for expressing an opinion without actually saying a word—the possibilities of influencing a decision within the rules, or at least making the judges feel like maybe they owe you one the next time around—are limitless and very harmless so long as you remember to overact rather than over*react*. I try humor. If an opponent starts making an explanation that I consider ludicrous, my racquet might become a violin or a pitchfork. (I try to perform out of my opponent's sight, so if the gallery starts laughing, he thinks they're laughing at his appeal.)

Anyway, however the decision goes, far and away the most important thing is not to let it affect your play on the next point, and that's where Vic was a pro. His full concentration would turn to the next point, whatever happened on the point before.

Nor did he let a setback in a tournament daunt his confidence. With three weeks' dieting and training under his belt for the next event, the Gold Racquets,* Vic may not have been lean, but he was hungry. Still, his conditioning was somewhat suspect. Certainly relative to Anil's.

Again they met in the finals, and again Vic opened with a frontal assault, smoking his drives. Not hitting as hard as Anil, but keeping continuous pressure on him nevertheless. Apparently, Vic still felt he could break him by keeping up a wicked pace. But after splitting the first two games and losing the third, 15–7, Vic appeared played out. It looked like back to the old drawing board for Vic. But after the five-minute break, Vic was back in it and surged to 13, where Anil caught him. Vic set 3. They split points. Then they played the showdown point. What had gone before, it turned out, was important only because it brought them to this one point. It wasn't game point, but they got stuck into it, and this point became a test of wills. It went on and on. I'd seen Vic make dive gets before, but this was the only time I ever saw Anil leave his feet. What happened was, after mixing it up for what seemed several minutes but probably wasn't that long (no one was looking at his watch at the time), Anil finally got a loose ball on his forehand and powered one of his sayonara "short kills," headed for the nick short on the left side. But Vic, having anticipated this shot, had gotten a true "head" start, that is, he had taken a headfirst kamikaze dive into the nick. His head didn't nick, and since the ball didn't either, he was somehow able to scrape it back.

Anil hadn't anticipated this save and the only way he could get the ball back was to take what was probably his first headlong dive ever on the squash court. It was successful and it looked like the point was over, for Vic hadn't been able to get back up on his feet yet. But it wasn't over, for somehow Vic was able to reach the ball and volley it from the sitting down position.

We may forgive Vic if it was a weak return, hit so softly that it permitted Anil time to get back up on his feet and give it a thwack. Only to discover that Vic was now back up on his feet as well. So the point continued for several more strokes until Anil finally hit

*Held at the Rockaway Hunting Club in Cedarhurst, New York.

the tin. And at the first opportunity in the next point, Anil hit a bad tin to lose the game, 16–14.

Everyone was up for the fifth game, except Anil, who seemed drained and out of it and handed the game over 15–8 with numerous tins. He had to have the physical edge in that fifth game, but he seemed to have lost his stomach for a fight, or maybe, he never had it. That tussle at 14 all had taken something out of him. It wasn't a physical thing, for he was clearly in better shape than Vic. And when they had both gotten back up on their feet toward the end of that rally, he was in as strong a position to win that point as Vic was. But whereas Vic was able to keep his concentration, to keep going, to keep playing tough squash, Anil wanted out. The continuous pressure seemed, at last, too much for him.

With that point, Vic won not only the match but also the season. (And you might toss in a four-year reign over the amateur circuit as well.) The next time they met, which proved the last, Vic beat him 3–zip. That was in the finals of the Cowles. Anil had lost his *élan* and tinned out whenever it got close.

Anil, with dazzling displays of speed and power, had blinded the competition to the fact that if you kept after him, he'd make errors. But Vic kept after him and wouldn't let up. So, finally, Anil called it quits.

Vic was once again "King of the Mountain." More than the leading player, more than the player who wins most of the time, he was the dominant player.

Dominance is not just winning most of your matches. Dominance is getting competitors not to be competitors. Getting them to feel that they can't win, so what's the use. They may not acknowledge this in words, but it shows up in their play. It shows up on the big points at the end of games when they try totally unrealistic shots and thus beat themselves, or they tighten up and do nothing while waiting for the champ to take control. During Vic's rule, if you had a lead against him, you felt about as confident as a distance runner who had a lead on the world's record holder. If you're ahead, you don't figure you're winning, you figure he hasn't made his move yet, and you burn up a lot of energy checking over your shoulder worrying about when he's going to pass you.

The psychology of dominance is making your opponent feel he can't win, so he backs off at the moment of truth. Making your opponent feel if he's ahead, something's wrong.

This momentum of dominance happens all the time, at all levels of the game. Being a little better than a rival can translate to an unbeaten record against him that doesn't reflect the differences in your abilities if he comes to expect to lose and backs off in the moment of truth. Or you develop a thing about not being able to beat someone, who, in point of fact, is not that much better than you, but on the key points against him you act foolishly. He, on the other hand, is damned if he's going to lose to you, and puts something extra into the big points.

What gives an added fillip to the momentum of the dominance (maybe it's more than a fillip, call it a big push) is when there's something about the champion, in addition to his obvious skills, that seems to set him apart. With Anil the fact that he was Indian played on competitors' minds. A little slip of a fellow who moved so easily, never tired, and hit such a big ball—you had to wonder if there was something about his Indian build that made squash easier for him. Something about the way he was put together that gave him superior speed, stamina, and coordination. Superior to us big-boned, lumbering Anglo-Saxon types.

In Vic's case, his eccentricities gave him an aura of genius that definitely psyched the competition. And the fact that he stuck to himself increased the mystery about him.

So Vic was back. But what was back? Everyone expected to see tantrums on the court, but he never lost his cool and was better than most, indeed, very good, about "calling double bounces on himself " (that is, calling his ball down when he thought he didn't get it). And he complimented his opponents on their good shots. Still, he didn't swing galleries to his side. In fact, he had a knack for turning them off.

Why was this? Was it because he won all the time? There is a natural sympathy for the underdog, but champions can also catch the fan's fancy, as was the case with Anil Nayar. No, there was something about his manner on the court that made it difficult for people to identify with him. If you don't know someone, facial expressions have a lot to do with your impression of him. Consider Vic's "facial repertoire" on the court—you couldn't call the looks he gave "facial expressions," for they lacked any real communication. There was that trancelike blank look, which suggested that he had tuned everything out, even the squash. But obviously he hadn't tuned everything out or he couldn't function on the court. Or he would tell you nothing by overacting. After a tough point, he'd put on the face of pain of the last man in the last mile of the marathon. Obviously, he wasn't that tired, so by overacting he was masking just how tired he was.

And in the overacting department, after an error, he wouldn't say anything (I can't remember ever hearing him swear), but he'd look like he'd just double-faulted on match point. The only look he gave that you knew was for real was when, after losing a tough point, he took a deep breath and stuck out his lower lip, like a very stubborn small child. That look communicated determination. On the other hand, when things went his way (as often they did), Vic never showed any real pleasure. He carried all the Tragedy Masks around, but no Comedy Masks were in his kit. The closest he came to a smile was a smug, slight pursing of the lips that suggested he was about to make a wry comment, which he never did, for the squash court was no place for humor, it was a place of business.

The thing about Anil was, though he frequently looked preoccupied and his basic facial expression was one of concern and worry, when something right or funny happened, his face would break out in a total smile; not the smile of a shark who's just made his kill, but the smile of someone who's having a great time and hopes you are too. A kind of smile that evinced total pleasure at playing the game, but at the same time communicated a squash-isn't-everything fellow feeling.

The only time Anil got mad was when he accidentally hit an opponent with the ball. Vic, on the other hand, made it a point not to apologize when he hit an opponent with the ball. Don't get me wrong. Vic didn't go out of his way to hit opponents with the ball. He was no head hunter, never hurt anyone, and didn't hit opponents with the ball any more than anyone else did. But if, in the normal course of play, you came within his sights, he wasn't going to make an extraordinary effort to hit around you. Whether they chose to admit it or not, this was the attitude taken by most players in a tight match. But Vic differed in that if he wasn't trying not to hit you, he wasn't going to come out with a big apology when he did. He was being perhaps more honest and less hypocritical than most players who'll blast you, then make a big deal of apologizing—Philadelphia players, in particular—but his honesty in this regard didn't score points with the gallery.

Except for his play, Anil was totally unobtrusive on the court. He preferred running around an opponent to calling a let, but when he did have to ask for a let, he made it seem like an apology for being so fast he didn't give his opponent time to get out of the way. Vic was just the opposite. You noticed him much more than his play. In a tight point, if his opponent was in the way, he would push through him for a shrieky let. This, too, would upset the gallery (more than his opponent), for he looked the bully. But, in truth, he wasn't trying to knock his opponent down, he just couldn't stop. It was the momentum of will power at work.

If Vic's klutzy presence didn't delight the spectators, it certainly fascinated them. How could somebody with a duck waddle run like that be the champion in a game of movement? To all but the experts it was a mystery how he could consistently beat players who looked better than him.

Other players looked better, maybe, but Vic was the person everyone wanted to see play. He was the champ, and as such, he was the person whose presence gave legitimacy to a draw. He only accepted a few invitational tournaments each season, so tournament chairmen, however they felt about him personally, played up to him to get him to participate in their tournament. (And they didn't seem to mind at all that Vic didn't choose to attend the dinner dance and other nonsquash festivities of the weekend. As always, he would appear for the matches and disappear afterward).

The established champ was not of the establishment, and both sides had to come to terms with this. What developed wasn't what you would call "easy camaraderie" between Vic and the club types, but both made an effort to be polite, and, in fact, Vic was very "correct" in his exchanges with the establishment. Administrators would show him cufflinks they had awarded one another for service to the game, and he would comment on how they certainly deserved them. He played exhibition matches at junior tournaments. He bought a pair of $100 patron tickets at the nationals. And he gave very gracious winner's speeches when accepting trophies. Feet shuffling, eyes scanning the ceiling, looking like a schoolchild giving his first speech before assembly, Vic overcame his obvious discomfiture at public speaking to really lay it on about what a well-run tournament it was, and how thanks were due to the club and to so and so and so and so, without whose diligent efforts the event would not have been possible.

Vic was giving speeches now, but he still wasn't one to indulge in small talk, at least not in these settings. People like to hang around the winner. But Vic really didn't have much time for this sort of thing. Most conversations with him were, as before, like strained interviews, with long pauses and short answers.

Still, he was more outgoing than he used to be, and if not a light conversationalist, he nevertheless kept things interesting. One thing he started doing was spouting sayings in response to questions. A variation of the Jewish elder answering a question with a question. I don't know what got him on this kick, but these weren't chance comments that he made up on the spot, and he had obviously put in some time digging up these old proverbs and committing them to memory. When he started quoting proverbs, you could never tell what he was going to say, and, for that matter, you weren't always sure what he had said, after he had said it. But if he was seemingly eclectic in his taste for old proverbs, one area in which he had a one "tract" mind was in his politicoeconomic thinking. And that "tract" was Adam Smith's *Wealth of Nations*. Which is to say he never missed an opportunity in conversations and interviews to strike a blow for free markets and free enterprise. This was something new also, but obviously not a passing fancy.

People weren't sure what to make of his fervor for capitalism, but certainly his views in this area gave no offense to the Wall Street-based squash community. And, if one had difficulty at times following his arguments or slogans, his hair showed you where his head was at. Quite literally, for he kept it short, not a crewcut, but too short to comb. I was never sure whether he was making a political statement during the headband years or just didn't want to bother with his hair. Certainly, Vic did not appear to spend an inordinate amount of time on his appearance.

I'm no Beau Brummell myself. Clothes don't interest me. I tend to wear the same clothes over and over again, and what difference does it make, for if I put new clothes on, after fifteen minutes it looks like I've had them on forever. When people point out to me that my socks don't match, I've learned to respond, "Yes, and I have another pair just like this at home," but the truth is I hadn't noticed that my socks didn't match. (Of late, I've become more clothes conscious and I make sure I don't mix up my socks by buying only one color.)

What I am leading up to is, for me to notice that someone is not a snappy dresser is about as likely as Columbo commenting on the sorry state of someone's raincoat. But I must say it, Vic was no clothes horse.

Which is not the same thing as saying he was not concerned about clothes. He had to be to come up with some of the combinations he did. I dress not to be noticed, but Vic took to wearing sweat socks for mittens. At the luncheon reception after the nationals one year, he accepted the trophy in slacks, a nice sports jacket, and a very pleasing sweater, the V-neck of which revealed the hairy forest on his chest, which took the place of a shirt and tie.

On other occasions you might see him impeccably dressed from head to ankle, looking very much the president of his financial consulting firm in a conservative business suit, solid shirt, and muted tie, everything in place save for the pair of screaming white sneakers on his feet. His sneakers became his trademark.

Noting that Vic frequently wore nonmatching sneakers on the court, Herbert Warren Wind, in a piece he did on squash in the *New Yorker,* dubbed Vic "an accomplished eccentric." Part of this, I guess, was scoffing at the conventions of "clubland" and "polite" society. He felt ill at ease in this environment, so he made sure everyone else felt a little uncomfortable, too, when he was around. But I also think Vic knew that in any setting he'd be a character. By playing off his social awkwardness, and seemingly going out of his way to project a screwball image, he got control of the situation. Instead of being someone who, try as he might, was unable to fit in and conform, he was someone who was asserting his right to be different. You may think he was a little crazy, but he had you off balance, and since he was obviously going his own way, you had to approach him on his terms. You might laugh at some of the things he was doing, but you could never escape the feeling he was laughing at you, too, and maybe a little harder.

Vic made those of us who tried to understand him (instead of just writing him off as weird or offensive) into amateur psychologists. But the truth was, nobody could figure him out. I'd known him for almost twenty years, but all I knew was the phenomenon, not Vic.

How did I feel about him? Certainly, he fascinated me. And, in a funny way, though his return tended to put a damper on my own championship fantasies, I think I almost enjoyed renewing the ritual of losing to him again, for it took me back to my racquet youth and reaffirmed my sense of continuity in my racquet career.

I liked Vic, or maybe what I liked were the memories he brought back of my childhood. Memories of summers spent in little white shorts. Here I was almost thirty, and I was still competing against someone I'd played when I was eleven. I hadn't beaten him yet, but I was still trying, and our matches still stirred in me the same hopes and fears. How many "adults" get to play games with the same kid they played as a child?

I also thought it was kind of neat that the Jewish kid from Brooklyn, the son of a cop, could come in and take over this clubby sport. (Not everyone shared my enthusiasm.) I liked his assault on the establishment. I thought he was more interesting and there was a lot more to him than many of the types I had met within the squash community. He was making it on his own, and I admired that.

Over the years, when his name came up in conversation, I had been one of his supporters. But more recently, I was frustrated by his standoffishness, and finally, it dawned on me that he seemed to be doing pretty well on his own. A lot better than me, in fact. This was no longer the scholarship kid from Harvard that nobody understood. This was a prosperous businessman. This was a national champion. He didn't need me to stick up for him. I finally concluded, like most people who knew of him, that he was totally wrapped up in himself and had no interest in anything that didn't directly benefit him. I was sick of making the conversational overtures with him. I figured I wasn't going to hang around him anymore when he chose to appear. From now on it was up to him to take the first step, otherwise, the hell with him.

Vic, as noted above, went undefeated for the remainder of the 1971-72 season; but at the opener for the next season, the Lordi, the shadow he cast over the competition was practically as wide as it was tall. Which is to say, over the summer the only running he had done was to fat. This is also a very modest introduction, I believe, to the fact that I finally snapped his winning streak in the finals of this event.

Having resisted the temptation to open this chapter with a telling of this heroic feat, I will not indulge here in a prolonged description of the subtlety of my play on that occasion. I will not dwell on the fact that I gamely came back to win the second and third games after losing the first by a heartbreaking 1 point. Nor will I big deal the fact that with some dogged digging I came back from 9-13 in the fourth to win the game and match 15-14. Sure, there was fire in my drives and ice on my drops, and I covered the court like wall-to-wall carpeting, but what filled my sails was Vic's heavy breathing. Indeed, he hyperventilated the whole court.

But a victory over Niederhoffer is a victory over Niederhoffer, and I was very pleased. Vic disappeared from the courts, but when I saw him in the locker room, he had a big pucker of a smile on his face. And he volunteered, "I was just thinking of that long string of victories that came to an end today. How many years is it?" He pretended to be boasting about how many times he had beaten me, and what a shock it was that he had lost today, but from his tone it was obvious that what he was really doing was reminiscing for a moment on how far back we went.

I agreed that we had played a few matches over the years, but confessed that the series went back so far, I was a little hazy on who was ahead at the moment, though I did have a pretty good recollection of what had happened today. Then, returning to reality, I suggested the obvious, namely, that I'd seen him in better shape.

"Nah, you played very well," he responded, refusing the excuse I'd given him. And he added, "I'm glad your parents were here to see it. My dad will be happy for you, too, when I tell him."

I gave him a funny look, thinking he was kidding about the latter. Obviously, his dad would be upset when he learned that his "Vickie," as he called him, had lost one.

But Vic clarified, "No, I mean that. He's always liked you. He'll be happy to hear you won." And I remembered to myself how, the first time I played Vic, his dad, sharing a courtside bench with my mother, had given my mother a little pep talk on how what your boy needs to do is to learn how to win, to figure out his opponent's weakness and exploit it. Well, I'd figured out that Vic was out of shape today, and I'd make an extra effort to run down all his shots so as to extend the points. Maybe his dad would be happy to hear I won this one.

This signaled a change in our relationship, not in our playing relationship, mind you, for he resumed whomping me the next time we played, but we started talking a little more at events, and the formal character of our exchanges loosened up a bit. And he seemed to take an interest in my game. Now, after beating me, instead of accepting congratulations and walking off, he'd slip me a few thoughts on weaknesses he had found in my game. I was starved for constructive criticism and started pumping him for information the way I used to work over Barnaby. Now Barnaby, you recall, would, at the slightest prompting, talk and talk and talk some more. Not Vic. He'd offer a pithy thought or two and be off. But he seemed to enjoy the role of mentor, nevertheless. And like E. F. Hutton, when he talks, you listen.

But I really didn't get to know Vic's squash mind until I started practicing with him. He was reputed to do most of his practicing alone, but I knew he also played a bit with some of his teammates at the Harvard Club, so finally I asked him if he wanted to have a practice game.

Which he was receptive to, and once we decided on a mutually convenient evening, he said, "OK, see you eight o'clock at the Harvard Club." Eight o'clock? I would have played him at twelve midnight, if that's what it took, but accustomed to starting around 5:30 or 6 I was surprised at the lateness of the proposed hour.

The reason for this late starting time, I gathered, was to permit him to put in a longer workday. But what really threw me was, after we finished, he returned to his office. He had left his teaching job at Berkeley to devote himself to his business full time, and "full time" to him apparently means something different from what it means to most of us.

We settled into a routine of playing about once a week, sometimes starting as late as ten o'clock at night, and often as not, he'd return to his office after our workout. I learned that he puts in a seven-day workweek and never takes a vacation, unless you count the time he takes off to play in a weekend squash tournament as vacation.

The reason he would be so grossly out of shape at the start of each season was because he felt he could take only so much time away from his business, so once the nationals were over in February he'd cease all athletic activity for the next seven or eight months.

If Vic is all business off the court, on the court he's no less so. Prior to our sessions, 1 hadn't come close to realizing how much importance Vic gives to thorough preparation. I had thought that, except for a little solitary practice, which as much as anything reflected his desire to be alone, he got himself ready for the nationals by playing his way into shape in the early season tournaments. I figured that talent and natural competitiveness were what did the trick for him. That his mind was so good, he didn't have to spend much time studying for exams, so to speak. And I had thought that his evident genius for ball-wall racquet sports was the source of his cockiness about his squash game.

But in these practice sessions, he would, if anything, belittle his presumed talents. It didn't please him at all when, after he won a quick exchange, I complimented him on his fast hands. He's not one to take smug satisfaction in natural abilities.

No, his whole focus is on self-improvement—on improving the things he can improve through hard work. He is a disciple of the old-fashioned notion that "Practice makes perfect," or as he puts it, "No gain without pain."

Sure, we're not dealing with an average IQ here. He has a restless, inquisitive mind and is continually coming up with new thoughts on the game—new responses to situations, reassessments of old shots, little spins to add to serves, and so on. But he introduces these new twists in his game only after careful research and development. When he practices alone, the court is not just a backboard for drills, it's also his lab where he tests and refines new shots and spins.

At the start of our sessions, more often than not, he'd have a thought for the day, sometimes something basic, like remembering the importance of keeping the ball off the back wall; other times, something experimental and wholly unexpected, like the proposition that you can get a better angle on the around-the-corner hard serve (see Figure 3 in Chapter 2) if you drop the ball on the floor and serve it off the bounce.

It's fun to be the sounding board (and backboard) for his latest ideas—and *very* useful for my own game—but the thing that impresses me most about Vic in these practice sessions is not his quirky brilliance, but his unceasing attention to detail. He has a complete dedication to craft; he calls it his "businesslike approach."

A good example of Vic's attention to detail is his dedication to proper footwork. Vic would continually get after me for not making the extra effort to set up properly for my shots; for stretching and hitting the ball off my back foot while facing the front wall, when I had time to get there and get around.

Perhaps better than any other top player, Vic uses little positioning steps to line his feet up properly before he begins his stroke. Whenever possible he hits off a slightly "closed" stance—that is, turned sideways to the front wall with the front foot a little closer to the side wall than the back foot.

Most people learn early on the importance of "legwork" in squash. It's pretty obvious if you can't get to the ball, you can't hit it. What isn't so obvious is that, once you get there, it makes a difference how your feet are lined up. You can get the ball back with lazy footwork, and you can even hit some good shots, but the odds of hitting good shots consistently are much improved if you use proper footwork.

The reason footwork makes a difference is because good footwork enables you to lean into the shot without losing your balance, so it helps you achieve the twin objectives of power and control. If you are lined up in a closed stance and take the ball out front, you can get your body into the shot the right way simply by transferring your weight from the back foot to the front foot as you swing through the ball.

Tennis players will recognize the closed stance as the preferred way of addressing a tennis ground stroke. There is one important difference, though. Whereas in tennis you step toward the ball as you stroke it, in squash you should plant your feet before beginning your downswing. If your feet are moving as you strike the ball, it's like trying to shoot a duck when someone's rocking the boat. In theory, you could hit the ball harder if you were stepping into it at the moment of impact, but in practice the speed of a squash ball and the many tricky angles that must be played off the back and side walls make this extra movement too difficult to coordinate. The timing of the stroke is much simplified if you cut down the commotion with the feet by having them well rooted when you meet the ball. So in squash you get set for the shot by taking little tennislike positioning steps as you approach the ball; but once you are lined up correctly, you plant your feet like a golfer.

On the all too many occasions when you simply don't have time to get around in a closed stance, you should try to at least steady your feet before commencing your downswing, and, if possible, you should wind up by turning your torso away from the stroke so that you can rotate your hips and shoulder into the shot. Sometimes when you want to rush your opponent it makes sense to step into the shot off the wrong foot. But bear in mind, the majority of "racquet errors" in squash can be traced to faulty footwork. Vic convinced me of that.

The impressive thing about Vic's footwork is not that he sets up properly when he has plenty of time, but that in situations where most of us would cheat on our footwork, he makes the extra effort, and this improves his percentages.

Vic's footwork is all the more impressive when you consider what an effort it is for him to get from one place to another quickly. He's not an easy runner. He has to struggle to lug all that "apparatus" around the court. True, with his long legs he can take in a lot of territory with one step, but he doesn't have speed afoot. In a race to the front wall and back, he'd probably finish dead last among the top ten players. That's if you started the race with a gun. But when it comes to reading an opponent's drop shot, he's there first. Along with his remarkable anticipation, his superb balance and long reach enable him to make his spectacular gets.

Still, his movement is not poetry. People see him straining to get around the court with clodhoppery legwork, and ask, "How can he be any good?" But if they'd check out his feet as he's hitting the ball, they'd see the foundation for his excellence. It can't be easy for him, but through hard work he's disciplined his feet, and today there's even a gawky grace, if you will, to his footwork.

By paying extra attention to details, like the way his feet are lined up when he hits the ball, Vic has programmed out of his game, better than any other player, the little, seemingly insignificant unforced errors that are so easy to forget, yet so often add up to the difference between victory and defeat. He gives up no cheap points, and on more than one occasion has called attention to the fact that when it comes to giving away points, I'm a veritable welfare agency.

Our practice sessions last about an hour and usually consist of five or six games. Every so often we may do a drill—for example, he hits a rail, I hit a three-wall, he tries to get it back—but the majority of his drills he does by himself. During the warm-up he'll bounce his latest idea off me, but most of his coaching comes in the form of little comments here and there, usually at the end of a game. Here are some of the things that stick in my mind.

He's a showman in his own way, and I had thought he lived for the moments when he would make the big play with the flashy shot; but his instincts are conservative, and he continually talks of clearing the tin by a safe margin of at least 6 inches.

Along with his devotion to sound footwork, he's religious about slice, for the usual Harvard reasons. And when he analyzes a weakness in a player's game, it's often the observation that this player, when under pressure, comes over the ball on his forehand, thus increasing the likelihood that his shot will end up in the tin. He discusses this lack of discipline on the forehand almost as if it were due to a want of character.

When we first started practicing, he'd take me out of the play by backing me into a corner. I'd concede the point, and then he'd turn around and get on me for having let him overwhelm me. The knowledge that I'll quit on nothing, he explained, puts an important pressure on my opponent.

So I learned to run for everything, and sometimes I'd make a get I couldn't believe, one that would save the point and get us into an incredible rally. The kind of rally that no matter how it ended, ordinarily in practice after it was over, you'd roll your eyes at your sparring mate and say something like, "Wow, what a point!" You'd be pleased just to have taken part in it. But if I ended one of these marathons by tinning out with a nonpercentage shot, Vic would wail his disappointment that I had looked for an easy out instead of sticking with it. So I got tougher on the tough points, but then he pointed out that after winning a tough point I usually let up on the next one.

I came to appreciate that Vic's genius, as much as anything, is his ability to concentrate, not only intensely, but also for long periods of time. His attention span is such that he doesn't have to come up for air as often as others. This is evident not just in his play, but also in his practice schedule, for once he begins his season, he doesn't take a single day off. Some days he works his body harder than others, but he gets in the court every single day. He feels that if he misses even one day of practice, his game suffers. His belief in the need for continuous practice reminds me of Paderewski's famous quote: "When I don't practice one day, I notice the difference. When I don't practice for two days, my wife is aware of it. When I don't practice for a week, even the audiences know it."

Like most players, I find that if I don't take every third or fourth day off, I get stale. But that never-miss-a-day routine seems to work for Vic, though I will say that sometimes in our practice sessions he's very flat and I cut through him with little resistance.

Vic would get after me not only for not hanging in on the long points, but also for not exploiting my opportunities. He's not one to prolong a rally unnecessarily. When he gets his opening, he takes his shot. And because of this, playing with him doesn't strengthen my conditioning. I had thought that practicing with him would improve my fitness vis-à-vis the other players. That working out with the top player would make the lesser players no problem for me physically. But it's turned out that the lesser players are more likely to tire me out than Vic because, unlike Vic, they don't always put the loose balls away, which means that the rallies with them on average last longer.

Though Vic may focus on weakness—he's hard on himself and a "tough grader" in his evaluation of others—he's basically very positive and at heart an optimist. His criticisms of me have always been in terms of what I can be. I'd lose a game to him in overtime, and he'd say, "You should have won that game 15-9," and explain why. Far from demoralizing me, his criticisms have the effect of boosting my morale.

One final thing about our workouts: for all his talk of you're only as good as you practice and his insistence upon practicing under match conditions (we use a new ball every time and award let points to each other), I've always found Vic a lot tougher in matches. I'm batting at least .333 against him in practice, which is a tad better than my lifetime match record against him. And, PS, I've finally learned how to handle that criss-cross serve of his, and have started using it myself.

It is often said that the mark of the great athlete is the ability to make the difficult look easy. But the peculiar stamp that Vic has put on the game of squash is the impression he gives that "If a guy like that can be good, then anyone can." His gawky movements give the appearance of a less than superior athlete, and the statements that he makes reinforce the impression that a brilliant mind, hard work, and the will to succeed are the reasons for his athletic success. What is often overlooked is the fact that Vic is an extraordinary athlete, and not just from the neck up. His hands, as I have frequently noted, are the fastest in the business. What makes his "zero reaction time" volleys all the more extraordinary is the fact that he wields a racquet that is 1 ounce to 1½ ounces heavier than that used by any other top player. The reason he can make a bat seem like a baton is because he has massive forearms. The advantage that a heavy racquet gives him is that with his strength, he can generate a lot of power with a relatively short swing.

Vic is a big, strong man. Because his shoulders are steeply sloped, he is much more powerful than he may appear. The advantage to an athlete of having "slope shoulders" is that with the arms attached lower down, the punch comes more directly from the body. The slant to Vic's shoulders, which lowers his center of gravity, may also explain his remarkable sense of balance, which in combination with his reach, he uses to great advantage when scrambling to make a get.

Also not to be overlooked is Vic's superb eyesight. Not only does he have good eyes in the sense of visual acuity, but he also has "fast eyes." A mutual friend once told me that as an experiment, they played a little game in which they would flash different numbers of fingers to test each other's speed of vision. Vic, he reports, was extremely good at this. Then again, maybe all this proves is that Vic has fast fingers. At any rate, my overall impression is that if you put Vic through a battery of East German sports institute type tests, he'd test out as a highly talented athlete.

Not that there's much chance of ever getting Vic to take those East German tests. This champion of squash, after all, is also a champion of capitalism. In interviews with the press he never misses the opportunity to talk it up for free enterprise. On these occasions (and many others as well) he sports a button that says "Create Value." Inevitably the reporter gets around to, "I see you're wearing a button that says 'Create Value.'" To which Vic inevitably responds, "Yes, Biff, that's what free enterprise does, it creates value . . ." But before getting too deeply into a purely theoretical discussion of Adam Smith—this is after all a squash interview—Vic keeps it relevant and asserts that he, of course, plays "Capitalist Squash." Capitalist Squash? Yes, you know, as opposed to the other kind, "Socialist Squash."

The capitalist squash player is an individual. He works hard. He takes intelligent risks. He reaps the benefits of a businesslike approach. He gets what he earns and earns what he gets. The socialist squash player, on the other hand, doesn't want to assume responsibility. Won't put in individual effort. Can't stand on his own two feet. Wants something for nothing. And can't take the heat in head-to-head competition. Vic would beat a socialist squash player any day of the week that ends in y. And those Russians better not take up squash, they'd be useless. With their collective mentality they'd be lost in a sport for individuals. Just let me at a Russian squash player— (That little flourish about the Russians was attributed to Vic in a feature *People* magazine did on him.)

Forgive me if I confess that for the longest time I thought this routine was a put-on, like those two different sneakers. It wasn't until I got to know Vic that I realized how deep all this goes with him. Sure, there's some showmanship in his examples, but he's a fervent believer in what he calls the "freedom philosophy." He was converted from liberalism to "Milton Friedmanism" (my term) while working for his doctorate at the University of Chicago's School of Business. I guess he's really to the right of Friedman in his advocacy of totally doing away with government. (Vic doesn't do things by halves.)

This isn't the place to develop his arguments about the sanctity of private property and the desirability of submitting all public decisions to the marketplace, but I assure you that when I advance my "pinko" thoughts on the possibility that maybe some form of income tax should be retained and that, however limited, there is, nevertheless, a role for government, his arguments to the contrary are well rehearsed, and he's as ready to pounce as Bill Buckley on "Firing Line."

Think what you will of his theories, capitalism certainly works for Vic. In a relatively short time he has been able to build up a very successful business that permits him to be his own man and to dress and act as he likes, so long as he can put himself across in the marketplace. He's done very well in the business of brokering businesses, and who's to say he hasn't "created value" in the process?

How do you combat a capitalist squash player? Toward the end of the 1974–75 season, when Vic had been getting a lot of play in the press because the nationals were held in New York, which is where the press is, and when Vic had been doing a lot of "Create Value" sloganeering, I warned Vic that I had had enough of his capitalist squash and to stop it had come up with a secret weapon. This, he assured me, was not possible. But the next time we played a match, the semis of the city championships, I warmed up in a sweater despite the fact that the temperature in the court must have been well into the seventies. I lost the toss, but when I took off my sweater just before he served, to reveal the message that was printed on the back of my shirt, I felt the momentum shift to my side. I won the first game easily and nearly took the second. In fact, a point here and a point there and I would have won the match. A much better performance than usual against him. And what was the message on the T-shirt? DEFLATE BALLYHOO.

I guess you shouldn't make fun of someone's "religion," but Vic seemed to like the joke. That's something that most people (including the players) don't know about him. That he has a very good sense of humor. A little twisted, perhaps, like mine, but very funny, nonetheless.

People who know him as the grim competitor on the court and the all-work-no-play businessman off the court might be surprised to learn that he's a Monty Python fanatic and a Gilbert and Sullivan aficionado. In fact, when he was in graduate school in Chicago, he hammed it up as a policeman in a local production of *The Pirates of Penzance*.

Vic doesn't have a lot of time for a lot of people. He drives himself hard, and is a very private person. He doesn't reveal the fun side of himself to most people, but it's there, nonetheless. People who think, as I once did, that his world is limited to business and squash are wrong.

He dotes on his kid brother, Roy, and his two young daughters, Galt and Katie. An evening with his family for dinner is a lot of laughs. Vic takes kidding well from his friends and has a wry sense of humor about himself and people's reactions to him. In these private moments you learn that he's much more aware of social nuances than he ordinarily lets on. He's a born ham and in telling a story he likes to sit up in his chair and wave his arms in the air as he acts out each of the parts. In other words, when he's "on" (which he always is on these occasions), he can be thoroughly entertaining. The evening usually ends with his wife, Gail (every bit as outgoing and effusive as Vic is not, and easy to see, the best salesperson in his business), or him, at the piano for a little group vocalizing. Of late, Vic has become interested in the clarinet and he sounds pretty good on it to me, but he's most accomplished at the keyboard, where he can sight-read like a player piano. (Growing up, he was never permitted to miss a day of practice; when his family went on vacation to Florida, his dad rented a piano for him in a studio.)

On these occasions, I have gotten to know Vic's dad better. A very solid, thoughtful man, he gave me a much needed pep talk once when I was in the doldrums of my dissertation. Having himself gotten a PhD the hard way (that is, plugging away at it part time over a period of ten years while still on the police force), he was now a professor of sociology at John Jay College of Criminal Justice, and could assure me that no matter how difficult things might seem to me at the moment, dissertations do get finished and are worth doing.

Like everyone else, he is in awe of Vic's talents and drive, and once confessed to me, only half jokingly, "I don't know how I created him." He does recall how he started his "Vickie" off in ball-wall games at the age of six months. There was an empty swimming pool next to the courts where he and his wife used to play tennis, and they found that baby could be safely entertained while they had their game simply by putting him at one end of the pool with an old tennis ball and letting him push it to the other end. They'd check in on him every couple of games, and when he got the ball to the other end, they'd turn him around.

A former Brooklyn College quarterback, Vic's dad is a good athlete, but in tennis he insists he is nothing more than average, and the same goes for his wife. Vickie, on the other hand, he assures me, was a natural with a racquet right from the start. They lived only two blocks away from the Brighton Beach Baths, a sports complex which had something like twenty-five one-wall handball courts and thirty hand tennis courts—half-sized cement tennis courts that are scaled down so the game can be played with the hand. The Baths was the mecca in those days for these sports.

Starting at age six, Vic used to watch the great handball players of the era have at each other in the "Sweeps," which were held at the Baths every Saturday and Sunday. These were money matches in which doubles teams would vie for a pot, augmented by a percentage of the side bets from the one thousand or so spectators. Spectators who, as Vic recalls, held strong opinions and were not reluctant to share them whenever their team lost a close call.

Play was frequently interrupted by arguments over whether or not an "intentional block" had occurred. In those days it was within the rules in one-wall handball for a player to block an opponent so long as the player was standing there already and didn't move his body. If the obstructing player did move his body, it was ruled either an unavoidable "hinder," in which case the point was played over, or an "intentional block," with the point awarded to the team interfered with. Many altercations erupted over rulings, and, as Vic recalls, sometimes players got so mad at decisions they would grab the referee and start shaking him, or a team would simply sit down and refuse to continue until the referee was replaced.

But the greatest violence, according to Vic, occurred because there is no penalty for blocking a return that was headed for the front wall. All that happens is the point is played over. This meant that many players, who preferred taking pain to losing a point, would step in front of an opponent about to hit a putaway. And the striker, seeing his winning shot thus denied, would try to discourage use of this tactic by winding up and hitting the ball as hard as he could at the offending wall of flesh, sometimes following through with a fist for good measure. These blows would smart, particularly since the players didn't wear shirts (the standard garb for handball is bathing suits and sneaks), and they would raise welts. But it was all part of the game, and after a "good" match, the worthy gladiators' backs would look like checkerboards from all the black and blue marks. The crowd, as Vic recalls, seemed to enjoy this "Roman Circus" atmosphere.

By the time Vic was ready to join the fray, wooden paddles were starting to come in. Hand tennis was giving way to paddle tennis,* and the handball courts were frequently in use for paddleball. It was in the latter that Vic first showed his gift for ball-wall games.

Since paddleball evolved from handball, it is not surprising that the preferred technique in this game is to use two forehands, by switching the paddle from hand to hand. (The logic behind this technique is that a second forehand extends the reach beyond what would be possible with a backhand, and since in the one-wall game there are no side walls off which to play the ball on the rebound, reach is of critical importance.) I mention this tradition of switch hitting because it explains why Vic, who played paddleball before he took up tennis, started off in tennis with that most unnerving second forehand.

Before long Vic was so much better than most of the people he came up against in paddleball that, to keep things interesting, he would frequently play with only one hand, sometimes the right, other times just the left. (A routine, you may recall, he used to pull on his squash opponents his freshman year at Harvard, before Barnaby went to work on him.)

And sometimes, I understand, a little money changed hands as well. But the Niederhoffer money match that locals still talk about today was a showdown between Vic and a man in his thirties who was a former national handball champion and who many considered to be the best one-wall paddleball player. There were others, however, who thought that Vic, despite his relative youth, was the best player around. That youth in this case might be considered a disadvantage is understandable; Vic, after all, was only eleven at the time.

There was a big crowd for this event and a lot of heavy betting, spurred by the fact that the two players represented different clubs. Vic's uncle, Howie Eisenberg, who is only a couple of years older than Vic (and was to go on to become a national handball

*Paddle tennis is not to be confused with platform tennis, which is sometimes mistakenly referred to as "paddle tennis." The two games are quite similar, but in real paddle tennis, the ball may not be played off the wire fence.

champion himself), was part of that crowd. He told me about that match and said it was the funniest damn sight, to see this skinny little eleven-year-old kid, using his skinny little eleven-year-old body, as best he could, to block out a fully grown man. (A man, by the way, whose competitive temperament was such that he once broke his wrist punching a metal post after he lost a critical point in handball. That injury, sustained when he was twenty, aborted what many thought to be a very promising career in pro baseball. He was generally considered to be the best all-around athlete in the area.)

I asked Vic's dad about that match. He shook his head and said he was embarrassed to say it happened, for if he had known the match was to take place, he would have stopped it. He felt an eleven-year-old shouldn't have all that pressure on him. Maybe not. But if we are to believe this much of the story, we might as well believe the ending . . . that Vic *won the match.* I've never observed pressure to have a negative impact on Vic's performance. If anything, he seeks it out. Indeed, now that he was back in New York, he resumed buying himself in the Cowles Calcutta.

Chapter 6
THE SOFT BALL GAME

"The Black Marshmallow"

By the end of the 1972-73 season I was starting to consider myself a pretty good squash player. Why not? During that season I'd finally scored a victory over Niederhoffer, I'd had the best league record in New York, I'd gotten my first seeding in the nationals—number three—and though I lost in the quarters of that event, I'd beaten Ralph Howe (3-zip) to get there. I figured, "Satterthwaite, you are now a player to be reckoned with." The events of the summer of 1973, though, caused me to think again.

It had seemed like perfect timing to me that at the very moment I'd established myself at home, an opportunity should come along to represent the U.S. in a major international contest. Our national squash association had decided to send a team to the 1973 International Squash Rackets Federation team championships, and I was chosen to play on that team.

It was the first time that the U.S. had sent a team to this event. The International Squash Rackets Federation (ISRF) was the brainchild of the Australians, but the English, fearful that the Aussies were trying to take over the game, latched onto it as their own idea and promoted its formation in 1966. Along with Australia and England, the charter members were Pakistan, India, Egypt, New Zealand, and South Africa.

India, Pakistan, and Egypt may seem improbable places for squash to have taken root, much less flourished, but the British military at the height of the British Empire built squash courts for their officers, wherever they happened to be stationed. The uniforms have since changed, but the military connection lingers, for today the heads of the squash associations in these three countries all have impressive military titles.

In recent decades national teams representing the abovementioned seven countries visited one another. Typically, there would be a series of team matches and then the visiting side would compete in the host country's national championships. The idea of the ISRF was to help promote and organize these tours and to hold world team and individual championships every two years. The first such match was held in Australia in 1967, shortly after the founding of the ISRF.

The U.S. did not join the ISRF at first. These countries play the English version of squash, which differs substantially from the game we play over here, and we refused to join their "international" association until they recognized our North American ball, court, and playing rules as an official version of squash for international play. The North American game, after all, was played in the U.S., Canada, and Mexico.

Why their game should differ from ours stems from the fact that squash was not standardized in England at the time that it was introduced over here. In fact, it wasn't until 1922 that a committee was formed over there to standardize their playing rules, court size, and equipment specifications. Up until then, court size was determined as much as anything else by space available, and balls of varying size and rebound were in use.

Ironically, though the British invented the game, by the time they got around to standardizing it over there, it had already become well established and organized over here. In fact, our first national championship, held in 1907, preceded theirs by sixteen years. But the game that had evolved and become accepted over here was now quite different from the game that became official over there.

The differences between the two games, though not as great as between cricket and baseball or rugby and American football, were (and are), nevertheless, real. The English court is 2½ feet wider than the American court and the tin is 2 inches higher. The playing rules differ principally in the method of scoring; in their game you play to nine points but can only score points when serving. If the receiver wins the rally he wins the serve, but the score remains unchanged.

But the real difference between their game and ours is in the ball. Theirs is much squishier than ours. The walls of their ball are so thin you can easily flatten the ball between your thumb and forefinger. Because it is more easily compressed, it leaves the racquet at a lesser speed than the firmer American ball would, given a comparable swat.

But the real cut in speed comes with each rebound. Even an American ball loses a good deal of speed every time it strikes a playing surface. But the softer English ball loses even more speed than the American ball* when it rebounds, and, furthermore, it seems to "stick" to the walls and floor longer in the process of rebounding, I guess because it flattens out more. Whereas the American ball takes a long, low, skidding bounce, the English ball sits up. Unlike the American ball, it doesn't come to you, you have to go to it. But it "hangs" so you usually have time to catch up to it.

What this means is a lot more running. It's tougher to put the English ball away, so the points tend to be much longer, and frequently the play takes on an essentially defensive character. Whereas our game rewards shot making and quick reactions, theirs puts more of a premium on retrieving and fitness.

It came as something of a shock to me, having played all my life with the zippy American ball, to discover just how soft the English ball is. I dug a little into the history of the two games and learned that while nobody knows for sure why our ball is hard (maybe it was pepped up under the influence of squash tennis), we are reasonably certain that the English squash ball has always been soft.

The story goes that sometime late in the eighteenth century the inmates of London's Fleet Street debtor's prison (whose entertainments were necessarily of the intramural variety) discovered the pleasures of thwacking a ball against a wall with makeshift racquets, and thereby gave birth to the game of "rackets."†

The rackets ball, made of tightly bound strips of leather and cloth, was hard like a miniature baseball. The "court" was open to the sky and used one or two walls.

---

*The American ball that we were using at the time was firmer than the "seventy-plus" ball that we now use, thus the differences between their ball and ours were even greater then than they are today. Still, the seventy-plus is a "hard ball" and is much closer to the old American ball than it is to the English ball. In what follows I use the terms, *hard ball, American ball,* and *seventy-plus ball* interchangeably.
† The British spell racquets with a *k* in place of a *qu*.

Rackets soon achieved a certain vogue as an adjunct to public houses (taverns). Again, these courts were one or two wall affairs (though sometimes a second side wall was added), and again they were open to the air.

Curiously, this pastime of debtors and drunkards gained admission into the very upper-class British boarding school, or "public school," Harrow, where a court was first built in 1822. Once again, it was a closed society that played the game, but this time at the other end of the social spectrum. How this came to pass, nobody seems to know; the connection apparently was not emphasized at the time. It would not unduly strain the sociological imagination to conceive of a descent from public school to public house to public institution. But the trip the other way remains a subject for future doctoral dissertations.

The game caught on, not only at Harrow, but at other public schools as well. At first the courts were open at the top and had less than four walls, but in the 1830s the Royal Artillery built a covered court and, thereafter, the roofed-in, four-wall court became the standard, as rackets became the game of the ultraexclusive schools, clubs, services, and universities.

Rackets enjoyed its greatest popularity in the 1860s and 1870s, particularly at Harrow, where students had to wait their turn outside the court. So that, once on the court, they wouldn't have to waste precious time warming up, and to pass the time while they waited their turn outside the court, the students at Harrow made up a little warm-up game, which consisted of rallying against a portion of an exterior wall. So that a missed ball wouldn't stray too far in the field behind them, they used an India rubber ball that had been punctured to deaden it. Squashy, you might call it! Another version has it that they rallied against a wall in a nearby courtyard, and used a squashy ball so as not to break any more of the master's windows. Either way, soon four-wall "miniature racket courts" were built to accommodate this "warm-up game." Thus the birth of what was then called "soft or squash ball rackets."

Squash was played almost entirely in schools until the 1890s, when some private courts began to be built. Then in the early years of this century, club courts started going up. But it wasn't until after the Great War that squash rackets eclipsed "hard" rackets in England because the latter was becoming too expensive. Squash courts took up less room and were cheaper to build than rackets courts. Because the squash ball was less lively than the rackets ball, squash courts ended up being about a quarter of the size of rackets courts. And the rubbery consistency of the squash ball meant that the playing surfaces didn't have to be the strength of prison walls. (To stand up to the punishment of the hard rackets ball, rackets courts had to be made of polished stone or an expensive blend of slate composition.)

Britain sent a squash team over here in 1924 and one Captain Gerald Robarts won our national championship. That was their first international competition. It was also, for some reason, the last time they sent an official team over here. We sent a team over there in the mid-thirties, but that was the only time we sent an official U.S. team to an English squash-playing country until the 1973 ISRF championships. From time to time various clubs would send not-too-serious "social sides" back and forth, but these teams were usually composed of players who were past their prime and picked for compatibility more than ability.

And so it was possible for a lad like me to grow up playing squash here with only the vaguest of notions as to what the English game was about. In fact, most of us hit the English ball for the first time in the spring of 1969, in a tournament in New York, put on by an Englishman.

Quentin Hyder, a British psychiatrist who was himself nuts on squash and had recently moved to New York, organized and bankrolled a tournament played with the English ball, but on narrow American courts, as there were no English-sized courts here then. The devout son of two medical missionaries, he appeared intent upon doing a little missionary work over here. His goal, he claimed, was not to win "the colonies" back, but just to expand the squash season, which he certainly did. In addition to his annual "Hyder" tournament, he organized interclub English-ball league play, which began after the regular season, and intercity team matches that involved New York, Boston, Philadelphia, Toronto, and Montreal. He also persuaded the Bermuda squash association to hold an annual fall tournament on their wide English courts for the leading American and Canadian players. And having achieved that, he got the Bahamians to host a sun 'n squash outing in the spring.

Quentin did a superb job of finding and creating events. My only complaint was that he used his office stationery for his squash correspondence. There's nothing wrong with that and it's done all the time, but the return address on his stationery was care of "The

Christian Counseling and Psychotherapy Center," an organization with which he had a professional affiliation. Which again was fine and certainly his business. My objection was that sometimes he sent these letters to my place of work, with the result that the day of their delivery I felt myself the recipient of many long and sympathetic stares.

So English squash now bracketed the "real" season. A number of us tournament types used it as a way of easing into and out of the season, though *easing* is perhaps a poor choice of words for an activity that required so much work. Anyway, it was recognized as a great way to play yourself into shape in the fall, and in the late spring it was something to do.

Playing "English" before and after the season was a way of playing more squash without going stale. Those of us who played in the Hyder events introduced the English ball to our home clubs, and soon some B and C players were playing with it too. And it was about this time that a number of clubs, particularly those that were in cities and didn't have tennis courts, installed air conditioning in their squash courts with a view to extending the squash season through the summer. Squash was becoming more popular, so there was more pressure on the courts during the season and some of this was spilling over into the off-season. Also, many of the new people taking up the game were not tennis players and so they were content to hang around the squash courts as long as they were playable. Air conditioning didn't bring the court down to winter temperatures, but it did make it more comfortable, and the slow English ball was a natural for these warmer temperatures, since no matter how heated up the ball got, it never got too fast.*

While some of us were getting acquainted with the English ball in these various Hyder events, the then president of our U.S. association, W. Stewart Brauns, was looking into the possibility of the U.S. becoming involved in official international competition beyond the annual U.S./Canada Lapham Cup match. The latter was a social thing—"five good players, five bad players, and five drinkers," is the way Brauns aptly described the fifteen-man teams that each side fielded. But how about real competition against the countries that used the English ball?

---

*The modern American ball, the seventy-plus ball, has been designed to play well in hot courts, and since its introduction it has killed off much of the summer English-ball play. Still, those who like a change of pace switch over to the English game.

Brauns investigated the possibility of coming up with a compromise game, which would reconcile some of the differences between the English and the American games, but the system of scoring seemed the only area where either side would consider making concessions. Court size is a larger problem, but the big issue is the ball. A true compromise would require either the adoption of a vastly pepped-up English ball or a significantly sloweddown American ball. But that wasn't in the cards. Both sides seemed content with their own games as they were, and Brauns concluded that for the foreseeable future, the countries that used the British ball weren't going to change their game, and we North Americans weren't going to change ours. And so for the time being, the best that could be hoped for was that we would become better acquainted with their game, and they more familiar with ours. After all, in tennis you have many different surfaces ranging from grass to clay, why not variety in squash?

What came of all this was the decision to enter a U.S. team in the 1973 ISRF championships. We were an official entry, but Brauns made it clear to the ISRF that the fact of our entry was not to be taken as an endorsement of the English ball as *the* ball for international competition. In point of fact, when the U.S. and Canada joined the ISRF in 1969, one of the conditions we set was that the ISRF constitution be changed to recognize our ball and playing rules as the official game for North America. In 1971 the rules of the association were changed to recognize our ball as an official ball, without reference to geography, and the next year the rules were further modified to specify that the official ball of the host country would be used for the ISRF championships. You can imagine all the memos and meetings that this sort of business requires, but in the end those "concessions" didn't change the fact that the ISRF championships would continue to be played with their ball. In fact, in recent years the English ballers, in official communications (particularly those directed at the U.S. and Canada), had taken to referring to their ball as the "international ball."

Stewart warned us that we'd be hearing this and urged us not to refer to it as such—that would be conceding too much. On the other hand, calling it "the English ball," as we were accustomed to doing, Stewart explained, wasn't quite accurate either. For one thing, we had to acknowledge that this ball was used outside England. And, for another, the ball that they were now using in most events was an ever so slightly pepped-up version of the "English" ball. It had been developed in Australia several years back and was referred to colloquially as the "Australian ball." Furthermore, to call ours the "American ball," as we were in the habit of doing, would be too limiting, for our neighbors to the north and to the south also use our ball. So ours, properly speaking, isn't the American ball, but the *North* American ball. But to avoid unnecessarily stirring up rivalries concerning international geopolitical squash boundaries, Stewart recommended we call theirs the "soft ball" and ours, the "hard ball."

And as for the championships, Stewart warned us they'd be calling them the world championships, though, in point of fact, they were the "ISRF championships," and nowhere in the charter or anywhere else were they officially designated the "world" championships. To call an event played with the soft ball the "world" championships would be giving too much away, so we were to be careful to refer to it in conversation as the "ISRF" or "soft ball" championships.

We were happy not to yield on these points as we were not too high on our chances, and so the fact that this was neither our game nor the only game could bear some repetition.

Only one member of our team, Dinny Adams, had had any international experience with the soft ball. The summer before, he had journeyed to South Africa to see some animals and to play the circuit there, which attracted some of the world's leading soft ball players. When he returned, he reported that he'd been totally outclassed, and then further shared his experience with us by winning both the fall Bermuda tournament and the spring Hyder event. Though ranked only number twelve in our game, none of us could yet hit the soft ball hard enough to rattle him the way we did with the American ball. That split second of forgiveness that comes with the slower ball gave him the little extra time he needed to get set up. And if he could get set up, he could go to work on us with his placements. Well I knew, for this New York lawyer ran me ragged in the finals of the fall 1972 Bermuda tournament.

Number two on our team was another former Harvard player, Jay Nelson, who was now working in New York as a securities analyst. Jay was really the first American to apply the fitness approach to top-level hard ball squash. At Harvard, where he skipped his freshman year, he recalls he spent most of his time goofing off in the "butt room." Barnaby's gift was for making players "better than they were," but Jay loitered at number five or six on the team. For some reason Jay didn't get turned on until several years out of Harvard, when he decided to see how good he could get in squash. To do this he not only quit smoking, but, as if to atone for years of sloth, he also put himself through a vicious running program, long before distance running became a national craze. He didn't neglect his stroking, but his basic strategy at the time was to be the "fifth wall" in the court and send everything back. He liked the physical challenge of a long, tough point, and so it was no surprise that he preferred the soft ball. Until Dinny went to South Africa, Jay was considered the best American soft ball player.

We didn't have soft ball rankings; the team was picked based on performance in the Hyder events. Tom Poor and I, ranked sixth and fourth, respectively, in hard ball the past season, rounded out the team. Like me, Tom was up for anything called squash. Over the years, he had played more tournaments than anyone else on the circuit. Perhaps envious of all the titles he won (over and over again), some people accused him of a little "trophy hunting." Well, no one could accuse him of that this time. The Canadians, who had sent a team to the 1971 ISRF championships, which were held in New Zealand, had come home with no team victories and just one individual win, at number three against India. It was obvious that we, too, would be in over our heads; the question was how much of a struggle could we put up before going under.

Except for Dinny, who had taken that trip to South Africa, our only exposure to world class soft ball players was in the hard ball game. The Khans and Anil Nayar, who had grown up in the soft ball game, we observed could hit our ball exceptionally hard, were cat quick, and never seemed to get the least bit tired. And strengthening the impression that the soft ball game was very "physical" was the performance of the Australian team that toured the U.S. for the first time in the winter of 1972.

Whereas the Khans and Nayar were flashy, explosive athletes, the Aussies were Steady Eddy, methodical "grinders." They all played the up-and-down game to perfection. Every now and then, they'd toss in a drop shot or a wide-angled roll corner, but there was little change in the tempo of their play or the expressions on their faces.

This was not a social visit; they came to play squash. They dutifully got up and sang "Waltzing Matilda," but they seemed impatient with the numerous cocktail parties held in their honor at each stop on their tour. They didn't talk much, and when they did, it was about squash.

At first the Aussies were put off by the unfamiliar angles and speed of the ball, but it didn't take them long to settle into their unimaginative, but error-free, groove. They all won some matches here and there, frequently coming back from down 1-2 or love-2 in games. But the player who really made an impression was Cam Nancarrow, who was rated number one in the world in amateur soft ball. This tall, sandy-haired lefty seemed half-asleep on the court. He parked himself on the T in a peculiar slouchy, splay-footed stance. His eyelids drooping, he looked about as alert as a basset hound on sleeping pills, yet somehow with a step and a stretch there was nothing he couldn't retrieve. And he had excellent ball control with a very nice, fluid stroke. But the thing that was most disconcerting about him was that during his matches he would slowly chew on a piece of gum without ever losing a beat. It was as if he were digesting our game, which apparently he was, for by the second week he had picked up a wicked three-wall nick.

Only two weeks after arriving, Nancarrow wore out our own "grinder," Jay Nelson, en route to the semis of the U.S. nationals, and the next weekend he won the Canadian title. This was some squash player.

The successes of Nancarrow, Nayar, and the Khans made me curious to learn more about the soft ball players and their game. I was also curious to see how we'd do in their game. Maybe we were out of our league, but this trip to the ISRF championships wasn't meant to be a George Plimpton-type misadventure. We were squash players near the top of our game, accustomed to winning. The soft ball wasn't our game, but just maybe we'd catch on. And it would be fun to represent the U.S. in a foreign country. But there was the rub. The foreign country where the 1973 championships were to be played was South Africa.

I had then, and I have today, real uncertainties as to whether or not an athlete should participate in an event played in South Africa. Their policy of apartheid is totally repulsive. Is it right to play games in such a country? Is it right to play representatives of white South Africa anywhere?

In general I am in favor of keeping international politics out of attempts to bring together scientists, artists, or athletes. And if you lay down the rule that any country that violates human rights should not be permitted to participate in international contests and exchanges, then no such events would be possible. There could be no participants. Every country to a greater or lesser extent violates human rights. Certainly athletic competition against the Soviet Union would be out of the question. And yet I think that, all things considered, the more exchanges with the Soviet Union, the better.

So what is to be done with South Africa? White South Africa complains that a hypocritical world singles South Africa out for special treatment. Well, from everything I read before I went there and saw while I was there, they are a special case. As far as I'm concerned, there's nothing else happening in that country other than the attempt by a white minority to exploit and "keep in their place" a nonwhite majority. There are some brave souls in South Africa who are trying to bring about change, but apartheid (which they're now calling "separate development") is the central fact of their political, economic, and social life, and until it's done away with, nothing else much matters there.

What then are the responsibilities of an athlete from another country invited to compete in South Africa? The fact is that international sports federations have had a liberalizing influence on South Africa's racial policies as they apply to sports. South Africans are incredibly sports minded. They are so desperate to compete against athletes from other countries, they have been willing to make concessions in sports that to date have been unthinkable to them in other areas of their life.

Black and white South Africans are now permitted to compete on the same teams in certain circumstances. I don't consider this a great leap forward, but it is a step in the right direction. Sharif Khan, who as a "non-European" would be forced to suffer the policies of apartheid if he lived in South Africa, was invited to compete in a series of South African squash tournaments the summer of 1972. He went on the understanding that there would be no restrictions placed on him, and apparently they honored this commitment. I believe their reason for inviting Sharif was to prove that they could host an international squash event involving "non-Europeans," without incidents that would embarrass the participants.

The charter of the ISRF requires that the host country of the ISRF championships send invitations to all ISRF members, and so South Africa was required to extend full and unqualified invitations to Egypt, Pakistan, and India. The governments of these countries would not let their squash associations send teams to South Africa, but at least South Africa was forced to accept on paper, anyway, the policy of permitting "non-European" athletes to move about without restrictions during this event.

I persuaded myself that since South Africa had made this concession to the ISRF, it was all right for me to participate. Obviously, whether or not I personally played there couldn't have made less of a difference to the South Africans or the policies of their country. So what it came down to was how I felt about being a participant.

Well, I went. But I was never comfortable with the fact of my participation. I was nagged by the thought that this is no place to be playing games. Ordinarily when I travel I like to throw myself into the country I'm visiting. When in Rome, do as the Romans do. But I had no desire to do as the South Africans do. I spent most of my time distancing myself from the South Africans or arguing with them. I love traveling, but this turned out to be the wrong place for me to be. I was mad all the time—mad at the South Africans and mad at myself for being there. Nevertheless, I stayed to the very end, which says something about the incredible pull the squash had for me.

In South Africa the Boers call squash "*muurbal*," which translates to "murder the ball." But the real killer turned out to be the altitude. Johannesburg, where the team event was played, sits on the world's richest deposit of gold, a mile above sea level, and at that height, until you get acclimated, you feel like you've got an iron band around your chest when you go to take a deep breath.

We started going for deep breaths there at the start of August, two weeks before the team championships were to begin. Six teams were entered in the championships, which was set up so that each team played every other team. They made a pretty big deal of this event. A team host met us at the airport. We were provided with a team car, room and board, and a daily allowance to cover additional expenses. Scaffolding had been put up above the sides of the exhibition court at the Wanderer's Club so that over five hundred people could watch the major matches. Reflecting the South African passion for sport, this private club had fields and facilities for every English sport I'd ever seen or heard of.

Courts were assigned to each team for morning and afternoon practice sessions. During those practice sessions we got a chance to have a look at the players on the other teams. Watching them work out, the curious thing about their play was that it seemed like a lot of nothing was going on. The points were longer, certainly, but not a whole lot happened in them. Most of the play was up and down the walls, with occasional straight drops and wide-angled side wall/front walls. But these short shots were seemingly not attempts to put the ball away, but just to run the opponent. These soft ball players were not nearly as aggressive as we were about bringing points to a conclusion. They were playing points—keeping score, anyway—but it looked more like they were going through drills at half-speed. I assumed they were saving themselves for the big matches, and so didn't take this "slo mo" stuff too seriously.

What did impress me was their swing, which I immediately set about trying to copy. I knew the soft ball players took their racquets back high—I'd seen the Khans, Nayar, and the visiting Aussies do this in the American game—and I had started trying to take a bigger backswing myself, when I played English. But what surprised me was the extent of their soft ball windup. The high-backswing stroke they used with the hard ball, it turned out, was only a cut down version of an even bigger stroke they used with the soft ball.

At the peak of their swing, the soft ball players have the shaft of the racquet parallel to the floor, as in a golf swing. This extra windup increases the arc of the swing and hence the speed of the head of the racquet at the moment of impact. With the slow bounding soft ball they have enough time to do this, and the added windup is the only way to put some smoke on that ball. They crack it not by muscling it, but by whipping the racquet head through a huge arc.

As in the traditional American squash stroke, the wrist is cocked so that the racquet is at right angles to the forearm, and the elbow bent so that the forearm is at right angles to the upper arm. Obviously, not all players swing exactly alike, but the only significant variation among orthodox soft ball players seems to be whether or not they let the elbow fly on the backswing of the forehand. Some keep it tucked in pretty close to the body, always pointing downward; others let it fly, taking it back like a bird flapping a wing. But in both styles, on the downswing the elbow is brought in close to the body as it passes in front of the belly.

I say downswing, but by the time the racquet head meets the ball, the racquet is moving through a horizontal plane. The fact that they take a high windup doesn't mean they swing down on the ball. What they do is swing down, and then through the ball so that, as with the Harvard stroke and every other sound stroke, the racquet is moving through a horizontal hitting zone at the moment of impact. What the big loopy windup does is add to the speed of the head of the racquet, but it doesn't have anything to do with the direction the racquet head is moving at the moment of impact. The follow-through of the soft ball stroke differs from the various American swings in that it is high. In fact, the racquet head at the conclusion of this swing is pointed toward the ceiling. What keeps it safe and controllable is that, unlike a wraparound tennisy follow-through, it is in close to the body and in this sense is contained. This unchecked follow-through permits them to swing with more force, and also to lift the ball well above the tin for length. With a squishy ball, the problem is not keeping a drive off the back wall, but getting it deep with force. The face of the racquet may be slightly open at the moment of impact, but no conscious attempt is made to cut the ball on drives, as this would attenuate the power. The ball is hit almost flat on power drives. Everything in the soft ball stroke is oriented toward making a ball that's mush on the racquet move quickly. The wrist is given more scope with the soft ball than with the American ball. It is snapped with greater force on the forehand, and is even given a little play, though not much, on the backhand.

Another source of power that the soft ballers draw on is the hips. A good rotation of the torso is always important, but particularly so in the soft ball game, since with the slow ball there is more time to set up for the stroke, and more need to. The good soft ball players wind up with the body as much as they do with the racquet, so that, though they are turned sideways to the front wall for the stroke, their rear end at the peak of the backswing is practically pointing toward the front wall.

Another thing we noticed about the soft ball technique is that while their swing is more furious than ours on the drives, it's more gentle on the drops. Touch is achieved by sort of cradling the ball with a slow, stiff-armed stroke so that the ball is almost carried on the racquet. Pushed drop shots seem more effective than firm, crisp ones, which tend to sit up or pop up out of the nick. In fact, in the soft ball game a drop shot that is hit softly and hugs the side wall, like a mini rail shot, is often safer than a drop that is aimed for the nick, but will jump up if it doesn't catch the crease quite right.

Since the South African championships began several days after we arrived, we didn't have too much time to perfect our latest versions of the soft ball swing before testing them against international competition. Most of the top players were entered in this singles championship, which served as a warm-up for the main events. Dinny had not arrived yet, but Tom, Jay, and I were entered in it. I am pleased to report that down 2-1, I fought back to score our first international overseas victory, against a highly underrated local player in the first round. Tom, alas, succumbed to a former South African champion, who was the captain of the South African team. The fact that Leo Melville last won that national title in 1961 and now in his forties was only a nonplaying captain of their team was bad for our morale. Jay picked things up a bit, though, with a solid victory over another underrated local. Jay and I got a taste of the real thing in the second round, where we met the top two British players. Jay played former Cambridge Captain Philip Ayton, and I had a go against former Oxford Captain John Easter. As in the practice sessions we'd observed, they were in no rush to put the ball away. Instead, they ran us silly. They seemed to be toying with us. We picked up a few points here and there, but mostly we got tired. Maybe it was the wide courts and the altitude that we weren't quite adjusted to yet. Only time would tell.

We had plenty of time to rest up and digest our early experience, for the South African championships lasted an entire week, and, of course, we didn't. Soft ball tournaments in general take much longer to run off than ours because they never play more than one round a day, and in the major tournaments they schedule rest days between several rounds. This is necessary, I suppose, because the matches can be incredibly draining, but it also means that in order to play the amateur circuits in the soft ball countries, you have to take a substantial amount of time off from work or find a way to make squash your principal occupation without being declared a pro. Many of the participants in the ISRF championships seemed particularly adept at the latter.

Our first opponent in the ISRF team event was Australia. They had won the previous three team and individual ISRF titles and, though their top two players, Geoff Hunt and Ken Hiscoe, had declared themselves pros after the last championships and hence were ineligible this time around, the Aussies were still the team to beat.

Playing number three, I had what proved to be the dubious honor of leading off. My opponent, Mike Donnelly, was a late arrival and had not played in the South African championships so I had not had a chance to scout him. Nevertheless, I won the serve and the first point, on a cross-court backhand drop that nicked. But then things started to go against me. To this day I refuse to believe the London *Times* report that my match lasted only eight minutes. (Six minutes playing time, if you subtract the two one-minute breaks after the first and second games.) Somehow, that London *Times* article got circulated among my squash friends back in New York, and I had to spend a year telling people it must have been a misprint; and even if it wasn't, did they think they could have done any better. I'd say the match was at least twice that long. But it is true that I made no effort to prolong things out there. Easter had convinced me in the South African nationals that it was hopeless for me to try to hang in on the long points. I just wasn't fit enough to go the distance. And so I decided to go for broke. I came out shooting, aiming everything—volleys, drives and drops—into the short nick. I think my scores were 1, love, and 2. Something like that.

Next up was Dinny, who, because of his victories in the Bermuda and Hyder tournaments, was stuck with being number one. None of us envied him his top position for it meant he had the least winnable match, particularly here, where he faced the redoubtable Cam Nancarrow, who had just added the '73 South African title to a long list of credits that included the Australian and British amateur titles. I don't have the minute count on this match, but I do know Dinny got one less point than I did. I know this because it emerged after the matches that to keep their concentration, the Aussies had each chipped a little money into a "low man pool" for the evening. And the player who held his opponent to the fewest points and thus won the pot was Cam Nancarrow.

The final match of the evening between Jay and their number two, Dave Wright, was a little less humbling. Jay knew he couldn't last, but instead of going for the quick winner, he tried to play the game the right way, that is, he kept hitting for length with only occasional side wall/front walls and drops. He didn't win many points, but he played a number of long ones, and at least looked like a serious soft ball player.

He impressed the editor of *The Australian Squash Player*, Doug Mason, who told us later that in a radio broadcast he and the team had taped to report home on Australia's progress at the championships, he had told the listeners that the name, Jay Nelson, is one they'd all learn, if Nelson ever had the opportunity to spend a season competing in Australia. And what kind of impression had I made on Mason? He allowed that he was only a club player and had been out of action for the past year because of a heart attack, but he was keen to have a game with me and suggested we play some time, schedule permitting.

The Americans were clearly no longer a threat. After the match the Aussies, who up to now had been grim competitors and stuck to themselves, loosened up a bit and gave us a few pointers. Dave Wright told me that going for quick winners was a losing proposition in the soft ball game, as if Donnelly hadn't already proved that to me on the court. But the interesting thing he said is that the idea of a short shot in their game is not to put the ball away but to work the opponent. It's possible to run almost anything down that's short in the court, so there's no percentage in trying to put the soft ball away with these shots. But it is possible to work your opponent, and he took me out on the court and showed me the premier shot for doing this. They call it the "working boast" and for good reason. It's like our three-wall nick, except it doesn't make the third wall and so it doesn't nick. A three-wall nick would be nice, but with a slow ball in a wide court the nick is almost impossible to make and certainly not a percentage shot. So they use the "working boast" instead, which is intended not to put the ball away but to run or "work" the opponent.

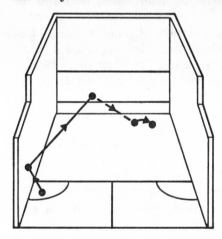

FIGURE 15: THE WORKING BOAST (IN A SOFT BALL COURT)

Strategically, it's used like the American three-wall nick—you set it up by hitting a few rail shots to get your opponent leaning toward the wall. And it's hit with a full windup so it looks like it's going to be a drive. But unlike the three-wall nick, you fully expect your opponent to get the working boast back. What makes the shot a killer is when you take him deep on the next ball. As with the three-wall nick, you make your opponent cover the diagonal. The working boast is a standard shot in the repertoire of all soft ball players, but I always think of it as a particularly Australian shot because "working the opponent" seems to be what squash is all about for the Aussies. They view squash more as a test of stamina than of strokes. This attitude is not simply a result of the fact that because the soft ball is tough to put away the game necessarily becomes something of a fitness contest. It goes deeper than that. The Aussies as a people are vigorous sportsmen who like to work up a sweat. Their athletes have always excelled in fitness sports like distance running and swimming, and in the finesse sports they usually have a conditioning edge on their opponents too. The years they dominated Davis Cup tennis, they rarely lost fifth sets. And these days they don't lose many fifth games in squash.

The Aussies changed my thinking on conditioning. Before I went to South Africa I ran three to five miles every other day for a couple of months. Since I was doing this in addition to playing squash, I figured I was really getting in shape. But obviously, I'd figured wrong, for I was getting exhausted in the middle of first games over there. And so were my teammates, who also had trained on three-to-five-mile runs. It didn't make sense until I talked to Lionel Robberds. An alternate at number three, Lionel was the captain of the Australian team. The program also identified him as a former Olympic coxswain. I've often suspected that coxes could never push themselves as hard as they drive their crews. Lionel proved me wrong. The stopwatch that he carried around, it turned out, was not a good luck charm from the Rome Olympics but something he put to practical use on himself. When I asked him about that stopwatch, he introduced me to the concept of interval training.

Lionel explained to me that there are two kinds of training, aerobic and anaerobic. In aerobic training you use the oxygen you take in during the exercise; but in anaerobic training you don't. It's the difference between distance work and wind sprints. When you run distances you continually process the oxygen that you breathe in. But when you go flat out in a wind sprint, you quickly develop an oxygen debt, and after a short while must stop, or at least slow down, so that you can recover.

Squash requires a good deal of anaerobic conditioning. It's an on-and-off kind of activity. You play a point, stop for a moment, play a point, stop for a moment, and so on until the end of the game, when you get a little longer time to rest. You need the kind of conditioning that enables you to go flat out for a tough point, and then recover quickly so that you can do it again. But running long distances, even at a fast clip, doesn't develop this ability the way wind sprints does. All it takes in squash is one or two points that are tougher than you are accustomed to and you're in trouble. You don't get enough time to recover and the next point you go even deeper into oxygen debt.

Robberds explained to me that he and his compatriots use distance work as a way of "getting in shape to get in shape." During the off season they run between three and ten miles every day or two. This provides the basic foundation; if they skipped this phase of their training they wouldn't have the strength to really put out when it comes time to do a series of sprints. After a month or two of this kind of training they phase out of distance work and into sprint work. Robberds and some of the fellows "like" to run quarter miles; others do sprints in the court. The idea is to run as fast as you can a predetermined distance that takes you between forty-five seconds and a minute and a half to cover. If you go for a shorter time you don't get the training effect you need for long squash points, but if you try to go longer than a minute and a half, you can't go flat out. They rest for thirty to forty-five seconds and then do it again. The goal is to be able to do a number of repetitions without a loss of speed and without increasing the rest interval.

I've learned over the years not to trust what people tell me about their conditioning programs. What they say is usually a boast. They either want you to believe they do very little, hence their accomplishments are due to great natural talents, or they want to intimidate you by leading you to believe they're even fitter than they are. The Aussies, I suspect, incline to the latter. Anyway, the Australian view seems to be that if you can do between sixteen and thirty-two consecutive quarter-mile sprints, without letting up, you should be in pretty good shape to play their game.

No doubt about it, the Australian squash players are dedicated athletes. Their culture has a lot to do with it, but there's another factor at work as well. And that's the commercial squash center. Until the mid-fifties all squash played in Australia was in private schools and clubs. As elsewhere in the world, squash there was a game for the well-to-do. But then a couple of enterprising souls decided to build courts that could be rented. The idea caught on and soon pay-and-play centers were popping up all over. The idea was simple; anyone could come in off the street and rent not just a court, but also a ball and racquet, and even a pair of sneakers. Squash became a game for the masses, like bowling in the U.S.

Apparently, most of these squash centers are nothing fancy. Basically, what they offer is squash and a shower. The fancier ones have lounges for "squash socials," and some of the centers have nurseries that look after kids while their mothers play. Most of these places have three to six courts, and typically they are "Mom and Pop" operations, with Mom and Pop living in an apartment above the courts.

Play is year round, but the courts are never air conditioned, not even in climes where the temperature tops one hundred. Apparently Aussies don't expect such pampering. And by keeping things simple, the rates can be kept simple—maybe two American dollars to rent a court these days.

Cam Nancarrow told me about these centers when we got to talking about how he got started in squash. When he was a kid one of these facilities went up near his home. His dad went to check it out and came home with a racquet and a pair of sneakers that he'd won in a promotional raffle. Figuring he was too old to take up a new game, he gave the equipment to his son. A good all-round athlete who'd played a little tennis, Cam decided to give the game a go and soon became hooked. So much so that, though the court rates were inexpensive, he couldn't afford to play as much as he wanted. However, he persuaded a sympathetic manager to let him and his friends play for free when the courts weren't booked. The only problem was that no lights would be provided, since the way people paid for courts was by putting coins in a meter that controlled the lights. So Cam and his friends would hope for a sunny day. And what shots they would practice would depend upon the placement of the windows above the court that was free and the angle of the sun at that time of day.

With the commercial facility as the vehicle, the game took off "down under." In fact, for some time now more squash has been played in Australia than tennis. Though bigger than tennis in terms of numbers of participants, with limited galleries, the game has yet to become a big spectator sport there; and until quite recently there's been very little money in their pro tournaments. But no doubt the increased accessibility and popularity of the game, made possible by the commercial center, has improved the chances of attracting good athletes. And the commercial center also makes it possible for the dedicated player to keep close to the courts. Both Cam, who quit school at sixteen, and Dave Wright, who is a qualified electrician, though "amateurs," found jobs in squash facilities, "assisting with the management."

Since there were four people on our team and only three could play, we decided that each of us would sit out at least one match. I volunteered to sit out our next one. It was against South Africa and I didn't want to have anything more to do with them than I had to. Again it was three quick matches, nine quick games.

Next came New Zealand. This one presented possibilities, we thought. They, too, had been clobbered by South Africa. Playing at number three, I again led off. The guy I faced was a diffident soul. He would smile sheepishly when addressed, and hardly ever said a word. His teammates called him "Rowdie." He had abysmal strokes that resulted from a faulty grip. I don't lose to guys with strokes like that. I was determined to follow Wright's advice and try to play longer points. Which I did. I won the first couple of points and was so buoyed by the feeling I was outplaying my man that I looked for a teammate in the gallery to wink at. In retrospect, I'm glad I never delivered that wink, for after I got to 4-1 in the first game, the lights went out. Rowdie, who proved a very determined retriever, got me into a long, long point that was just too much for me. And that was it. I never recovered from it. I picked up a few points here and there, but I was just too tired to regain control of the play. The frustration was I felt I could beat him if only my conditioning were better.

Tom and Jay, playing the tougher number two and number one men respectively, also fell in three. So, after three matches, we had yet to win a game, and the prospects of doing so in the upcoming match against Great Britain were not rosy.

The British were clearly not up to the Aussies, but a powerhouse, nonetheless. At the time, commercial centers were just starting to go up all over England. It was too soon to feel the effects of this at the top of the game, and the four members of their team were public school boys in the British sense of the term. But they had some dedicated athletes on their team, and none was more dedicated than my opponent, Bryan Patterson. Like Rowdie, he was less than a classic stylist. He had a "broken wing" backhand and wasn't particularly quick. But he was terribly determined.

He had seemingly modeled himself after another British lefty whose natural talents caused little envy, but whose ability year after year to grind down the competition in the British Open taught a little respect. I speak of Jonah Barrington. Barrington, who was now a pro and therefore ineligible for the ISRF championships, had lifted his game to new heights by training in the mountains of Kenya before the British Open each year. The British Open, which is regarded as the world championships of soft ball squash, had been dominated by Pakistani and Egyptian pros since World War II. Barrington was able to "win the title back" by working out for an incredible six and seven hours a day. Some claimed it was the vindication of the fitness approach; others said he was ruining the game by setting an example that took the artistry out of it.

I've seen Barrington play, and it's true he's no stylist. He looks like he's playing with his wrong hand. And he's not particularly fast. But the thing about him is he doesn't slow down. Apparently, when he plays a big match, the first game he keeps his eye not on the score, but on the clock. He doesn't much care who wins it so long as he keeps it going for over forty-five minutes or something like that. The defensive play up and down the walls won't keep you on the edge of your seat, but the guts and determination of this little man are inspirational. At a time when every one else was despairing of the possibility of beating the Khans and their countrymen, Barrington said, "I can beat these guys," and went out and did it. His view was that the English were no longer tops in their game, not because of a lack of talent, but because they relied too much on talent. Though himself a graduate of the system, he was scornful of the British public school ethos of the amateur who, born to rule, succeeds because of his superior gifts.

Something of a carouser during his university days, Barrington became interested in fitness only after his doctor recommended some exercises for a back problem. He took up squash, first as a way to keep fit; but the game grabbed him and he started working at getting fit to play squash. It became a passion and, determined to make his mark as a squash player, he supported himself with odd jobs, which included a paper route that he ran. But his principal occupation was improving his fitness. With this in mind, he consulted a Sergeant "Bomber" Harris of the Royal Air Force, a fitness specialist who had trained the British badminton team with great success. And each year before the British Open, Barrington would take himself to the mountains of Kenya, to train at altitude.* Barrington would lose matches before and after the Open, but in the big one, he could push his sinewy little body to extraordinary lengths and grind his opponents down until style didn't matter anymore. And for all the talk of his not being much with a racquet, he was extraordinarily accurate up and down the walls.

What Barrington did was up the conditioning ante for championship soft ball squash. Aussie pro Geoff Hunt finally ended Barrington's five-year reign over the Open in 1974. Geoff told me he had decided he was damned if he was going to lose that title again on fitness, and so in his training program for that tournament he built up to thirty-two consecutive quarter-mile wind sprints. The Aussies don't like to get beat on conditioning. Interestingly, Barrington seemed to have had more effect on the Australians than on his own countrymen. The English team members in South Africa, with one exception, were classic public school amateurs. They were fit enough, but not fanatics like Barrington, and relied basically on their strokes to win. The one exception was my opponent, Bryan Patterson, who was a high school phys. ed. instructor by trade, but for the previous six months had taken time off to train for the team trials. Following Barrington's example, he spent his weekends training at "Bomber" Harris's fitness camp with the result that, though not much in the stroke department, he made the tail end of the team, and so he was my opponent at number three.

I know a bad backhand when I see one, and I went right to work on his. (Lefties for some reason never have strong backhands, and Patterson was a good example of this.) I found if I could glue the ball to the right-hand wall, he'd either make an error or send up a cripple. I was having a grand time out there, leading something like 7-1 in the first game, and then the lights went out again. He put me through what, I believe, Barrington calls a "pain bearer"—a tough point that tests your ability to take pain. I

---

*In point of fact, I don't believe there's any medical evidence to show that periodically training at altitude improves your stamina at sea level. But it may give you quite a psychological boost and psych out the competition, which is apparently what it did for Barrington.

flunked. From there on out I had an oxygen debt I couldn't finance, and as Vince Lombardi used to say, "Fatigue makes cowards of us all." Patterson really rubbed it in by going for a run after our match. My teammates, who had tougher opponents at one and two, also fell in three.

So, we were down to the last match and still no games. The Canadians at least had won that match against India in the 1971 championships. But there were no Indians or Canadians this time around. The Canadian government, at the last minute, had threatened to withdraw financial support from their squash association if they competed in South Africa. The Canadians scratched, but matches had already been scheduled. Filling in for the Canadians, informally, was a pickup team composed of an Aussie and a New Zealander, who had just missed making their respective teams, and a Dutchman, who laid claim to his country's national title.

In the soft ball game height is considered a distinct disadvantage. A long reach is small compensation for having to make an extra effort to get down to the ball. And in grueling soft ball rallies, there's a lot of getting down to the ball. Six foot three John Easter of Britain told me that for this reason his size works against him in long points. And Cam Nancarrow, assessing his build for squash, told me he was lucky to have arms that were so long he needed specially fitted shirts, but he felt at 6'2 he was 3 or 4 inches too tall. His thinking was that if he had shorter legs, he could turn more easily.

Well, the Dutchman was 6'5. "Tallie" the New Zealanders called him. But given my own level of fitness, I wasn't so sure I should attempt to draw him into long points to make him feel his size. By now our team had attracted a considerable following—clowns always do—and I was bombarded with advice from members of other teams who wanted to see the U.S. win something, so long as it wasn't something off of them. As so often happens when you get squash advice from a number of different people, it all added up to zero. For every person who said keep him deep, there was someone else who said take him short. I decided to play my own match. One thing I'd noticed was that like so many soft ball players, instead of hitting his backhand, he would scoop under the ball and pull it. So I decided to work his backhand over, particularly with cross-courts that would twist "Tallie."

The plan worked and once again I built up a nice little lead in the first game. In fact, I beat him to 8, and at 8-5 it looked very much like game U.S.A. But then we started one of those hand in, hand out, hand in, hand out routines and I couldn't seem to get that ninth point. The lights hadn't gone out yet, but they were starting to flicker as I put everything I had into winning that game point. But he tied it up 8 all and I set 2, not wanting to give him game ball on his serve. Again it was hand in, hand out, hand in, hand out. Then I pulled ahead 9–8, only to have him tie it up 9 all. Again, hand in, hand out, hand in . . . And then I popped him with the ball. I can think of more glorious ways for the U.S. to win its first ISRF game, but the manner in which I won that point didn't dim the sound of "The Star-Spangled Banner" as it played in my head. I would have preferred it to be a game against an official team, but in life you have to settle for what you can get, and as it turned out that was all we could get the entire series. One game.

At the conclusion of the series, which, as expected, Australia won, our team host drew me aside and asked me in an it's-OK-to-tell-me kind of way, "Come on now, what's your real ranking back in the States?" He seemed incredulous that a player of my standard could be number four in such a large nation. And the events of the past few weeks, I must say, had done little to reinforce my own image of myself as a squash player of some standing. I had to keep reminding myself (and anyone else who would listen) that this wasn't the game we played back home.

It was called squash, but it wasn't squash as we knew it. It was more like a squash player's nightmare. You're out there supposedly playing squash, but everything's a little wrong—the tin's too high, the court's too wide—and when you hit what looks to be the ball, nothing happens. It's a black marshmallow.

It's like that dream where you're running as hard as you can, but you're not moving. You get your opponent out of position, but you can't put the ball away. And when you finally do win a point, it turns out you don't get the point, just the serve. And you're getting more and more tired. Now I ask you, is this not a squash player's nightmare? No, say the soft ballers. A nightmare is finding yourself in a narrow corridor, which is masquerading as a squash court. They tell you it's squash, but the ball's so hard it plays like a golf ball on concrete. You're in each other's way all the time, and before you can get into any real rallies, your opponent's put the ball away with some fluky shot.

The two games are different. In my opinion, soft ball is a terrific game, but hard ball is a better one. The soft ball game is a challenge and you can learn something from it. I think the soft ball swing with the big windup is superior to the one I originally learned because it enables you to get power without muscling the ball. When playing with the hard ball I don't wind up quite as much as I do with the soft ball, and my follow-through is not quite as high, but basically it's a soft ball swing that I use these days.*

Because there's more time between strokes, playing with the soft ball helps you develop the habit of lining your feet up properly for every shot. And playing with the slower ball gives you more time to work on improving the accuracy of your drives. Which is a must, since if you catch the side wall on a rail with the soft ball, it totally ruins the shot.

And playing a succession of fifty-stroke points requires not just marvelous conditioning, but terrific mental discipline also. But the conditioning is the big thing, and I must say, these fellows taught me the value of recovery exercises, not just for their game, but for ours as well. Like most amateurs of my era, I had been brought up to believe that training was for people who lacked skill with the racquet and who therefore always found themselves on the running end of points. But the truth is, "shooters" have to be in every bit as good shape as runners. If you get fuzzy from fatigue, you can't hit your finesse shots with consistency and accuracy. What happens is you start cheating on footwork and stop getting down to the ball and leaning into it. A runner can be a little groggy, all he's trying to do is get the ball back respectably. But a shot maker has to be fresh and alert to execute properly. And a shooter has to cover the response to his initiatives, which often means a mad scramble.

Before I went to Africa, like most American players in those days, I viewed squash as basically a test of strokes and strategy, and of mental toughness. To the extent that it was a physical contest it was a test of raw speed. But stamina was not a legitimate

---

*Now that we've switched over to the "seventy-plus" ball, which is a little slower than the old hard ball, all the top players are now using basically a soft ball stroke because there's more time to wind up and there's more need to, to make the ball travel. While the seventy-plus is a little softer than the old hard ball, it's still very much a hard ball, and, as with the old hard ball, the reverse corner and three-wall nick are effective shots with it. Though we were playing with the old hard ball at the time that I was first introduced to the soft ball, the principal differences I found back then between their game and ours still apply today.

part of the contest. I'd get tired all right, and so would my opponents upon occasion, but the ideal that I carried around in my
head of what squash was supposed to be did not include "test of
fitness." I wanted to win, so I tried to hang in when I was tired.
But I wasn't as tough as I might have been because I never fully
accepted the physical challenge. I wasn't playing squash to prove
that I could take pain and outlast my opponent. I took no pride in
that part of it.

But a dose of international soft ball and exposure to the atti-
tudes of these dedicated athletes changed my thinking. I came to
recognize that squash, not just theirs but ours as well, is, among
other things, a test of fitness. And not only did I come to accept
this as a fact of squash life, but I also acquired a taste for the
physical challenge. Henceforth, part of proving myself a squash
player was proving myself fit and able to take the pain of tough
points without letting up.

However, the conversion was not total. I felt then, and I feel
now, that soft ball squash places too much emphasis on fitness.
There's more to the soft ball game than just finesse, but in my
opinion you have to pay too high a conditioning ante to get into
the soft ball game at the championship level. No matter how
skilled you are with a racquet, you can't compete seriously in that
game unless you are phenomenally fit—much fitter than professional tennis players, hockey players, basketball players, and leading athletes in most other sports that test both fitness and finesse.

I find soft ball fun to play as a change of pace, and useful for
training, but in large doses it becomes very boring. There's too
much jockeying for position and too little decisive action. I soon
miss the exciting shots of the hard ball game. Some soft ballers tell
me that there are too many "fluky" putaways in hard ball. Sure,
there's some gambling that goes on, but you have to play the odds
intelligently to win in the hard ball game. The basic difference
between the two games is that in hard ball, if you get an opening,
you have a reasonable chance of putting the ball away, but in soft
ball the chances are all you can do is work your opponent.

It's fun to play a long point now and then, one that has several
lives, but a continuous diet of this stuff has as much intrinsic appeal to me as running on a treadmill. And watching championship
soft ball squash is the ultimate bore. In an exhibition, the top soft
ballers will fool around a little bit and show you a few shots, but
when the chips are on the table and the two players are evenly

matched, the game becomes a dreary exercise in defensive strategy. As they hit the ball up and down the wall, it's like the world sit-up contest. They go up and down, up and down, up and down, and you marvel at their ability to do this. You'd like to see the start of the contest and the end, but who wants to sit through the whole damn thing?

Because the soft ballers, as a rule, do better when they try our game than we do when we have a go at theirs, they sometimes make the argument that this is proof that they have a better game. In my opinion, which players win is hardly a test of which game is more fun to watch or to play.

Still, as a competitor, I take an interest in whose players win, and I'd have liked to have seen our team do better. The problem is, when you go to an unfamiliar game, you need an edge in fitness to make up for all the bungling you do in the process of getting adjusted. When they try our game, they have this cushion of conditioning to fall back on, but when we tried theirs, not only were we less fit than them, we didn't even have the minimum level of conditioning required to get into their game.

Though I admired the soft ball swing, I was not impressed by the racquet work, in general, of most of the players I saw. There were some excellent "stroke players," certainly, but most of the soft ballers had suspect backhands, and in most cases their feel for the ball was nothing special. After the team series I felt I had a pretty good feel for their game and wondered how I'd be able to do if only fitness weren't a factor.

Well, I found out. After the team event, in keeping with the original plan Dinny went to see some animals, Jay returned home to wife and children, and Tom and I journeyed to Durban for the ISRF singles championships.

The Cabana Beach Hotel, where the tournament was played, overlooked the Indian Ocean. It was about as close to sea level as you could get, so high altitude was no longer an excuse for getting out of breath. But Tom and I did get out of breath and we both lost in the first round. As expected, Cam Nancarrow won the title, but his opponent in the finals was a big surprise. Bryan Patterson, the number four man from England who I'd played in the team event, left a trail of upsets as he "Barringtoned" his way to second place.

But the interesting match, from my point of view, occurred in the first round of the "Plate Event," which is a polite term for the consolation tournament. There I met Derek Broom, who the year before had been rated number two in South Africa and had beaten Philip Ayton of Britain in an international "test" match. Ordinarily a player of this caliber would not find himself in a consolation event, but Broom had quit serious competitive squash and played very little the past year. He had entered the ISRF singles tournament only because it was held not far from where he lived. Woefully out of shape—in their terms—he lost in the first round, and I drew him in the "Plate."

What made this match interesting for me was he had all the skills of a world class player, but he didn't have that fitness advantage. If anything, I was in slightly better shape. So this would be a test of sorts, to see how I might do in their game if I had their conditioning.

Well, it was a battle. I got the first game, he got the next two. He got me down match point in the fourth, but I squiggled out of it and won that game to tie it up 2-2. It was at this point that my teammate, Tom Poor, did me a great disservice, albeit unwittingly. After the fourth game in soft ball squash there's a two-minute break, which may not sound like much, but it's twice as long as the break you get between the other games. As I was leaving the court, Tom met me with the words, "He's dead!"

I appreciated the encouragement, but what I didn't know at the time was that Broom, who was out of sight, was not out of hearing. A friend of Broom's told me the next day that after that fourth game, Broom was considering defaulting. He was dead tired and his business schedule would only permit him to play one more match anyway. But when he overheard Tom's unflattering assessment, he became determined to prove him wrong.

The fifth game was brutal. This was a clean match, but we'd been out there a long time, close to an hour and a half by now. We were both staggering and gasping, yet both unwilling to quit. Finally, I brought him to match point. But I needed some air bad. Since I had the serve, I decided to do something that I'd been doing with greater frequency toward the end of this match. I decided to serve a fault the first serve, so that I could get a little more time to get some air in and get myself together for this big point. I'd worked hard to get him down match point and I didn't want to blow it now. I was determined to put everything I had into winning this point.

Now in the American game, all I'd have to do is knock the first serve into the gallery. But in soft ball, if the first serve goes out of court (or into the tin), it counts as a double fault. But if you serve a fault within the court, under soft ball rules, your opponent can still play it, if he wants. After some experimentation, I had found that if I knocked the serve down my side of the court like a rail shot, my opponents wouldn't bother with it.

So I fired a rail. But this time Broom, who up to now had been quite willing to let these first serves go, and had seemed to appreciate the extra rest, was climbing up my back, hollering for a let point. To have gotten on me that fast, he had to have anticipated that fault down the wall and taken a head start.

If I was surprised that Broom was suddenly on my back, I was stunned that the referee would actually award him a let point. It's true that in the soft ball game referees are much more likely to award a let point when there is an obstruction than in our game, I guess because the court is wider and the ball is slower, so there's less excuse for being in the way. But a let point on this?

Broom went on to win the next three points for the match. I don't think I've ever been quite so outfoxed. I had thought I was being so clever, faulting that first serve. Broom told me afterward that he had been waiting for the right moment to spring that move. Apparently, there was more to this soft ball game than just fitness.

Chapter 7
THE KHAN PHENOMENON

"Sorry for English . . ."

What do you think about when you have a match against Hashim Khan? Hashim Khan, the greatest squash player who ever lived. Hashim Khan, the founding father and head man of the Khan squash dynasty. Hashim Khan, the legend. Hashim Khan, the living legend. Hashim Khan, my first-round opponent in the 1973 Boston Open.

Well, for one thing you think about his age. I mean how old is he, anyway? The program lists his date of birth as July 1, 1916, but it would have been a trifle more accurate if it had said something like, "Born same day as neighbor's cow." As I understand it, around the time of Hashim's birth not many records were kept at Nawakille, Northwest Frontier Province, India. And for that matter, I'm not so sure that many records are kept there even today, except for one. And that's a sign over the railroad station that reads: "Hashim Khan's Village."

I know about the sign because I read his book, *The Khan Game.* In his first chapter (reluctantly, but at the insistence of his coauthor) he tells his life story, or, as he puts it, "This is story of my life—so far."

It's a story that would never make it as fiction, it's too unbelievable. But when Hashim tells it, and tells it in his very affecting, "telegraphic" English, as he does in his book, the communication is so direct, you have to believe it. Believe everything except his date of birth. Westerners want to know the facts and figures; they want to know "the stats"; they want to know how old he is. Hashim wants to please, he doesn't want to give offense. So he says he was born July 1, 1916.

But what is age? We tend to look at age as determining performance. But for Hashim it's the other way around. Performance determines age, and, looked at this way, he seems to have stopped the clock. Most athletes are obsessed with age. Not Hashim. Legends aren't rooted in time.

If you're going to play someone, and that someone has written a book, as a general rule it's probably helpful to have read his book. What better way to get insight into how his game works? "As a general rule" this is probably so, but Hashim's book, particularly his first chapter in which he tells of his rise from obscurity, makes you wish you'd waited until after you'd played him to read his book. Still, it's must reading for anyone hooked on squash.

In case you haven't had a chance to read it yet, here are a few of the details of his remarkable life, just to give you an idea of what I was up against. Mind you, the story is far more effective when told in Hashim's own words, but for that you'll have to consult the original.

Hashim was born too poor to know poverty, let's say in 1916. His tiny village, Nawakille, was a fifteen-minute walk from Peshawar, a sizable city ten miles east of the Khyber Pass. The British troops who guarded the pass were quartered in Peshawar, and Hashim's father was a steward at one of the officers' clubs. As I have mentioned, wherever the British stationed troops they put up squash courts for the amusement of the officers, and Peshawar was no exception. The courts at the club where Hashim's father worked were open to the sky, and it's a lucky thing they were, for if they hadn't been, the calluses today on Hashim's right hand most likely wouldn't be from squash. But the roofless court was Hashim's opening, for as a small boy he would sit perched on the back wall watching the officers play, and when the ball flew out of court, he'd fetch it. For this he received five rupees a month. A rupee was worth about twenty American cents.

And because the courts were exposed to the sun, the officers didn't want to play at high noon when it was "beastly hot." So it was during this time of day that the ball boys would climb down off the walls and, barefoot on cement floors, knock a broken ball around. Sometimes Hashim couldn't find anyone to play. So he would play Hashim versus Hashim. Always running, running, running.

"It is good to run as hard as you can like this. You find out what you can do. Then you play a real opponent and never touch your limit, you are surprised, everything is more easy. But I do not know these reasons when I am boy. I play alone because I am alone, that is all."

And sometimes when the moon is out, Hashim practices alone under the stars. He also spends some time in school but his mind wanders, "For a while I go to school, but it is like I am not there. I do not hear teacher, I do not see what he puts on blackboard. He thinks I am in his room, but I am in court, playing squash. I hear ball dash on wall, I see it bounce to me. I sit on floor in this school, yes, but my arm makes squash strokes."

Hashim quits grade school at age twelve, determined to become a squash professional one day. A native Indian can achieve this. He continues to hang around the courts, working as a ball boy, but gives his lunch money to the assistant pro to teach him strokes. Now instead of just running, he practices strokes. He stands in one place and hits the same shot over and over again.

"When ball begins to go again and again to that certain place where I aim, I go to a new position and start again. Almost every day I do this. After a while, it is like court moves inside my head, I can close my eyes and see everything. Eyes shut, I stroke and ball goes to that mark."

Just the other day I heard a story about an exhibition that Hashim played in Buffalo or Rochester not so long ago. His opponent was late getting to the courts because he had been snowed-in. The courts were very cold and Hashim felt it was incumbent upon himself to warm up the gallery while they waited for his opponent to arrive. So he went out in the court alone, turned to the gallery, and said with a bashful smile, "When court cold, very good time to play nick shot." And then, without saying another word, he proceeded to hit a nick shot from every conceivable spot in the court. Every shot he hit rolled out of the crack. Every one. Practice makes perfect.

The officers take notice of his skills and start paying him to play with them. He keeps the games close so they want to play again. But still he is not a coach. There are only a few such jobs in Peshawar, and he doesn't want to leave family and friends. So he must wait. Finally, in 1942 at age twenty-six (more or less), a coaching position opens up at the Air Force Officer's Mess and he gets the job. His life ambition is fullfilled. Now he can marry the girl his family has chosen for him and raise a family. He's very happy. End of story? Not quite.

Two years later in 1944 an All-of-India championship, open to both pros and amateurs, is organized in Bombay, and Hashim, who is now the best player in his area, is persuaded to enter. He is already twenty-eight, but this is only his first tournament outside of Peshawar, his first time in front of a gallery. In the finals his opponent has the best drop shot Hashim has ever seen, but, says Hashim, "I am light like a fly, 112 pounds only, and never before does he see me run . . ." Hashim wins and the officers at his club are very proud of him. They reward him by reimbursing him for his expenses.

He repeats in 1945 and 1946 but the next year there is no tournament because of the fighting. The British are pulling out and a new state, Pakistan, is being created out of the areas of India that are predominantly Moslem. The Hindus in these regions are fighting to get out and the Moslems who have been excluded are fighting to get in. Hashim is a Moslem and his region, the Northwest Frontier Province, is declared part of Pakistan. He keeps his job at the officers' club, but now he is squash professional for the Royal Pakistani Air Force (RPAF). By 1949 things have settled down enough to resume sports competitions, but Hashim is no longer Indian and so doesn't enter the All-of-India championships. Instead he enters and wins the first Pakistani championship. That same year an Indian professional gets to the finals of the British Open, and a high government official from Pakistan who sees the championships gets it in his head that there should be a Pakistani entry in this Wimbledon of squash. Hashim is persuaded to go the following year, though nobody gives a thirty-four-year-old Pakistani much chance in this company.

Hashim recalls, "My game is simple at this time. I drive very hard and low, cross-court, and sometimes I play soft drop shots, that is all. But speed on my feet I have this, I can get to ball. Also I think fast. When I am up front in court and [opponent] tries to pass me with ball, sometimes I surprise him . . ."

Hashim does more than surprise a few opponents. He stuns the entire squash world, for he wins the British Open, considered the world championship. Coming on the heels of Pakistan's partition and independence, this is more than a squash victory. Though it is an Egyptian he beats in the finals, what he has done, in effect, is beat the English in "English games," and Pakistan is very proud.

He returns home to a hero's welcome—a party and a gold watch in Karachi and a special Royal Pakistani Air Force plane ride to Peshawar, where schools are closed so children can see him ride through the streets in an open car, a garland of flowers around his neck.

"Never I think a squash player can have so much honor . . . . They think I do something good for Pakistan and it helps make them glad to be Pakistani. They want to show me thanks."

In 1951, another win in the British Open, and following that a goodwill tour of exhibition matches in Australia and New Zealand. A Royal Pakistani Air Force plane flies Hashim from place to place. He plays fifteen, sixteen people a day; one week he plays 350 games. He hurts all over, but he does not complain, does not turn down games.

"Newspapers say I am good ambassador for Pakistan. I am glad to hear this. This is idea of matches, to make more people think good about my country."

When he returns home, he is made a lieutenant in the Royal Pakistani Air Force. A special position is created for him—lieutenant instructor in squash and tennis at the new RPAF school—and the president of the country signs his commission. The idea behind it is to give him an easy job with a nice pension when he retires. He sets his own hours and a "bat boy" is assigned to him to do chores and run errands.

Hashim feels he must do something more for Pakistan, so he wins five more British Open championships, his last in 1957 at age forty-one. And to carry on the tradition he trains his younger brother, Azam, and nephew, Mohibullah, who later become Open champions too.

While he is still champ in the English game, he visits the U.S. in 1954 to play in the first U.S. Open. After only a few days of practice with our ball, he makes the finals of this event, but loses to Henri Salaun. The match is only three games, but each game the score is closer, and the third game is determined by one point. The feeling in the gallery at the time, I'm told, was that if he'd won that point, he would have won the match.

In 1956 and 1957 he returns to the U.S. with brother, Azam, and cousin, Roshan. The Khans dominate the tournament; Hashim wins. In 1960 he is offered a club pro job in Detroit. The money is very good. What should he do? "If I am alone with my wife, certainly I stay in my country. But I already have ten children, seven boys, three girls . . ." Moving to the U.S. will enable him to provide them with a good education.

Hashim does not wish to be ungrateful or disloyal to Pakistan, which he knows has done much for him. "But I think: I do something good for Pakistan, also. It is in record. I can go and record stays. And when I go it is not like young player with many wins left going. I am forty-four."

So he moves to the U.S. But on one point he is very mistaken. That bit about not having many wins left. In 1963 he again wins the U.S. Open, and in 1964 at the age of forty-eight he is still able to win the U.S. Pro championships. And these were not to be his last squash victories.

In this brief biography I've mentioned only a few of the titles Hashim has won, but there are many others, such as the Australian Open and Australian Professional championships. And when you add them all up, nobody has won as many major titles as Hashim Khan. Nobody comes close even. Now, when you consider that he didn't enter his first major championship, the British Open, until he was thirty-four (or thereabouts), the whole thing gets a little eerie, and you start asking just what are we dealing with here. Granted, his year of birth has never been confirmed, but the feeling in the squash community is that he is older than he lets on. Perhaps four or five years older. Nobody considers him prematurely bald.

You look at Hashim's record and his approximate age at the time of his major accomplishments and you might be tempted to conclude, "Well, that just shows you what a minor league sport squash must be, if a little old man can win all those titles." Herbert Warren Wind, the highly respected veteran sportswriter for the *New Yorker,* sees it differently. In a piece on squash in the spring of 1973 he said of Hashim, "The more I think about it, the more firmly convinced I am that the greatest athlete for his age the world has ever seen may well be Hashim Khan."

Certainly Hashim has to be considered in these terms. But I'll tell you something. If you've heard about Hashim, about his marvelous accomplishments and incredible athleticism for his age, but have not seen him, the first time you do see him you might think some impostor has shown up. Several years ago he stumped the panel of the TV show "To Tell the Truth."

At first glance, Hashim does not look the Olympian he is. The best you could say for him is Pablo Picasso in squash shorts. He stands only 5′4 and is preceded by more than his reputation. In other words, he carries what would normally be described as a sizable beer belly were it not for the fact that as a devout Moslem he does not drink. Western food!

But look again, and you'll see there is a nobility to his bearing. He carries himself—all of himself—with pride. He's a simple, unassuming man, but there's no way for him to hide his enormous chest. And that chest, along with his noble eagle's beak, and, I guess, his sense of who he is, combine to give him the presence of a natural aristocrat. And there's a certain timelessness to his handsome face.

It would be one thing if he were losing his hair, but since all traces of it have long since been erased (except for what might be generously described as a horseshoe at the base) and since he looks so well without hair, his polished pate gives off a glow of triumph over the indignity of this aging process. Another thing that contributes to his look of agelessness is the fact that he has no wrinkles, save for the creases along his smile lines. And when he smiles he reveals not only a beautiful set of teeth, but also a man who is very happy with his lot in life.

You might think from his bashful smile, his broken English, and his distant origins that in our world when he's out of the squash court, he's out of it, period. Well, nothing could be further from the truth. Hashim's genius is not only for playing squash, but also for playing the part of Hashim Khan, grand old man of the game. I can't imagine anyone doing it better.

I remember the night before our match at the 1973 Boston Open. I entered the reception room and immediately spotted Hashim, who I'd met several times before but I was sure wouldn't remember me. He was sitting in a far corner, chatting with another Khan. True enough, he didn't seem to notice me.

Uncertain how to approach the great man, I pretended not to see him, but slowly worked my way toward his side of the room, figuring that after a while, I'd reintroduce myself. But as I was doing so, the other Khan suddenly spotted me. He quickly nudged Hashim and tossed his chin in my direction, as if to say, "That's Frank." Hashim asked him something out of the side of his mouth. The other Khan squinted hard at the draw for a moment and then jabbered something back. The exchange was in a language I wasn't meant to understand, but I did make out the word *Washington* in the response.

Hashim then popped to his feet, and with a big smile and a hand extended in my direction, Hashim called over to me, as if suddenly recognizing an old friend, "Hi, Frank, how's Washington?" Hashim is very sensitive to the pleasure a squash player feels when his presence is publicly acknowledged by Hashim Khan.

Just possibly Hashim didn't remember me. Even so, I appreciated his attempt to fake it, and, to his credit, Washington was the right connection. I was, as the draw indicated, once again back in Washington, once again on a consulting assignment. But more important to the moment, the last time I'd seen Hashim was in Washington, about six months before this. I won't say we shared the spotlight, but we did both participate in a court-opening ceremony. I played a couple of games against a local amateur to warm up the gallery, and then Hashim played his nephew, Mo, in the feature match.

The "match" was strictly show biz, with each game determined by one point, and with many shots hit from behind the back. But the best show was Hashim as guest of honor at the banquet that night. After dinner he gave his little speech that always begins, "Sorry for English, hope you me understand . . ." He knows he's got them in the palm of his hand with that one. For with his delightful, present tense English, spoken in high-pitched, prophetic tones like the wise man on top of the hill that he is, he can grip an audience like a squash racquet—firmly but with a light touch.

He claims he doesn't know what people want to hear and so opens the floor to questions about his life and game. An hour or so later, he finishes up by assuring the assembled dignitaries that, indeed, these are the best courts he has ever played on. Now maybe they will be some day, but on that particular day the lights were giving the ball a double image and the floors were slippery as ice.

But, as Hashim would say, "Idea of exhibition is make people happy," and no new courts are officially opened until the grand old man has played an exhibition on them and pronounced them the best anywhere.

Hashim's diplomatic observations on courts remind me of a response he gave to a question once put to him by *Racquets Canada* magazine. The question was: "Which country has the best squash?" Hashim's answer: "All squash players gentlemen and my friend."

Should Hashim ever enter the "Heaven Open," these words

would make a fitting epitaph. But Hashim isn't a memory just yet. Sure, he's reached the age (and then some) at which most former champions wonder if anyone remembers what they did. An age where he could well be the honorary chairman of the event; get a front row seat. And if he wished to keep active, he could referee a match, say a few words at the awards ceremony, and maybe present the trophy. But Hashim confers prestige by playing, which brings us to Saturday morning, the 1973 Boston Open.

By the time we took to the court that day it was late morning and the crowds had had time to gather. For the first several years the Saturday matches of the Boston Open were played at the more intimate Harvard Club, but because of swelling interest, all matches were now played at Harvard University's Hemenway gym on the two exhibition courts, whose steep galleries could accommodate three hundred-plus spectators per court. And this was one of those plus days. Which was fine by me. I like galleries and the bigger the better.

So what do you think about when you're playing Hashim Khan for the first time? Like I said, the matter of his age has to cross your mind. I don't care how good he once was, just what can a guy who's giving sixty a push (albeit a healthy one) do against a highly ranked player, thirty years his junior? After all, I was the number four amateur at the time. And poor old Hashim, it had been nine years since he won his last pro championship. These days he had to settle for the vet pro title. Nevertheless, many people thought he was still the best player in the game—for one game. But matches are 3 out of 5.

The one thing that was obvious to me was that I'd have to make him work out there. No easy points. But beyond that I didn't have any ideas. You can watch someone play, but you don't really know what he can do until you get in the court with him. And this is particularly so when you're dealing with Hashim, for he's such a spectacle it's hard to take in exactly what it is he's doing to his opponent. You spend so much time asking the question—how can a guy that age, and, moreover, a guy who looks like that, be competitive—that you don't get around to answering it, if indeed there is an answer. Two peculiarities of style I had noticed were huge steps and huge swing. I figured that those big steps he took, which were so big they were ludicrous in proportion to his dimensions, had something to do with his ability to get from here to there quickly and with little effort. And that his gigantic, full-bodied swing, which he used on his drives, enabled him to get the ball moving with little effort from his aging arm. But just how much speed and strength were left in the old boy, and what did he do to compensate for his waning physical capabilities?

I'd say I was more in awe of the moment than fired up with strategy. Here I was going into the court with the greatest player in the history of the game. Which is not to say I didn't want to win. The fact that this was a chance to establish a winning record against Hashim Khan had not eluded me. What a squash boast that would be: "Yeh, I played Hashim Khan once. Had a nice little game, but couldn't take the heat when I turned it on." If I could beat him, I might just be the only person to have a winning record against him. Think of all the "indirects" that would give me; I could claim indirect victories over every player he'd beaten, i.e., over every major player of the last thirty years.

Sure I wanted to beat him, but even if I didn't, at least I would have had the experience of trading a few shots with the genial old master.

The first game was a let's-see-what-he-can-do kind of game. They had said he was still the best for one game, but what they don't tell you is which game, and it was obvious to me that the first game was not his game. Or so it seemed the first dozen or so points in which I built up a nice little lead. Hashim was slow to limber up, or maybe he was just plain slow. That's what I thought until two-thirds of the way through that game I found myself short in the court with a loose ball on the forehand side. I sensed he was creeping up behind me, anticipating a drop shot. So I let him have it right in the belly. I slammed it as hard as I could, right at him (via the front wall). Bull's eye, right into his gut. Whoops, wrong gut. He's got his racquet on the ball and volleyed it away for a winner!

Now I want to tell you, that was the fastest "think fast" reaction I ever saw. The only other player who comes close in the speed of hands department is Niederhoffer. Well, I can't say that Hashim hadn't warned me, for he did say in his book, "I think fast. When I am up front in court and [opponent] tries to pass me with ball, sometimes I surprise him . . ."

The curious thing about that shot was not only his reactions but also the way he used his racquet for this volley. It was the damndest thing, for he held his racquet vertically, head down, and looked for a moment like a Ping-Pong player using a pen-hold grip. Liberties of genius!

I didn't like to see those fast reactions, but I could sort of understand them. Speed of hand is apparently something you don't lose with age. Or at least not markedly so. Arthur Rubinstein can still fly around the keyboard, and he's over ninety.

But how about his legs? (Hashim's I mean.) They say when a baseball player gets old, he gets old in the legs. The same is true for squash players.

The next time I found myself with a loose ball, short on the forehand side, a little wiser, instead of knocking it right at him, I smacked it down the wall. Buried it. But no, Hashim guesses right. His racquet becomes a shovel and he exhumes it. Now how did he get that one? "Always I watch wrist, see where goes ball . . ."

So another thing I learned that first game was about Hashim's anticipation. He still has the best first step in the game, and if he takes off in the right direction, with those long strides of his, he seems able to hopscotch to most anything.

Then there was the matter of the crowd. It became apparent to me early on that they weren't all there to see Satterthwaite play, and even fewer of them were there to see Satterthwaite win. I mean, where's the drama in the healthy kid beating up on the smiley little old man with the potbelly? What kind of entry would that make in *Ripley's Believe It or Not?*

A nice guy like me isn't used to playing the heavy, but on this particular day a nice guy like me was wearing the black hat and was having second thoughts about my fondness for galleries, three hundred-plus ones in particular. What I'm getting around to is every damn time I hit the tin (and I did start hitting the tin after he made a couple of those incredible gets) the crowd roared its approval. And they were particularly appreciative of the setup I smacked into the middle of the tin to hand over the first game.

What I took away from that first game was a determination to mind my own business out there. Forget about Hashim Khan; forget about the gallery. Block everything out and just play squash. Good thoughts, for the second game was clearly mine. And one thing I did notice was if I could catch him going the wrong way, in other words, if (and the emphasis here is on the conditional, *if*), if I could surprise him with a shot that caught him zigging when the ball was zagging, so to speak, then he was completely out of it, almost gimpy legged. He had very little capacity to recover from a misstep. In this respect he had the legs, if not of an old man, certainly not of a young man. The trick, of course, was to get him going the wrong way.

So, game two, Satterthwaite.

Game three, however, was nip 'n' tuck. I nipped a few quick points here, he tucked a few away there, and what it came down to was overtime with me serving. I remember trying to slip a real floater in, tight along the forehand wall. I remember this because the old fox let the serve drop to shoulder height, then volleyed the damn thing for a three-wall nick. First time I'd seen that one all day. It didn't roll out of the nick, and possibly, had I been looking for it, I could have scooped it back. But I wasn't looking for it. That shot slowed me down a bit, and he knocked off the next couple of points for the game.

I lost that game and was now down 2-1, but it was Hashim who had his back to the wall, quite literally. As soon as the game was over, Hashim signaled for his towel and slumped down on the floor, back against the side wall, legs spread-eagled, feet splayed. During the game there had been no indication that he was hurting, but now the mask drops and he has that how-can-I-go-on look of gasping and grimacing that one often sees on faces of prize fighters between rounds. As he toweled the sweat and agony from his face, belly heaving in sympathy with his chest, he looked sixty-five and I looked a good . . .

The fourth game had a now or never quality to it. I lose it, I lose the match. He loses it, he's in a fifth game; and if he's the best in the world for one game, the fifth game doesn't figure to be the one.

After five minutes of making faces in his towel, he seemed refreshed and ready to go for the fourth. So was I.

This one started well for me. I got in a few good cuts at the ball—and I don't care who my opponent is, if I'm smoking my drives, he's not going to take charge. But the exchanges I remember from that game were not with racquet and ball.

Long about the fifth or sixth point I knocked one down the left wall and Hashim barreled into me. I can't recall ever having had a head-on collision with Larry Csonka (though I don't suppose I would if I had), nor to my knowledge have I ever tried to tackle Franco Harris. But I can tell you this, Hashim Khan is one solid individual. Bump into him, or rather, get bumped by him, and you get a pretty good idea how big he is through the shoulders, the back, and the chest, and you learn that a belly can contribute to momentum.

"Let point," he demands. The elder statesman wants a let point? I turn quickly to protest with a "he's-got-to-be-kidding" look of anguish on my face. The referee turns him down. Hashim shrugs his shoulders and protests, "He not clear on that." He smiles at the appeal judges but they echo: "No let point. No let point."

All of a sudden the match has taken on a new look. Namely, it has taken on the look of a match. Up to this point I had played hard, but I had also tiptoed about in the great man's presence, minding my P's and Q's, while he tended to the T. But with that let point appeal, it became obvious that the adorable, cute, smiley little old man was also a feisty old—— That even now his instincts were still those of a competitor, and could not be turned off just because he's no longer the player he once was. That he was built for winning. How do you think he got to the top anyway? But this was a side of Hashim I hadn't seen before and certainly never experienced.

I felt he'd pushed things a bit far with that body check and let point appeal, and that got my blood up. I was damned if I was going to get "Khanned" by that cute little old man/elder statesman routine. If he wants a match, he'll get it. Several points later he mishit a ball, and now it was my turn to crash into him.

"Let point!" I demanded. (Something I would never have asked for, no matter how grievous the offense, earlier in the match. Or at least I wouldn't have asked for it in that tone of voice.) The referee and judges turn me down. I smirk at the ref and roll my eyes at Hashim, who is shaking his head. Now, neither of us are losing our tempers. As always, Hashim keeps an even head, and, as almost always, so do I, but neither of us is going to give an inch. Sometimes an incident, or the makings of an incident, can put you off, but I'm playing well now, well enough to win the fourth game, which I do.

During the break Hashim once again slumps down against the side wall, and I have to keep reminding myself that the match is not over yet. There remains the "technicality" of the last game. This obviously is the game to run him. To keep the ball in play as long as possible. Nothing funny, just make him work for every point. And no errors.

So I opened up hitting the ball with consummate caution, resolved to keep it going and to make no errors. But Hashim had it in his head that this wasn't the way the fifth game was going to be played. I discovered that you can't make Hashim play a long point unless he wants to. And he doesn't always want to. Or, as he puts it in his book under the heading, "Strong Attack," "Yes, I gamble, I take chance. I do not care to play up-court, down-court many, many strokes, waiting for opponent to make some mistake, so I can get cheap point. I try quick as possible for kill. Maybe I make mistake myself, yes. Of course. Many times I hit tin, I miss crack. This is gamble, this is joy game. When I start to have fear to make mistake, then I think I am ready to stop this game!"

What Hashim doesn't tell us in his book is that the turning point in the finals of his first British Open came at 5 all in the first game, when he hit one hundred-plus successive strokes at his opponent's backhand. His opponent couldn't take the plus. He blew mentally as well as physically, for they didn't play that way then. Up until then, squash had been a game of beautiful angles and of subtle strokes and strategies. Hashim won that point and the final score was 9-5, 9-0, 9-0.

Of course, he was a lot younger then. Today, like an aging pitcher who has lost his fast ball, he stays alive by throwing a lot of stuff. But the real point is that Hashim does whatever he has to to win. In the fifth game against me, at the age of whatever, the "joy game" was his best shot at winning, so "joy game" it was.

Joy game *for him* it was. For me it is "sad game." By not attacking and just keeping the ball going, I ended up feeding him balls he could set up on and do something with. I realized this when he started putting them away. No dummy, I try to adjust by swinging over to the offensive, but by now I am too jumpy and my attempts at quick kills are quick tins, the sound of which elicits Pavlovian roars from the gallery, who are loving what they are seeing, for what they are seeing is the little old man doing it again.

His lead builds and I revert to careful play. But Hashim will have none of this. He's nicking now like an old razor, and it's match, Khan.

I've been fed to the legend to keep it alive. Well, at least I had the experience of playing a real match against Hashim Khan. In retrospect I treasured those let point flare-ups for they meant he had really put out against me, and I admired the fact that at sixty he still wants it.

As a postscript to that match, soon afterward Hashim had to lie down, wrapped in blankets. He wasn't feeling well and had the chills. I like to think it was because he was totally spent from our match, but some one had the bad manners to tell me it was because he had a cold. At any rate, Hashim's a pro and the show must go on, and several hours later he was back up on his feet, out on the court playing his second-round match against Niederhoffer. Hashim lost, but he did take the first game—and Niederhoffer doesn't give away games.

I must add that I did play him again, in the spring of the following year. I mention this match because this time I won. What I did on this occasion was right from the start, tune everything out and play my own game. I put out of mind the fact that it was Hashim (as best I could), I ignored the crowds, and I did not indulge in speculations on whether or not he was tiring. The result was I won it in four.

So the classic Khan/Satterthwaite confrontation stands, for the moment, at an inconclusive draw. I will point out, though, that in terms of games won, it's Satterthwaite 5, Khan 4! Not bad, even if The Great Handicapper in the Sky did spot me thirty years.

Incidentally, after I beat him, every time he saw me for the remainder of that weekend he called me "Champ." What a grand old man!

Chapter 8
THE WOMAN'S GAME

"A Show with Heather McKay Becomes a Showdown"

I didn't know whether to be flattered or insulted, but Heather McKay asked for me. She was meant to play an exhibition against Sharif Khan on a top woman vs. top man card, but she indicated she'd prefer to play me.

As it was relayed to me, she was afraid Sharif, not knowing his own strength, would possibly overwhelm and embarrass her. She felt I wouldn't. Or was it she felt I couldn't? At any rate, she felt more comfortable playing against me. We were friends. We'd hit the ball around before. She knew I was sympathetic to how she felt about competing against men, and so things wouldn't get out of hand playing me.

Frankly, I was reluctant to get involved in this. I liked the cause—the exhibition was a fund raiser to send a team to the Maccabean games in Israel in the summer of 1977—but we were already into June and I hadn't played competitively for six weeks. I was still playing three or four times a week, but I hadn't done any training, namely court running, for a couple of months. I'd decided to take a break from competition, and accordingly had turned down a tournament that normally I would have played in several weeks before. I just wasn't up for it, and my conditioning was nowheresville.

Then again, an exhibition is not a match, it's a show. It's meant to look like a match, but the results don't count for anything. If the players are pros, the pressure they feel is to keep the thing entertaining for the paying customers. Ordinarily, you don't have to be in such hot shape to put on a good show. But this wasn't your average exhibition. For starters, they wanted us to play with the soft ball, to give the sponsors a look at the ball that would be used at the Maccabean squash event. And because this was McKay's ball, the thinking was that she might be able to give me a better game with it.

Now, as I have suggested, the soft ball is not my ball. And it was even less my ball at the time, because with the introduction of the "seventy-plus ball," I'd quit playing with the English ball over the summer, and, in fact, had not played with it for a couple of years. If you add "out of practice" to "out of shape," you get "not ready."

But the real issue was: "Not ready for what?" It may seem inconceivable that the number four ranking pro in North America, which is what I was at the time, would manifest some concern (however slight or passing) about a game against a woman; but I'd be less than honest if I didn't allow that the possibility that I could come out of this less than a winner did cross my mind. Really, it was a no win situation for me. If I beat her, I'm a bully; if I lose to her, I don't look so good either. The latter possibility, I must say, was a larger area of concern to me than the former. Principally because of a story that was going around that Heather had gone five games with Gordie Anderson several years back in an exhibition with the soft ball. At the time he was the reigning Canadian amateur champion (in the hard ball) and a former member of the Canadian team that went to the "world" soft ball championships in New Zealand. It's not unusual for exhibitions to go five games (and often as not they come down to extra points in the fifth game), so I checked with Gord for the real story. And the real story, according to Gord, was that after letting her in by easing up the first couple of games, he had to fight like hell to get the match back under control. "You don't have to fake it to make it a good exhibition with her," were Gordie's words to me.

Now if Gordie had had to struggle to keep things in line, what would I have to do? I'd only beaten Gordie once, and that was with the hard ball and when I was in what I choose to call "top competitive shape." We'd never played with the soft ball, but I liked my chances against him with that ball even less.

I'd played Heather once before myself, but that was just a couple of practice games with the hard ball. It was an informal practice session the day before she played in her first tournament ever in the U.S. The event was the 1977 Bancroft Women's Open, which for the first time brought together the top women in the world in both the hard and soft ball games. It was held in January in New York and they played with the hard ball.

I was Frank Satterthwaite, journalist, that weekend, as I had been commissioned by *Women'Sports* magazine to do a profile on McKay. The women's game had been around a long time, but it was new to me because the courts in New York had only opened up to women in the past couple of years, and so it was only in the last year that the women's circuit had started making stops here. I thought it would be interesting to see what the top women could do, and in particular to find out what Heather McKay (pronounced McEye) was all about. So I lined up a magazine assignment that would give me an excuse to hang around a women's tournament and ask a lot of nosy questions.

When I played Hashim I thought he was the greatest player in the history of the game. I'd never heard of Heather McKay. Now that I've learned something of the Heather McKay story, I think I'd have to say that, without a shadow of doubt, Hashim Khan is the greatest *male* player in the history of the game. As for who is the greatest player, Khan or McKay, well, I wouldn't want to get into that.

One statement I will make is that Heather McKay has the best racquet record in the history of sport. If it seems like I'm going out on a limb a little there, consider this: since first picking up a squash racquet in 1959, McKay has lost only two matches. As of January 1977 when I interviewed her, she had played in fourteen Australian championships and fifteen British championships and she'd won them all. You can add to these the Canadian championships and also toss in the World Open while you're at it, but when you're dealing with someone who has a lock on every major women's championship (and appears to have swallowed the key as well), it's not the wins but the losses that become interesting.

Here and there, there have been hints of fallibility. Why in 1977 she actually lost *a* game in the British championships, but previous to that she hadn't lost a game in competition since the 1968 Australian championships, when she lost one. The only other game she lost in the British Open was in 1964, which was a bad year for she also lost one in the Australian nationals that season. But ever since the first couple of years, when she had to endure a few struggles, what it's come down to is not even games lost, but *points* lost. When she returns from a championship, that's the question people ask, "How many points did you lose?" In the inaugural World Open championships, played in Brisbane, Australia, in August 1976, she lost 15 total. Four in the finals. Now this was in the soft ball game, using English scoring, so it was possible to lose rallies without losing points, just the serve. But if McKay has a weakness, it may be her serve return, for she doesn't get to use it very often.

Where did she come from and how did she get so good? Here's the story I pieced together from press reports and interviews.

Heather McKay, born Heather Blundell, grew up on the outskirts of Canberra, Australia, in a little town called Queanbeyan, which is certainly bigger than neighboring Cootamundra, though possibly not as big as Wagga Wagga. Most likely she'd still be there with her "mum" and dad and ten brothers and sisters, perhaps still selling papers and pencils at the local news agent's office, if a couple of squash courts hadn't gone up a half mile from her home in late 1959, shortly after she turned eighteen. Courts rented for only four shillings a half hour (about eighty American cents in those days), and Heather and five other members of the Queanbeyan girl's field hockey team decided to play this game to get fitter for hockey. Heather, who was also the local women's tennis champ, could handle a racquet and had remarkable stop/start speed, and soon she was playing only against men, one of whom persuaded her to enter a local tournament at Wollongong. Only six months into the game, she surprised herself and the field by sweeping both the women's junior and senior events. This got her an invitation to the New South Wales championships, where she again won the junior event, but, alas, in the senior tournament, up 2–love in games and 8–2 in points (with 9 points for game and victory), she blew the lead and went down to the top seed in overtime in the fifth game. The greatest victory in Yvonne West's career, though, no doubt, neither of them realized it at the time.

Heather's showing in this one earned her the last spot on the New South Wales team, which meant a trip to Brisbane to play in the national individual and team championships. What an honor it was for her to be permitted to play in the qualifying rounds.

"I couldn't believe it all. It was less than twelve months since I had taken up the game and there I was in Brisbane playing for the Australian championships."

What a surprise it was when she toppled the South Australian champion in overtime in the fifth game in an early round. And what a shock it was when she dominated the finals, winning it 3-1. Before she left, some of the girls at Brisbane presented her with a straw broom in recognition of her "clean sweep."

That's what they said, but maybe the real message was they hoped she'd return to Queanbeyan, get married, settle down to housework, and forget about squash. Instead, she moved to Sydney, which had become squash boom town. Rent-a-court facilities that made squash inexpensive and readily available were opening up there, seemingly every day. (Just as bowling alleys were going up over here, but with one important difference, the demand there continued to exceed the supply.) She became a receptionist at one of these centers in early 1961.

Up to now she had received no serious coaching, just a few tips and pointers here and there, and so had had to rely on her ability to retrieve to win matches. But in Sydney she could get the coaching and practice games she felt she needed. That year she won the Australian championships without loss of a game and in December was off for an assault on the Wimbledon of squash, the British Amateurs.

Then it happened, another loss. Four days after arriving, she lost in the finals of a warm-up event, the Scottish championships, to the British title holder, Fran Marshall. A tough five-gamer in which she broke both her racquets, but not in ire! And apparently not in vain, for she did seem to learn something from the match, as the next week in the finals of the North of England championships she beat Marshall 3-1. Another learning experience, for when they met the next time, in the finals of the British championships, Heather 3-zipped her. And ever since then, it's been a matter of points lost.

A matter of points lost, until she entered that Bancroft tournament in 1977. Up to then all her competition had been with the soft ball. Even after moving to Toronto in 1975 to accept a club pro teaching job, she continued to play and teach with the soft ball, which was now catching on in Canada. And each year she returned to Britain to defend her title there. The British Amateurs went open in 1973, the year she turned pro, but the prize money—£100 or so—was nothing compared to the prestige. Since then the purse has increased maybe £50.

The 1977 Bancroft event, however, offered a $2,000 top prize, and this may have had something to do with McKay's decision to finally give the hard ball game a go.

Money in the bank? Not necessarily, according to Heather, who, at a press conference before the tournament began, went on record with *The New York Times:* "I'm world champion at soft ball, but I'm nobody at hard ball. . . . I've only played the American game six, seven, eight weeks. The first couple of hours were pretty grim. The speed is different, the angles are different, and you have to adjust your strokes. The American court is smaller, there's even a different scoring system. You name it, it's different."

Just how different the two games would turn out to be for McKay, we'll see in a moment. But first a look at the competition.

The top domestic seed was Barbara Maltby of Philadelphia, the number one ranking U.S. player. Voted the best woman athlete at the University of Pennsylvania in her senior year (1970), Barbara, who excelled in field hockey, basketball, and baseball, didn't take up squash until she got out of school. But once into it, it took her only three years to make the finals of the national singles.

Invited by a friend at work to have a hit, she fell in love with squash the first time she played it. "I was looking for a sport to play now that I was no longer involved in school team sports," she told me. "I discovered squash and right from the first hit I enjoyed it so much I couldn't think of anything else. While at work [as a technician at Penn Medical labs] I wished I were playing squash, so I decided that's what I should be doing."

Her husband, Lewis, who she helped put through law school, was now a trial lawyer and that gave her the flexibility to quit work and concentrate on squash. She joined the Cynwyd Club, outside Philadelphia, because that's where the best women's squash was played in her area and because that's where Bramall was.

Norm Bramall is known as *The* coach for women's squash. And for good reason. In the past twenty-five years he has turned out six national women's champions, and if there's any question what part he played in their development, consider this: he saw five of them hit their very first ball. It's unlikely that any other coach in any racquet sport could top that one.

When Barbara learned I'd never met Bramall, she suggested I at least give him a call, to get the expert's view on the women's game. So I got what, indeed, sounded like the "voice of experience" on the other end of the phone.

We talked first about his own background. Bramall has been associated with the Cynwyd Club in Bala-Cynwyd, Pennsylvania, for the past fifty-five years, first as a player and then as the pro there. He also taught tennis at Haverford College for forty-one years. As a tennis coach he had Vic Sexias on his Junior Davis Cup squad. Like former Australian Davis Cup captain Harry Hopman, Bramall is a great believer in the benefits of squash for tennis, and recalls that Margaret Osborne duPont, who played number four on his women's squash team at the Cynwyd Club and later went on to win the national women's tennis title three times, claimed that squash improved her reflexes for tennis. DuPont was never a national squash champ, but her tennis partner, Margaret Varner, with whom she represented the U.S. against England in the annual Wightman Cup women's tennis challenge series, did win the squash title, four times. A rodeo rider from El Paso, Texas, Varner seemed an unlikely national squash champ. But through her tennis friendship with duPont, she was introduced to squash, and through squash to Bramall, who in one year had her winning the national title.

While it's true that the University of Texas today has a huge twenty-one-court squash complex where women can play, the woman's game has not been traditionally associated with Texas any more than the men's game has. The first women's nationals were played in Boston in 1928 at the Harvard Club. Somehow in the mid-twenties in Boston the wives and daughters of members of exclusively men's clubs were able to gain admission to squash courts on off hours.* The first few championships were played in Boston, but since then the women's nationals has rotated pretty much between Boston and the Philadelphia area, with occasional stops in between. I say Philadelphia *area,* for, with the exception of quirky Boston, until very recently the women's game has been played not in the cities, but in the country clubs in the suburbs.

Over the years suburban Philadelphia has been the focal point of women's squash, and the interclub league for women has been very active. But women squash players have not been taken seri-

---

*You might think that Brahmin Boston would be the last stronghold of male chauvinism. But you have to consider the women there too. Consider, for example, one Abigail Adams Homans, who on a snowy evening in Boston many years ago sought refuge at her husband's club only to be told at the desk that she could not check into a room unescorted by a male. Well, she went right back outside, hailed a cab, and had the driver escort her to her room. Is it any wonder that house rules or no, the women in Boston gained access to the courts at the men's clubs?

ously by the men, particularly by the pros. Norm Bramall at the Cynwyd Club has been the exception.

Bramall is quick to point out that he didn't see Varner hit her first squash ball, and that she was such a natural with a racquet she could have won the squash title with a Ping-Pong paddle in her hand. Or with a badminton racquet, anyway, for in addition to playing for the U.S. in squash and tennis, she also played on a national badminton team, making her possibly the only person to represent the U.S. in three different racquet sports.

So what was the secret with the others?

"Their hard work," he replies. "Willingness to do what I call 'acceptable homework.' Every time we'd begin a lesson I'd ask them, 'Now tell me what you've been doing for homework?' That's the great thing about squash, you can practice alone in the court. All my champions spent a lot of time alone in the court, practicing."

And what did they practice?

" 'Make the walls your friend, not your enemy,' that's what I always tell them."

I had the feeling his pupils, indeed, had heard that phrase on more than one occasion. Bramall was very patient with me as I attempted to milk that phrase for every drop of possible meaning. He's clearly a kindly old gentleman and I'm told that patience and a positive attitude are two of his outstanding virtues as a teacher. I had trouble communicating to him that I, too, was something of an expert on squash, and so our discussion of this precept was a bit rudimentary. But I take it what he means is hit the ball tight along the walls to good length, and don't let it break into the middle. The up-and-down game. Good basic stuff.

So that's the secret to the women's game, befriending the walls?

No, he teaches men and women the same basic style. The stroke and strategy are the same for both. Of course, each player, man or woman, is an individual and has to be taught a little differently. But the basic concepts are the same for all.

Any difference between men and women?

"The women can't run as fast or hit as hard, but other than that the game is the same for both."

He went on to explain to me in his unassuming manner that if he has a talent as a coach, it's his ability to recognize talent. He can pick the ones who are going to make it right from the start. Sometimes even before the start. He spotted one of his prize pupils while driving past a game of girl's field hockey. He pulled over and after the game persuaded her to give squash a go. She became a national champion.

And what does he look for?

"Speed afoot and the heart to dig for balls. You can't teach this."

His latest hopeful, Barbara Maltby, certainly has those qualities in abundance. Running was what she did best in her school sports, she told me, and she found the quick stops and starts of squash came easily to her. Watching Maltby in action against the other women, I'd say she has a very sound all-round game, and has befriended those walls, but the something extra she has, relative to most of the other women, is her ability to cover court.

And Maltby does her homework. Every day she puts in an hour or so by herself in the court, plays a practice match or two, and maybe takes a lesson. She also does some off-court work. She has gotten herself a coach for conditioning, Ralph Hippolyte, the volleyball coach at Penn, who has designed for her not only a running routine, but also a cardiovascular-oriented weight-training program. After describing for me in some detail her conditioning program, she asked me, as one tournament player to another, what I did to improve my fitness for squash. I guess she was looking for tips. Well, I must confess that, after hearing what she did, I felt compelled to exaggerate the rigors of my own off-court routine.

As is the case with all the top women, Maltby does most of her practicing against men. (Bramall noted that one of the major reasons for his women's success was the willingness of the B league men at his club to play them.) Now that the Philadelphia men's B league permits women to enter a team, Maltby also plays real matches against men. The women's team hasn't fared so well, but Barbara, who plays number one, came out on top in all but one of her matches her first year in the league. It's clear she could make it as a low-A men's player, certainly, and, who knows, if given the chance, maybe she could be a very good A player. (Less than 1 percent of the men playing the game are rated A.)

She can't outrun her male opponents, nor can she, at 5'7, 120 pounds, outhit them, so she finds against the men she has to rely on accuracy to win points, and to keep out of trouble. The men, she notes, in a competitive situation tend to play closer and give up less court than the women do.

Maltby is a dedicated athlete. She works as hard on her game as anyone in squash. She'd like to win that Bancroft Open some day, but her immediate goal is to win the U.S. nationals. And her immediate obstacle is Gretchen Spruance of Wilmington, Delaware.

Maltby wins the tournaments leading up to the nationals, but somehow Spruance always wins the big one. The one year she didn't win it, 1975, she wasn't entered because she was busy having a baby. And, really, housewife and mother would be a better first description of Spruance than sports figure.

At 5'11 she stands out a bit, but her profile is that of your typical young suburban housewife on her way to the country club. She likes to sew (she makes her own squash dresses), and she likes to cook (chocolate chip cookies are her specialty). She has a part-time job selling plants, and a full-time job looking after her two and a half-year-old son, Jake. And one night a week during the winter, she and the other wives go watch their husbands play inter-club league squash matches, and afterward they all go out to dinner. Her banker husband, Halsey, plays number one on the B team.

In the summer she plays tennis once a day, and in the winter, squash—all part of the suburban routine in Wilmington, Delaware, where women have been playing squash for years. Of the squash she says, "It gives me a lift. After a good game I feel ready to tackle anything."

Ready to tackle the nationals, certainly. Spruance may play a couple of tournaments to warm up for that event, but she doesn't play the circuit. From September through March the other top women are weekend warriors in tournaments played throughout the Northeast. But Spruance, who likes her weekends with her family, doesn't warm to that routine. "The circuit isn't a magnet for me," she says.

Even though she always wins the nationals, half the time the women refuse to rank her number one. They can't rank her number two, so they list her under "insufficient data." They say it's because she doesn't play enough tournaments outside her region, but maybe there's a touch of envy involved also.

It's easy to get the impression that somehow Spruance doesn't deserve to win. Her strokes are anything but classic. After she won her first national title she thought it might be nice to learn something about the game she was champion of, so Gretchen, who had never had a lesson before, consulted one of the top teaching pros in the country (not Bramall). He hit with her for a few minutes, shook his head, and said, "Every time you hit the ball you do it differently. I don't know where to begin. I guess you better just stick with what you've got, it seems to be working for you." That was her last lesson.

She uses a funny grip, it looks like she just picked up the racquet and without further thought continued to hold it that way. She doesn't cock her wrist. Instead, she drops the head of the racquet and sort of pushes the ball. It looks different, but look carefully and you'll see it's a very safe stroke with a long, straight-hitting zone that provides plenty of margin for error.

Another thing that gets to the women is her court presence. She shows up for matches in frosted bouffant hair and chalky pink lipstick, looking more like she's participating in a fashion show than a squash tournament. Don't be fooled, this lady is one tough competitor.

Giggly and garrulous off the court, she's a regular motor mouth on the court—continually talking to herself, talking to the gallery, talking to the walls, talking to her racquet, talking to the ball. Talking to everything and everybody, except her opponent. And when she's not talking, she lets you know how things are going with her face. The other players think it's a psych, but Gretchen insists she's in her own little world out there and half the time she doesn't even know she's talking. Still, it has the effect of a psych.

There's a lot more to her game than meets the ear, for she plays position beautifully. She parks herself in the center of the court and uses her long reach to cut everything off. She has superb balance and remarkable agility for a woman of her height, and this enables her to take full advantage of her long limbs in stretching for the ball. And she volleys from instinct, sometimes it happens so fast she appears more surprised than her opponent. For all her size she's not a power player, it's just not in her nature; but she's very accurate along the rails, has a real tweaker of a lob, and can be very patient when necessary.

And she likes to win. A good example of her competitive spirit was her match against Maltby in the finals of the 1976 nationals. After blowing a match point on a missed setup to lose the fourth game 17-16, Spruance came charging back to win the fifth 15-6. *Sports Illustrated* caught the essence of Spruance with a picture of her making a belly flop get.

If Gretchen bugs some of the women on the court, they'd be even more bugged to know that she never practices by herself. She plays against good men once a day, and that's it for squash.

She's just an outstanding athlete. Like Maltby, she excelled in school sports; she was high scorer in both basketball and field hockey. But unlike Barbara, she has a background in competitive tennis. After she got out of the University of Delaware she played the national tennis circuit for a year and had wins over several second-echelon players, including Patti Hogan and Valery Ziegenfuss.

Tennis she worked on, but squash was just something she fooled around with as a kid. The courts were there and, being a good athlete, she sometimes played in an under-eighteen girls' interclub league. Her mother, Bunny Vosters, was a many-time national doubles squash champ, but didn't push her, with the result that Gretchen came to the game on her own terms.

Most of Gretchen's early squash games were with boys she was dating. She only started playing seriously when, after she quit the tennis circuit, her regular squash opponent and husband-to-be Halsey suggested that she try a few tournaments.

So she entered a local invitational tournament, made it to the semis, and based on this decided to give the nationals a go. She found herself in the finals of this one. She also found herself facing her older sister, Nina, who had won this tournament two years before in 1970, and was not only far more experienced but also had the psych of being the big sister going for her. The big sister won, but then she retired to babies and platform tennis, and the next year Gretchen took over.

It all seems so easy for Spruance. She fools around with squash, is persuaded to try a few tournaments, warms up in a local tournament, enters the nationals, makes the finals, and from then on she's the lady to beat. All this on one hour a day of practice games (in season).

No question about it, Spruance puts in less time than her competitors, who, in addition to playing practice games, also run, work out, take lessons, practice alone in the court, and play the circuit. Yet Maltby is the only player who can give her a match. Reviewing Spruance's scores en route to the finals of recent nationals, her opponents averaged about six points a game off her.

So how does Spruance do it? The one thing you keep coming back to is she's a superior athlete with a gift for racquet sports. Call her a country club player if you like, but, remember, she has to play the men at her club to get a decent game of squash or tennis. Those tennis workouts, incidentally, are all she needs to win the Middle States Women's Singles tennis title, a tournament she "owns" along with the Delaware singles and the national mother/daughter tennis championships.

She talks about how squash and tennis fit nicely into her daily routine. How great it is to get out of the house once a day; this way you enjoy the time you spend with your child. How important it is to get your daily exercise.

"I think I'll always have to play," she says. But then she stops herself to ask, "What's the point of doing it, if you're not going to be competitive?"

And that's the other thing about her, her competitiveness. She may not play that much, but when she does, she goes flat out. "I'm brutal on myself," is the way she describes her competitive attitude. And she allows that as the nationals approaches she thinks about it a lot. "I get pretty hyper around that time, particularly if I don't think I'm playing well enough."

Somehow she always is.

There seems to be more involved in the rivalry between Spruance and Maltby than just two great squash players going after the same title. Spruance represents The Woman, or, I should say, the Traditional Woman. She's a great athlete, but she doesn't want to come on like one. She has a lion's heart, but she likes to look like a pussycat.

Maltby, on the other hand, represents The Athlete. There's nothing frilly about her on the court. No makeup, certainly. Everything she wears is functional, including both a sweatband and a headband, the latter to further secure her straight hair that is pulled back and held with a rubber band.

Both players give 100 percent on the court, but off the court Maltby trains, as noted earlier, to the point of lifting weights. Spruance, caught up in a suburban routine, has other priorities off court. And as for lifting weights, I doubt the possibility ever crossed her mind, and if it were suggested to her, no doubt she would quickly reject it for fear it might develop "unsightly muscles."

As far as I can tell, there's no great animosity between the two. They hardly ever see each other except in the court for the finals, and they describe each other, to me anyway, with great respect.

The animosity is between their rival supporters. Those who root for Maltby say it's because she works harder, and, therefore, deserves to win. And those who support Spruance find her very "stylish." But I have a feeling that what's really at issue here is a conflict in views over what role sports should play in a woman's life. How much should a woman give herself over to a sport? The traditional answer has been, "Not all that much." But that view is changing, and Maltby personifies the change that is occurring in women's squash. Related to this is the question of how feminine a woman athlete should strive to be. Or, asked another way, what concessions, if any, should a woman athlete make to femininity? Indeed, what's feminine? The trend may be toward female muscles being "in," with the calf muscle the most exciting female feature. Anyway, these are tensions in the women's game, at the club level as well as the top.

Spruance's supporters weren't running the 1977 Bancroft Open, with the result that the national champion found herself the number two domestic seed behind Maltby. This meant she would meet McKay in the semis.

As I mentioned before, Spruance likes to park herself in the center of the court. When she gets out front, she knifes volleys into the nick and slips in near-impossible-to-read forehand roll corners. But in their match McKay didn't let Spruance get out front. She hit the ball so soon and hard, she had Spruance pinned to the back wall. Poor Gretchen got shelled so bad she looked more like she was tending goal than playing squash. The game scores of that match were 5, 10, and 3.

Gretchen is a shooter, but in the finals McKay took on a different sort of player in fellow Australian Sue Newman. Newman, who is number two to McKay in the world in soft ball, is a very physical player—a heavy hitter and a tireless retriever. This burly lass looks like she can bench press a lot more than McKay (she could probably clean and jerk McKay in the bargain) and she trains with a stopwatch in her palm. Her dad, a motor mechanic, quit his trade to convert his garage into one of the first squash courts in Sydney and his very personable daughter helps with the family business.

Newman reached the finals with a win over Maltby in the semis. With her broad shoulders and big soft ball swing, she just hit too hard for Barbara, who fell in three. But in the finals, again it was three easy games for McKay. Newman told me afterward that the reason McKay is so tough to play is because "she's there that much faster, and so there's no time to stop and think about what you're doing. You go out there to attack but end up on defense."

That's the thing that impressed me about McKay that weekend, her quickness to the ball. She's so quick, I can see how even if she didn't have a great swing (which she does), she'd still be too much to handle.

Part of this is, of course, the anticipation that flows from controlling the play, or, as one undone opponent put it with a shrug of her shoulders, "I knew she knew where I was going to hit every ball." But it's not just that. She also has super acceleration and, when caught off base, she can suddenly shift directions and recover from a misstep with an ease no other woman seems capable of. The top women players remind me of veteran male players in that they can cover court quite nicely so long as they start off in the right direction, but if they take a wrong first step, they're finished. Heather, however, is different. She can scrape and scramble if she has to.

Not that she has to do much scraping and scrambling, for over the years she's mastered a superb swing that masks the variety of her repertoire, and, because of its golflike windup, enables her to crack the ball without muscling it. The soft ball players all use a high, wraparound backswing, but somehow McKay times her stroke better than the rest, and when she leans into an I-mean-business drive, the court echoes with the sound of the ball smacking the front wall.

For someone who hits that hard she's not all that big. She stands about 5'6, and in street clothes her narrow face, thin shoulders, and trim figure give the impression of someone much lighter than her 133 pounds. However, her business suit (always a skirt for freedom of movement and to retain her femininity) reveals a pair of sturdy legs and the fact that, as with all right-handed racquet athletes, her right side—shoulder, arm, and leg—is more developed than her left. But save for a slight list to the right, her upper section and back appear quite ordinary, not what you'd expect from what might be the world's greatest athlete. Her power appears concentrated in her thighs and torso.

The best way to describe McKay in action is to note that she plays like a man. Period. She looks feminine—with her small face and dark brown hair clipped functionally, she has almost a pixie presence—but for some reason she has the speed and strength of a man. She's got a rifle arm that enables her to strike the ball with greater severity than any other woman, and she covers court just like a very fast man. True, she can't accelerate or change directions quite as well as the very best men, but she uses the stretch as well as any squash player I've ever seen, male or female.

Inevitably, when you see a picture of McKay in action (in a squash magazine or hanging on the wall of a club), it's of her stretching out for a ball in a near full split. The fact that she can stretch like this is remarkable, but the thing that always impresses me in these pictures is that she is executing this maneuver with the apparent ease of a figure skater in a low glide. Like a fencer thrusting home, she's in a controlled split, not a desperate lunge, and it takes superb balance and extraordinary strength in the legs to do this.

She's all business on the court, but if you catch a glimpse of her face while she is hitting, you can see the beginnings of a little smile. The smile of a hunter about to pull the trigger? Between hits she walks (never runs) to the T with a rolling "jock's gait"—shoulders thrown back and elbows out like a gunslinger. It's an appealing toe-dragging swagger and I'm sure she's unaware of it. Perhaps this walk of hers is simply the result of the fact that she's somewhat bowlegged and pigeon-toed, but I suspect that it really is body language for "this is my turf."

What training regimen separates the superchampion from your run-of-the-mill everyday champions? Hours and hours of practice? Single-minded specialization to the point of obsession? Not for Heather.

Ever since first picking up a racquet, she's rarely put in more than an hour of work on the court per day. Sometimes drills, other times just play. "One hour, five games. That's it. If I've done what I should have done, I'm pooped."

Nor does she, like so many superstars, tiptoe about in mortal fear of injury, careful to shake hands with her left hand. Far from it. For athletic diversion and as a change of pace from the one-on-one of squash competition, she returns to her first love, field hockey, playing in leagues wherever she happens to be located. And that's a big stick she carries. In 1967 and 1971, the two years when the Australian national squash championships didn't happen to conflict with the interstate field hockey tryouts, she was named to the All-Australia field hockey team. Squash, which she had taken up to get fitter for hockey, ironically, delayed her receiving full recognition in the latter. And there's no telling how good the Queanbeyan women's tennis champ might have become in tennis if she'd toured and received coaching as she did in squash. But after taking up squash, she found there wasn't enough time left for tennis.

One thing about her squash workouts: with no woman around who can give her a game, or rather who can take a game, McKay does all her practicing against men. Ever since she got past that beginning stage with the Queanbeyan field hockey players, she has developed and maintained her talents playing against men. However, leery of the unwilling male opponent who "either will not try or will win at all costs, because he doesn't want to lose to a woman," she refuses to enter men's leagues or tournaments. (I suspect her attitude on this reflects, as much as anything, the Australian view of a woman's place.)

Without "real matches," it's hard to know how she would stack up against the top men. She did once, in an exhibition, beat the British amateur men's champion, who spotted her 3 points a game and the right to score points when she was receiving as well as serving. The Australian press reported her five-game overseas victory without mention of the handicap. The press, which would vote her the 1967 winner of Australia's highest sports honor, the Australian Broadcasting Commission's Sports*man* of the Year, had come to expect miracles from this woman.

It's not all ice cream and beer, mind you. McKay does train. Her partner in this is her husband, Brian, whom she married in 1965, and who is also a pro. They met in a squash center in Sydney, where he was teaching weekends and evenings. After they married, he quit his job at the lathe as a fitter and turner and the two went into the business of managing squash centers. He did the teaching and she, still an amateur, ran the desk. After she turned pro in 1973, they became a teaching team. Though squash was booming in Australia, most of the centers were small operations, and none could support two full-time teaching pros. So in 1975 they came to Canada to share the squash professorship at the Toronto Squash Club, a very successful seventeen-court commercial club in downtown Toronto.

Their day at the club is mostly taken up giving lessons and managing the pro shop (and those lessons are no help to Heather's squash, for she can beat everyone in the club, including the men's champ, 3-zip), but every other morning they get in a couple of miles of roadwork and some calisthenics. (Interestingly, Heather, who covers the court like wall-to-wall carpeting, doesn't have track speed. Or as husband Brian puts it, "She couldn't disappear on a dark night.") When Heather is pointing for a tournament, they step up the roadwork and calisthenics to every day and load on some wind sprints and stationary bicycle riding.

But McKay is no trophy hunter. She plays in five or six tournaments a year, the big ones. This may explain why she's been able to keep on top for eighteen years. She's not "squashed out." "I never play enough to get bored, so I look forward to games," she says.

Does she ruin those tournaments she enters? Reduce them to "ho hum" contests for second place, and reduce opponents to the humiliation of scraping for points in a desperate struggle not to get "zipped"? McKay, let it be noted, does not give away "courtesy points." Her competitive credo is simple, "I try to win as quickly and easily as possible. If I started to give away points," she adds, "I believe my opponents would lose respect for me. Now they know where they stand. They know damn well that they'll earn every point they win."

I wondered if her opponents took such a positive attitude toward it all, but typical was the comment made by Jane Cartmel, number two behind McKay in Canada. She recalled that in a finals in a soft ball tournament against McKay, "I won one point, and I felt like I'd won a game."

Opponents insist they find the excellence of her play and her court behavior inspirational.

"She's the ideal," exulted one whipped opponent.

"She shows you how good a woman can be," rejoiced another thoroughly crushed competitor.

And as for ruining tournaments, her opponents point out that Heather gets welcome publicity for squash. Journalists who might not ordinarily show up for a squash match will turn out to see McKay. And her personal honors—that ABC award in 1967, the Lindy Award for Australia's Outstanding Athlete of 1968, Member of the British Empire in 1969, and a Hall of Fame medallion struck in her honor by the Helms Foundation in the U.S. in 1973—these firsts for a squash player, they point out, are good for the game.

For all these honors, other players find her "a natural person," one who likes a good laugh, doesn't put on airs, and, off the court, just wants to be one of the group. A straightforward and honest person, except when it comes to Liar's Dice, a game she plays almost as well as squash. A game in which, "you keep a straight face and you lie as much as you can without getting caught," she confides with a laugh.

This ability to bluff, she admits, may have something to do with her dominance in squash. "If I play a tough point and get a little tired, I try not to let on. I figure if I'm hurting, they must be hurting too." This, and, "Right at the start I try to get their best shot back. What happens is, if they, say, play a drop shot, and I get to it, they get discouraged and then they stop playing it, and that suits me to a tee. Ooops, I guess I'm giving away a secret there."

But she adds, "I don't try to beat them by trickery. The whole idea is to get them so out of position that eventually the winner will set itself up." Well, that's all there is to it, fellow competitors.

As I watched the women play that weekend, I was looking for "the women's game." Looking for a style or approach that women used and men didn't.

I concluded that there's no distinctive style of women's play. As is the case with the men, there is a full range of kinds of athletes—some women are quick and jerky, others, smooth and deliberate. You have power players, shooters, retrievers—all the different approaches you see among the men. And the stroke women use depends upon where they come from. The soft ballers use the golflike windup; top fiver Lisa Griffin Drake, who learned squash as an assistant pro under Mo Khan at the Harvard Club in Boston, chokes up on the racquet just like Mo; and Barbara Maltby has a Philadelphia stroke, which she learned from Bramall at the Cynwyd Club. They use a squash stroke, not a *woman's* stroke.

The only difference I noticed in shot choice is that the women don't use nearly as many three-wall nicks as the men. The three-wall nick is really the premier putaway these days in the men's game, among the top A players at least. But very few women hit it, and those who do do so sparingly, almost by accident it seems. Possibly it's a tougher shot for women to hit because it has to be hit very firmly to make the nick, and the women as a rule don't hit as hard as the men. But the top women certainly have enough strength to hit this shot, and, in my opinion, it's the toughest shot in the game for a woman to retrieve because it requires a mad dash to the front wall ending with a long, low stretch. The get is ordinarily made a fraction of a second before the ball bounces twice, and that fraction of a second is the difference in speed between a man and a woman.

One of these days, one of the women is going to master this shot and go to town with it, and then all the others will start using it. That's what happened in the men's game. The shot existed, but no one used it much until the Khans came over here and discovered that the "working boast," which they used with great effect in the soft ball game, didn't work so well on the narrow courts; but the three-wall nick, which was hit in much the same way, was a good replacement for it. They started working everyone over with that shot and suddenly it was in vogue among all the top tournament players. But the women haven't "discovered" it yet. Playing against each other they hardly ever see it, and when they practice against men, they play mostly B and C players who haven't mastered this advanced shot.

One shot that the women hit much better than the men on average is the slow lob serve. They seem to take more care with it, and possibly they have better touch, with the result that they float some real tweakers. I got Spruance to give me a few pointers on the slow serve, but it doesn't come easily to me.

I think Bramall is right. The difference between boys and girls (in squash) is that the men hit harder and run faster than the women. Obviously some women are faster and/or stronger than some men, but at the top of the game, the men have an overwhelming advantage in terms of brute speed and strength. And women seem to have a lot more difficulty twisting and turning and changing directions than men.

So the action in women's squash is not as explosive, nor are the points quite as long, but this is not to say that their matches do not make a good spectator sport. A good match is a good match, and when you have two players with contrasting styles going neck and neck, it's exciting.

And another thing top women's squash offers the spectator is that men can learn from it as well as women. In fact, the average man may learn more from watching the top women play than from following the top men because he is less likely to be overwhelmed by the women's athleticism. The speed and reflexes of the top men are so superior to that of the average man that the club player has difficulty relating what the top men are trying to do to what he can do as a player.

But since everything is a little slower in the women's game, it's possible for the club men's player to see himself on the court, and to get a feel for what he might be able to do with improved stroking and strategy.

Of course, if he ventures on the court with one of the top women players, he might also get a feel for the ball if he doesn't know what he's doing. That's what happened to the wrestling coach at Princeton when I was there. He wasn't all that good a squash player, but he liked to grapple for the T, and every now and then he'd stop by the courts after wrestling practice to pick up a little game. After one such outing, he took an awful lot of razzing in the showers, because he had a rear end full of purple welts. These ball marks smarted; the reason he received little sympathy was because his opponent that day had been B. Constable, and the *B* stood for Betty!

I say B. Constable because that's the way she was always listed on the court assignment sheet. In those pre-coed days, women were not supposed to be in the gym, where the courts were located. But coach Conroy was sympathetic to Betty's plight. There were no women anywhere who could give her a decent game. Consequently, for several weeks before she was to defend her national title, he would, at the designated hour, look both ways and then let her into the gym through a back door so that she could practice with the team. These days she's the highly successful coach of the Princeton women's squash team, and it's rumored that they're now letting her enter the gym through the front door!

In my day the most stimulating games that men and women played on college squash courts occurred at Harvard. There, some of the dormitories had courts attached to them, and though women were supposed to be out of the dorms by a certain hour, no such restrictions were placed on the courts. All of Princeton's courts, alas, were in the gym.

Betty, who could have played number three or four on most Princeton men's teams, was the only woman I'd ever played half seriously in squash until I played a couple of practice games with McKay the day before that first Bancroft hard ball tournament in January of 1977.

McKay was mighty impressive in that practice session. It was like playing someone who was on the tail end of the men's national amateur rankings—maybe, eighteen, nineteen, or twenty. When I picked up the pace and cut down her reaction time, she couldn't keep up, and I could pretty much score points at will. But I'll tell you this, when my three-walls didn't nick, she dug them out; and if I gave her a loose ball in the center of the court, she'd back me out of the middle and put the ball away with a man-sized drive down the wall. I beat her pretty badly the first game and a half, but then a crowd started to gather and I didn't want to look like a bully or demoralize her the day before her American debut. So I let up a bit, but made sure to win the points at the end of each game.

Naturally, the next day the rumor was circulating that she'd beaten me in practice. I kidded her about it, and, to my surprise, she became very embarrassed and wanted to know who started the rumor so she could set that person straight.

She's as modest and unassuming as any person can be, but I think the real reason she wanted to set that person straight is because she takes great pride in her record. She knows every match she's won, and the time and place of every point she's lost. Sometimes she will playfully quiz an interviewer, to make sure he's got the facts straight. She'd never say it, but she knows damn well she has one of the greatest records going in the history of sport, and that's enough. Unlike most of us, she doesn't need any exaggerations or embroidery. She has too much pride in what she's accomplished, to take credit for anything she hasn't done.

When I first met her I mistook her small town shyness for standoffishness. But I quickly learned this is a champion totally without pretense or airs. She's polite to everyone, and if she likes you (the odds are she will), she's quick to warm up and likes nothing better than to "yuk it up" with a good elbow-in-the-ribs laugh.

She's a natural person, but there's no such thing as a world champion who's "just plain folks." In an interview, she's very helpful and straightforward, and gives attentive answers to questions she must have been asked a thousand times before. But she's also very canny; she tests you before she parts with her opinions. And there are certain areas, like her schedule for retirement and for raising a family, that she politely lets you know are none of your business.

I asked her if she thought the competition in squash was up to what it is in other, more major, sports. That got her back up. "It makes me cranky when people ask me that one," she fired back. "Those other players are damn good," she pronounced with a toss of her head and a proud nod.

Such flashes of pride gave hints of a very competitive makeup, and I wanted to learn more about this side of her. Granted, she is physically superior to her competitors, but dominance in a sport is never just physical.

From talking to her I could tell there was something special about her drive and willpower. But an athlete is tested not by talk, but by action. And ultimately, that's why I consented to play her in an exhibition. At first, I resisted it because, as I said, I was out of shape and out of practice with the soft ball, and I have my pride too. But then I realized that my lack of preparation might even things up enough to make this a golden opportunity for me to test her champion's mettle in the heat of play. I'd had the experience of a hotly contested match with Hashim Khan, thanks to the fact he spotted me thirty years; now, so long as the match didn't become too one-sided, maybe I could find out firsthand what McKay was like when pressed.

Another thing—I'd had a chance to go through her press clippings, and a theme that runs through them is that this could just possibly be the world's greatest athlete.

What a fantasy. Me, competing seriously against the world's best athlete. Sort of like a baseball fan finding himself on the mound with the count 3 and 2, pitching to Babe Ruth.

Then again, I didn't want to wake up to the reality of losing to her, thereby assuring myself a place in sports history comparable to that occupied by the guy who was pitching the time when Ruth, according to legend, pointed to a place in the stands and then socked a home run there.

Much as I admired her, I didn't want my name showing up in McKay's future press clippings as the male pro she once beat. The fellow who was organizing this event, however, assured me that this fund raiser was a private party to which the press would not be invited, so I needn't worry about not being in shape or how the match came out. Just keep it light, he told me, make a few jokes and put on a good show.

So imagine my surprise when Heather showed up at the University Club in New York that June evening in 1977 with a sportswriter in tow. Genial Jack Batten, who was ghosting a book on squash for Heather, had flown down with her from Toronto, hoping this match would, as he told me, "provide some interesting material."

Nor was it reassuring to learn just before our match that when Heather had been tested for strength at Lenox Hill Hospital's Institute of Sports Medicine earlier in the day, her right leg had literally knocked the needle off the chart. It was the strongest female right leg on record there. This surprised her, she told me, because, unlike the ballerinas, who were second to her but considerably stronger than the other women athletes tested, she had never done any special exercises to develop her legs.

So what was my plan going into this match? I wanted to keep the match fairly close, but keep it under control. Gordie Anderson had gotten himself into a spot of difficulty because he had taken it too easy at the start. The lesson was, if you let her in, you're asking for trouble. My plan was simple. I'd play hard at the beginning, get control, and then maybe back off a bit so the paying customers could see Heather do something. All the while keeping it light, without being disrespectful.

In accordance with my plan, I really laced into the ball the first couple of hits in the warm-up, just to let her know who was in charge. But damn if she didn't send it back just as hard, perhaps harder. I couldn't believe it. Clearly she wasn't as strong as me. And I could hit the American ball considerably harder than she could, but, evidently, she timed her English stroke much better than I did.

So much for the chest beating during the warm-up.* A more immediate problem was the gallery. The University Club has a big one, and a big one was necessary because nobody wanted to miss this spectacle. And as the gallery started to fill up, there was the inevitable razzing from my "friends," who shouted their comments into the court.

I had the good sense to smile faintly throughout this, acknowledging the wittier comments with a lift of my left hand. There are times when no matter how clever you think your retort might be, it's best to realize you're in a compromised position and outnumbered. However, when somebody suggested my slip was showing, I interrupted the rally, walked to the back of the court, and politely offered the handle of my racquet in the direction of the person who had made that "observation." And with my other hand, I beckoned him into the court to take my place. That was the end of the comments. End of the comments from the gallery, that is.

She won the spin for serve, but just before she opened up, I

---

*Incidentally, several teaching pros have since told me that when a man plays a woman for the first time, he almost always overhits. Upon reflection, I suspect this is not just an attempt to gain strategic advantage by overpowering the weaker opponent, but also reflects some deeper, more primitive need of the male of the species to show off his brute strength to the "weaker sex."

turned to the gallery and announced that the huge blister, the size of a silver dollar, on the ball of my left foot, had drained quite nicely. That thanks to an excellent program with weights after the operation, I had now recovered at least 80 percent of the strength and flexibility in my right knee. That yoga was definitely helping my troublesome back, and that the infrared lamp had been doing wonders for the painful tendinitis in my right elbow. So I really had no excuses . . .

The first game I didn't need any excuses. I was totally in command and took it 9-3. Heather, on the other hand, seemed strangely out of it. She was making what appeared to be nervous racquet errors and was not moving as well as I knew she could for my short shots. During the break, as we were toweling off, I noticed she was breathing heavily and seemed very tight. Now in a match, this would be the cue to go for blood and put her away, but this is an exhibition, right? So I decide to back off a bit.

I hang back deep in the court and let her run up a little lead—up to 5-love at the start of the second game. OK, enough's enough. I really turn it on.

She wins that game 9-3. That's the last time I worry about keeping this exhibition close.

Now I don't want to get down 2-1 in games. I don't care who you are or who your opponent is, if you get down 2-1, you can lose. Particularly if your conditioning is suspect. So right from the start of the third game I go to work. And with a lot of work I get to 8-6, one more point and I've got the game and can relax again. But the referee starts awarding her penalty points, claiming that the several collisions we have are my fault, and that I'm not getting out of her way enough when it's her turn to hit. Now it's true I'm not making extraordinary efforts to give her extra room, and she does crash into me a couple of times en route to the ball, but by the standards of the American game, anyway, I'm giving her enough room. But this is the English game, and because the softer ball is slower, there's less excuse for not getting completely out of the way. I know the refs are stricter in that game and certainly this ref knows the English rules. In fact, before the match it was I who suggested that Brian McKay should ref it. I had thought it was a nice gesture. But now, I'm getting a little ticked, having those points given to Heather, and I wonder (irrational thought) if the whole thing isn't a setup. Hubby works it so wifey wins. They've worked as a team for years, haven't they?

No, Brian's right, I'm not clearing to the satisfaction of the English rules. But after he awards her a second or third let point I call up to him, "Hey, Brian, you're missing a good match!" Not the kind of comment I'd risk making to a referee in a serious match, but this is meant to be a show. Isn't it?

He is not amused and several points later, with the score tied 9 all and Heather serving, he awards her yet another let point, which gives her the third game, 10-9.

Now I'm not at all amused. And as we leave the court, I'm shaking my head and muttering to myself over that last let point. Heather overhears me and hits me with an Eliza Doolittle "Awwwnnn, I'm telling you, Frank, ten out of ten times that would be a bloody let point!"

And I shoot back, "Come on, Heather, no way." Then I catch myself. What's going on here? We sound like a couple of guys in a bar arguing over whether or not a baseball player on the tube was safe at home. This is no way to talk to a lady.

And Heather is a lady. But there's evidently a lot of tomboy in her too. Along with four sisters, she also had six brothers and a father, who in his day had been one of the leading rugby players in New South Wales. It's obvious that the men dominated a very athletic household and she learned how to fend for herself, rough-housing with them.

I didn't pursue the argument with her over that let point, but as I toweled off, I thought to myself, "Well, you played her to find out just how competitive she was. I guess her combativeness in that little exchange pretty well sums up what a tough cookie she is, when she gets into a match."

I also started to think about my own situation. I'm down 2-1 in games, and if I fall behind at the start of the fourth, I'm in real trouble. Lose one more game and my picture could end up in her book, maybe on the cover as well.

I rise to the occasion that fourth game and play brilliantly, if I say so myself. She has a power stroke and great accuracy, and on more than one occasion she has jerked me around with fakes, but my big advantage over her is I'm quicker to the ball. By pressing forward in the court and taking everything early, I can do to her what Sharif does to me—pick up the pace so much that racquet skills are no longer a determining factor. And that fourth game, I get on the ball so early, there is no time for her to react. I am just too quick for her. Maybe she is tiring too. Anyway, I knock it off,

9-1, and so long as I get an early lead in the fifth game, I've got things back under control.

I get that lead. Three-zip. And when I make it to 7-3, I'm no longer in any rush. I've got the match in my back pocket. So I relax a little—always a dangerous thing to do—but this is an exhibition and so long as she's not in a position to beat me, why worry.

The score gets to 8-6. I've got the 8, so I've got her match point. Well, I'm sorry, but the show's over, folks, it's time to end the match. But she refuses to exit.

The show really started at that point. It was the most extraordinary finish to any match I'd ever played. This show with McKay became a showdown. The score locked at 8-6. I had 9 match points on her, and each time I tried to win the final point, she made a sensational get or shot that saved the match and won the serve back for her. And I couldn't afford to lose more than a couple of points or I'd lose the match. So the pressure was on. I'd win the serve back, have her at match point again, and figure, well, this time I've got her. But she'd make the most extraordinary get and there I'd be, receiving serve again, and having to win the next point or I'd be in danger of losing the match.

We'd been out there for an hour and a half, but the emotional seesawing—now I've got it, no I don't; ah, this time I'll win it, dammit, I didn't—was the thing that was really getting to me.

With the English scoring system, the score can stall like that. It's frustrating as hell to keep earning the serve but be unable to advance the score. And when you stall at match point, the unresolved tension is unbelievable. It's a little like the trick Victor Borge plays at the piano when he keeps bringing a tune to the end—you think—but then instead of playing the last chord and resolving the tension in the harmonies, he goes off on another little tangent. He drives you crazy with his false endings. Well, that's nothing compared to the exasperation of stalling at match point, for this is no little tune, this is a sports contest in which the outcome is a matter of considerable personal interest.

I knew I wanted to win, and it had become abundantly clear that Heather wasn't going to hand it over. It wasn't the English scoring system that was denying me that last point, it was McKay's refusal to yield.

And when after 9 match points and 18 hand in/hand out rallies, Heather finally scored a point to make it 7-8, I thought "Oh, Jesus, here she comes."

"Heather, you're forgetting the script," I quipped. The gallery appreciated the comment, but Heather was not in a joking mood. Punchy from exhaustion, all I had left was my sense of humor, which I used in a show of bravado. But I was too tired to get out front, pick up the pace, and take control of the rallies. However, I dug in and won the serve back. But again the score stalled. Now with the score at 8-7, every time I lost the serve I had to win the next point or the match would be all tied up. The pressure was unbelievable. And there's nothing that can break you spirit more than having the ball on the one-yard line and not being able to score. I'd had 9, 10, 11, 12 match points on her, and still I couldn't put her away.

What was going on? Here she is playing a man, in an exhibition, with no title and no extra money at stake. She's been out there for 1½ hours and has had numerous match points against her. And still she refuses to yield! Her athletic talents and squash skills are wondrous, but this incredible pride and determination transcend even them. I'd gone into this match hoping to learn more about McKay's competitive makeup. Now I'm wishing I was studying it from the gallery, for I'm getting that sinking feeling of the inevitability of defeat—a feeling that, I'm sure, all her female opponents down through the years must have experienced.

On the next point, off McKay's serve, I volley a cross-court drop into the nick. A risky shot, a shade above the tin, but it's a winner, and I've got her match point again. Match point for the thirteenth time! This time we get into a sneaker-squeaking scrambled exchange, and she happens to cross in front of me as I'm hitting the ball. As you know, the rule is, if you hit your opponent with the ball and it would have gone directly to the front wall had your opponent not been in the way, then you win the point.

I won that point.

Epilogue
THE SEVENTIES-PLUS

"For the Many, If Not the Masses"

Several years ago Rod Gilbert, who was still playing hockey for the Rangers, was having a game of squash with one of his teammates at the newly opened Uptown Racquet Club in New York City. Actually, what with all the hip checking and blocking, it was more like they were playing hockey without skates (or pads).

A member of Uptown's staff happened by, and, horrified by what he was seeing, politely called down into the court as soon as there was a break in the action. "Excuse me, sirs, but did you know that in squash you're supposed to get out of each other's way, and if someone does get in the way, instead of trying to knock him over, you play the point over?"

"Yeh, we know, kid," responded Gilbert, "but we like it better this way."

Soon after the Broad Street Squash Club opened in the financial district of Manhattan, a rather shapely woman stopped by the desk, asked a few questions, shrugged her shoulders, turned around, and walked out. Owner John Halpern, who was busy selling his new club to prospective members, happened to see this and tore himself away from the business at hand to follow this stunning woman out the door, onto the street, and practically into the cab she was in the process of entering, to find out if there was anything he could do for her.

She said she'd arranged a game with the pro but he was not there. It seems that there had been some mix-up with the bookings, and her name, Yvette Donen, had been put down for the wrong hour, and the pro was out for lunch. Halpern apologized, explained they were still working out the bugs, and with his sharp eye for "business" offered to hit with her.

She accepted, and Halpern's gallantry was well rewarded, for she turned out to be pretty good, and certainly no less statuesque in her form-fitting squash clothes. After their game, Halpern used that old line, "Haven't I seen you someplace before?" To which she responded, "Perhaps you know me by my stage name, Yvette Mimieux."

These stories, of course, wouldn't be told if they hadn't happened, and they wouldn't have happened if squash in the U.S. were still the sole province of private boys' schools and men's clubs. The big development in squash in North America in the seventies has been the emergence of the commercial squash club. Now that commercial squash is going great guns, it seems strange that it took so long to get here. It's been almost twenty-five years since the first commercial courts wents up in Australia in the mid-fifties. And though squash was a remarkable business success there, it wasn't until the sixties that England went on a court building binge, and not until the early seventies that things started to happen over here.

The first commercial squash courts in North America went up in Mexico about 1970. There's a great tradition of ball-wall games in Mexico City, which is derived from the Basques of Spain. Until squash came along, the most popular of these was *"frontenis,"* which is like playing squash tennis on a jai alai court. But space is now at a premium in this growing city, and, since you can put a dozen or more squash courts inside a single *frontenis* court, squash is more practical and a much better business proposition. In 1964 there was one squash court in Mexico; now nobody knows for sure how many courts there are, but the estimates range from 1,000 to 2,500 squash courts in Mexico City.

Commercial squash next struck in Toronto, Canada, where a seventeen-court complex, the Toronto Squash Club, went up in 1972. Since then over fifty commercial facilities have opened in the Toronto area, and centers have started going up all across the country.

The first pay-and-play courts in the U.S. were put up in 1973 in Berwyn, a suburb of Philadelphia, by Paul Monaghan, an architect who played squash at Merion. And soon after the Berwyn courts opened, Harry Saint, an ardent C player in New York who was working in computers at the time, opened his Fifth Avenue Racquet Club, consisting of seven courts near midtown, which could be rented for half-hour periods. At the time there were maybe 2,000 squash players in the metropolitan area. Now, five years later, a conservative estimate would be 40,000 squash players. A dozen or so entrepreneurs have been putting courts up all over the city with the result that there are now more squash courts than tennis courts in Manhattan.

Five years ago I knew everyone in the business in the U.S. and Canada, but now commercial courts are popping up everywhere, and I can no longer keep up. The surprise to me is that courts are going up not just in the Northeast corridor but all over, including the Far West (Seattle, San Francisco, Los Angeles) and the South (Atlanta, Fort Lauderdale, New Orleans). In fact, I made my pro debut playing an exhibition as part of a court-opening ceremony for a new club in that great squash town, Greenville, South Carolina!

With squash becoming a business, you could expect to hear from the old "capitalist squash player," Vic Niederhoffer. Vic, who won the North American Open as an amateur in the winter of 1975, turned pro at the start of the next season. From the vantage point of today's very active pro circuit, it would seem the obvious thing to do, but at the time there were only two or three "open" tournaments that a pro was eligible to play in. This meant that, unless Vic could get something going for the pros, he ran the risk, by turning pro, of being locked out of the mainstream of competition. Given his love of competition, it was a courageous decision.

It proved a very good decision for him and for squash. Vic really came into his own from that moment on. He had always been a fervent believer in capitalism and in squash, but all his talk about "capitalist squash players" beating "socialist squash players," though never dull, didn't mean very much to most of us. But when he turned pro, he finally made a connection between capitalism and squash that made a lot of sense.

With business beginning to take an interest in squash, Vic started talking about all the things that business could do for the sport. He suddenly became very inspirational for those of us who thought the time had long since come for the game to open up. Indeed, Vic became the champion of the new era of open squash— open to the pros and open to the public.

When he turned pro in November 1975, he released a statement that was picked up by *The New York Times,* in which he made a very compelling and cogent case for the benefits to squash of financial incentives for top players and the benefits of "open" competition—competition that is open to all players, be they pros or amateurs. He made the point that the phenomenal growth of tennis in recent years can be traced to the opening up of competition and the decision of business to invest in this sport.

Vic, in his early years, was not always what you'd call "a credit to the game." Whatever excuses you make for him, the fact remains, when he first started out, his court behavior was sometimes pretty awful. And he made few contributions off the court.

But he grew up. He became one of the best sports in the game; few players call double bounces on themselves as often as he does. And in recent years, he has been the source of most of the positive ideas and efforts to promote the game. In my opinion, he matured a lot faster than the game. While squash associations were burning up precious time debating ways to exclude pros from their championships, Vic was espousing sensible ideas that anyone outside the game, not caught up in the amateur traditions, would see as the only way to go.

It took me a season to follow Vic's lead, but I was the next amateur to break ranks and turn pro. I had hoped that the national squash association would see the light and do away with their "amateurs only" provision. I made a lot of noise about this but heard only the echo of my own voice as it bounced off a brick wall. Finally, with no little encouragement from Vic, I made my decision.

I believed then and I believe now that the top players should have a professional commitment and be actively involved in the promotion of the game. But on a more personal level, I also felt that the time had come for me to make more serious career commitments. I couldn't continue to let a hobby have the upper hand. Playing the squash circuit was fun, but it was also becoming increasingly expensive as the tour expanded, and it was distracting me from getting settled in a career.

I decided I had to either give up competitive squash completely or make it into a business. But I couldn't continue to fool around as an amateur. One fortunate thing that happened to me on the career front about this time was that in the process of writing my PhD thesis, I discovered that writing was almost as engrossing for me as squash, not as much fun, certainly, but every bit as challenging. And when I completed my degree, I decided that instead of pursuing a career as an academic or a management consultant, I wanted to take a shot at becoming a writer. I was able to line up some magazine assignments, but writing is a tough nickel when you start out, and I'm not a man of independent means. So it was squash to the rescue! By turning pro, I figured I stood a chance of making enough money through tournaments, exhibitions, and clinics to get my career as a writer off the ground.

You believe all this? All this stuff about the only reason I continued to play squash was because it supported my career as a budding writer? I'm not so sure I believe it. Sure, this was the reason I gave myself, but deep down I think, more than anything else, what I was looking for was an excuse to continue playing competitive squash and the pro angle *cum* writing gave me a new lease on my squash life. It gave me an excuse to continue in the game. That's how much control I have over my "habit."

When I turned pro, I went the full route and joined the North American Professional Squash Racquets Association. At the time, Vic and I were the only members who didn't know how to string a racquet. When I first joined, I must say I was afraid that some of the club pros—all of whom were hard working and many of whom had been dedicated to their profession for years—would view me as something of a dilettante, or worse, as someone who was trying to cut into their money. But the president, Jim McQueenie, a delightful, canny Scotsman who still rolls his R's after twenty years over here, welcomed me into the fold. And, perhaps reflecting the zealotry of recent conversion, I became one of the most outspoken advocates for pros getting their fair share. I was elected to the board of the pro association the following year, 1977, the year that Vic was elected president.

With Vic at the helm, the pro association was a very exciting place to be. He lined up some sponsors for new tournaments and negotiated better deals for the pros as the circuit started to open up. He urged tournament committees to set aside several slots in their tournaments and hold qualifying events so that players, amateur or professional, who didn't have high rankings would get the chance to play their way into the draw. But the most significant thing he did, I believe, was to encourage the adoption of the new "seventy-plus" ball.

The seventy-plus ball, originally designed for summer play in courts where the temperature was over 70 degrees, had been around for a couple of years. A smaller ball than the then standard hard ball, the seventy-plus was made in the mold used for the English ball, but with the walls made thicker than the English ball so that the seventy-plus was significantly harder and zippier than the English ball. The result was it retained the basic playing characteristics of the old American hard ball, but unlike the old ball it wasn't much affected by changes in court temperature. This meant you could hit reverse corners even in hot courts. In terms of shot choice, the only difference was you could hit more offensive lobs and volleys with the seventy-plus ball than with the old hard ball.

The seventy-plus was an instant success, particularly with beginners. If given a choice, they reached for the seventy-plus instead of the clunky old hard ball because the seventy-plus was a little slower and a lot lighter, which meant it was easier to catch up with and hit. And, interestingly, from all reports beginners also seemed to prefer this ball to the English ball because it didn't need to be warmed up as much, and because you didn't have to swing so furiously at it to make it travel. It became apparent to the squash center owners that using the seventy-plus ball year round would make the game easier for beginners and thus bring more people into the game.

The pro association, under Vic's leadership, was the first group to adopt this ball. Since the seventy-plus ball required more running than the old ball and Vic was not as fast or as fit as he used to be, he was clearly going against his own best interests as a player in advocating the adoption of the seventy-plus ball. But his basic argument was whatever will help bring new people into the game and make it grow is the best way to go.

Down through the years, no one had ever accused Vic of being a riveting orator, but, ever full of surprises, he proved to the pros he knows how to run a meeting—all views are aired and he's able to jolly things along with humor. Really, he knocked everyone out the way he conducted his first pro meeting. People came out of it saying, "I didn't know Vic could be so outgoing and had such a good sense of humor."

Frankly, I'm a little worried about Victor these days. He's becoming distressingly normal. Fortunately, he hasn't totally lost his whimsical side, but gone are the outlandish outfits and comments that once were his trademark. Could it be that Vic's gone establishment?

I picked the right time to turn pro. The pro game has really blossomed the past couple of years. Whereas in the old days prize

money came from the patron's tickets, now businesses are starting
to provide purses in exchange for having their names affixed to
titles of tournaments, or at least getting mentioned in the advertising of the tournament.

Since there are many more tournaments that offer prize money
than there used to be, and the money is getting much better in
these events, the pros are now putting a lot more time into improving their games. As of 1978, Sharif Khan is still the only full-time
touring pro, that is, he's the only pro without teaching responsibilities or other career commitments. Because he's much in demand
for exhibitions as well as for tournaments, he has a busy schedule
year round as he crisscrosses North America. And when you toss in
his endorsements, he does quite nicely as a touring pro. A life of
just playing squash may seem a lark, but he lives with the pressure
of having to win all the time, to maintain his earnings from prize
money and to keep himself in demand for exhibitions.

Sharif is the only full-time playing pro to date, but the trend is
toward young teaching professionals doing less teaching and
spending more time on their own games.

The guy who is pushing Sharif the hardest these days, and,
who, I believe, best exemplifies the qualities to be looked for in the
next squash champion is New York's own Stu Goldstein. He's a
hard worker, terribly fit, and totally dedicated to improving himself as a player. An outstanding junior tennis player in the East, he
might have become a touring pro in that sport had he not thought,
quite mistakenly it turned out, that someone who is 5'5 can't make
it on the modern tennis circuit. Anyway, he was introduced to
squash in 1970 at the State University of New York at Stony
Brook, Long Island, which only the year before had begun fielding
an intercollegiate team. He didn't know a lot about the finer points
of the game, but he could handle a racquet and had a good pair of
legs, which carried him to a number seven intercollegiate ranking
his senior year.

He graduated in 1973, just in time to sign on as Harry Saint's
squash pro at Saint's first commercial club in New York, the Fifth
Avenue Racquet Club, which opened that fall. Stu had one thing in
mind and that was to make himself the best squash player he could
possibly be.

I've observed over the years that if someone has a talent for the
game and really works at it—I mean goes at it like a Berlitz language course—it takes about three years to get very good. This was

true in Stu's case, for in 1976 he started to have some good wins, and in 1978 he became the first non-Khan in fifteen years to win the pro championships.

It didn't take him all that long to get there, but young players who aspire to future championships should take note that he didn't take any shortcuts either. He spent endless hours alone on the court refining his techniques. He also spent hours in the New York Public Library reading up on conditioning programs followed by leading athletes in other sports. Basically what he settled on for himself was a lot of running. I once asked him if he really thought all the running he does off court is productive for squash,* and he said, yes, he thought it was, and anyway, running is his "hobby." I've never thought of training as my hobby.

Even though he is now one of the leading players, Stu still conducts group clinics at Saint's three clubs in New York, and he gives an occasional private lesson. But most of his time—about five hours a day—is spent on his own game. Two or three of those hours are spent on physical training, which includes running of various kinds and cardiovascular-oriented weight training (light weights, lots of repetitions).

Cat quick, he is now one of the fittest players in the world. Like a flyweight boxer, he delivers a very quick punch, which enables him to sometimes put the ball away before you realize he's even taken a swing at it. And though he's petite, he has sinewy strength and knows how to take a big windup, which means he can power the ball with the best of them.

Champions have always been hard workers, but all too often in the old days the leading players, the amateurs in particular, would boast about how little work they did. It was like the old schoolboy trick of hiding your books if you heard anyone coming so you wouldn't get caught studying. In squash the ultimate was to win without appearing to work at it—the pose of effortless superiority.

That's not the way Stu operates. He puts himself on the line. He once said to me in describing his preparations for an upcoming tournament, "You can't pass the test if you don't study for the exam."

The most successful young pros today, far from concealing

---

*I believe in the old sports adage, "Train close to your sport," and so I spend almost all of my training time doing squashlike wind sprints on the court.

their hard work, if anything tend to exaggerate how much time and effort they put in. At least, speaking as a competitor, I hope they're exaggerating.

Except for Sharif, gone are the days when leading players would play their way into shape. The younger Khans are now starting to train systematically, but Sharif and his elders have a disdain for doing anything other than playing the game. To begin with, the Khans are built strong. It's an open question whether they were born that way or growing up in the court made them so. Anyway, if you grow up playing five hours a day against your brothers and uncles and cousins, who happen to be the best players in the world, and you're playing in a court that's open to the sky, with the sun beating down, the temperature 100 degrees, and the humidity thereabouts, who needs to train? But the Khans who live over here are now dispersed throughout North America, working at different clubs. A day or two before a major tournament, they might get together and play among themselves, but it's not like the old days. And so, it's going to be a lot tougher for them to maintain their monopoly. Sharif is still number one, and for my money the greatest player in the history of hard ball, but unless a cousin from overseas suddenly arrives (and don't bet against it), it will be difficult for the Khans to continue to rule.

I look forward to the day, which I think is not far off, when the prize money in squash is enough to support a dozen or more full-time touring pros who spend all their waking hours working on their games. When that happens, the caliber of play and depth on the circuit will be beyond anything we can imagine right now. But I also have to admit that I feel fortunate that for a little while there's been room for part-timers like me. Being a pro has certainly been the high point of my squash career.

I'm playing the best squash of my life, and I hadn't expected this to happen. I'm even covering court better than ever. I'm sure I don't have the raw speed I once did, but I run a lot smarter than I used to. That's one of the great things about squash, it's such a complicated game, you never stop learning. And as you get older, if you keep in shape, your improved knowledge of the game compensates quite nicely for a little loss of speed. Experience can make up for a loss of youth up to the age of forty or so, if you are willing to train a little harder each year.

And on the topic of youth, Mark Twain once remarked what a pity it is that youth is wasted on young people, who don't appreciate it. I think I've particularly enjoyed competing at the top of the game the last couple of years because I'm now old enough to enjoy the fact that I still have a little of my youth left in me. Maybe as long as you keep playing, no matter at what level, you always feel that way. I hope so.

The play is fun. It's also great to be part of the game in these exciting times. The game is growing and prospering on all fronts. At the junior level, squash is no longer played only at Merion and a few New England prep schools. Commercial clubs are running clinics for kids during their off hours and leasing court time to local schools, so more young people are getting introduced to the game, and almost half these kids are girls. In New York there are now tournaments for kids eleven and under. In Ohio there's a summer squash camp.

Squash has really caught on in the colleges too.* In my day there were only ten or so schools represented in the intercollegiates, all from the Northeast. Compare this to the draw of the 1977 intercollegiates, which had entries from over thirty colleges, including Berkeley, the University of Georgia, the University of Michigan, the University of Mexico, and the University of Western Ontario (in Canada).

Gone are many of the great and colorful coaches of my day, but from all reports, the caliber of coaching in general has improved. Schools that were once pushovers now have very capable coaches. Barnaby has retired (though you'd never know it from all the squash projects—talks, clinics, and books—he's busy with these days), but his successor, Dave Fish, who played for him in the sixties, is ably carrying on the tradition. And it's nice to hear Fish cite Barnaby the way Barnaby used to cite Cowles.

Perhaps the most exciting thing that's happening in college squash today is that women are now playing in great numbers. One reason for this is the Ivies have gone coed, but it also has to do with the long overdue emphasis that is now being given to developing sports programs for women in college. George Washington University now offers athletic scholarships to women squash players.

Along with what's happening in the colleges, the other big boon for the women's game is, of course, the commercial center. Right from the beginning these clubs have sought to attract

---

*According to the latest court survey, some 200 colleges now have squash courts.

women. At first the owners thought that, as is the case in tennis, housewives would help fill the off hours. But, in the cities anyway, most of the women squash players are career women who use the courts at the same time and for the same reasons as the men. And average women players are now beginning to compete against men in leagues and tournaments.

The old guard has not always been pleased with what's been happening to "their game," but amateur associations are now accepting the fact that things are changing, and they seem to have decided to heed Talleyrand's advice that "the art of statemanship is to foresee the inevitable and to expedite its occurrence."

Since all of the best amateurs have turned pro, except for the ones in college, the amateur associations have lost control of the play at the top of the game. But the United States Squash Racquets Association has gone out and gotten itself a sponsor for a national B- and C-level tournament that will in 1979 have something like four thousand entries.

What took some time for many of the traditionalists in the game to recognize and adjust to is the fact that the sponsors and center owners are the new powers in squash. For example, to make a financial go of it, commercial clubs have to book courts year round, and that's why squash is suddenly a year round sport. The marketing and investment decisions of businessmen who are interested in making a profit out of squash will, as much as anything, determine the future of the game.

And how does that future look? When I interviewed Heather McKay in 1977, she observed that commercial courts were starting to pop up all over North America, and told me, "Squash is starting to go over here like it did in Australia in the early days." And she predicted that "squash will grow a lot bigger than people at the moment will believe."

But how much bigger? I don't think squash will overtake tennis here, the way it did in Australia after commercial courts started going up. Tennis may have peaked, but you're still dealing with 20 to 40 million tennis players in the U.S. and Canada, depending upon whose estimates you believe and how you define a player (someone who plays twice a year or twice a month?). But what tennis has demonstrated is that a racquet sport can make it big over here.

Since squash is far easier to learn than tennis, provides more exercise in less time, and is cheaper to play,* it stands to reason that if squash is made available and is properly promoted, it, too, can become a racquet sport for the masses. In an article entitled "Squash Racquets, Anyone? Definitely Yes," John Radosta of *The New York Times* said of squash in November 1977, "Its growth resembles the booms in tennis, golf, and bowling in the last two decades." And the *New York Post* that same year ran a feature on squash under the headline, "Squash Craze Promises Profit to Club Operators."

The game is catching on. But there's another ball-wall racquet game that's also bidding for the public's attention: racquetball.

Racquetball is essentially squash played on a 20 by 40 foot, four-wall handball court. The rules are pretty much the same; the big difference is there's no tin and you can play the ball off the ceiling. The "boingy" ball takes a rather vertical bounce off the floor, which makes it easy to catch up to, and the racquet, which is strung, has a short shaft that makes it very easy for the beginner to connect with the ball. Boosters of racquetball claim that their sport will "bury" squash because it's much easier to learn. But now that we've gone to the seventy-plus ball, I'm not so sure that racquetball is that much easier to learn than squash. Anyway, the differences between learning squash and racquetball are nothing compared to the differences between learning tennis and learning squash. Tennis is a much tougher sport to pick up, and yet there are millions of very average athletes playing it. The popularity of a sport is not determined solely by how easy it is.

Since racquetball, like squash, is an indoor ball-wall racquet game that offers real fitness benefits, there's no doubt but that the growth of racquetball may hurt the growth of squash. However, racquetball has two disadvantages relative to squash. First, while it is easy to learn, once you get into it you discover that, unlike squash, there's not much to it. When the ball hits a wall it slows down tremendously and tends to angle out sharply into the middle, you can't use the walls the way you do in squash, so you don't have nearly as many shot options in racquetball as you do in squash. The pros at the top of the game are certainly great athletes, and they can handle a racquet, but by their style of play they've proven

---

*Squash court rentals in New York City are a third to a quarter the cost of commercial tennis courts.

that winning racquetball boils down to hitting ceiling balls for position and then driving kills into the crease, where the front wall meets the floor, for the point. If people quit tennis because it's too tough to get a decent rally going, they'll quit racquetball because there's too little variety and too much senseless running around in circles.

The problem with racquetball as a business, compared to squash, is the courts take up more space and are more expensive to construct—the latter because the courts are bigger and the ceiling is a playing surface. This means the economics of squash are better; courts can be rented at a lower rate and don't need as much usage to make a profit.

But the thing racquetball has going for it is momentum. Some very good businessmen got behind it about ten years ago, and they got the jump on commercial squash. The problem with putting up racquetball or squash courts is, if the business bombs, there are not an awful lot of things you can do with these empty courts other than tear them down. This means that investors want to see a lot of successful projects before they put their money into one of these clubs. Since there are more commercial racquetball courts than commercial squash courts, investors are more inclined to back racquetball these days, even though the economics of a squash project may make more sense.

Racquetball won't bury squash, nor will it make serious inroads into places where squash is already well established, like New York and Toronto, but it will limit the growth of squash in areas where racquetball gets there first.

It's obvious, if business gets behind squash and it's marketed correctly, squash can be a tremendous participant sport in North America, the way it is elsewhere in the squash playing world. What may not be so obvious, but I think is a very real possibility, is that squash could also prove to be a great spectator sport. I've never seen a major match when the gallery wasn't filled to capacity and then some. The question is how to expand that capacity. The glass back wall, which is now standard in all new exhibition courts, has helped some, but what would really be great is an all glass court, preferably a portable one that could be set up in places like Madison Square Garden. The technical problems are negligible—the glass has to be treated so that the ball doesn't slide on it, and the lighting has to be worked out so that the players can see the ball. A fish bowl court can be built right now, the question is who's going to pay for it? I'm told a portable one would cost several hundred thousand dollars to develop.

For the time being, the best that can be hoped for is that centers interested in holding tournaments will put in courts with maybe two glass walls. But the basic business problem here is the more space you give to galleries, the less space you give to courts, and galleries don't make money the way courts do.

The big play, of course, would be to get squash on network TV. I played a match that was televised locally in Canada, and I did the "color work" (expert commentary) for a match that was picked up by cable TV in New York. In both cases the matches were taped, so I had a chance to judge the product. Mind you, I'm a little biased, and, of course, it's easy for me to follow the action because I know the moves of the players, but I'll say it anyway, I was impressed. In both instances, the producers "went low budget," as they say in the trade, but the excitement of the game came through, nevertheless. What it needed was more creative camera work and editing and, most important, a lens with a faster eye than is normally used, so that the ball wouldn't now and then disappear. Again, it's only a question of money! Nothing out of the ordinary, just the standard sums that go into the standard sports broadcasts.

However, the network TV executives are convinced that people will watch squash only if they play squash. So they want to know the numbers, and when you cross your fingers and tell them there may be well over a million players now in North America in this fast growing game, they're not impressed.

One place where squash did sneak on network TV was in the so-called "World Racquets Championships," in which the champions of tennis, squash, badminton, racquetball, and Ping-Pong competed against each other outside their specialties. Sharif so thoroughly trounced everyone (including Bjorn Borg, who finished second), they rigged it the next year so he wouldn't win. (The second time around they wouldn't let him compete in racquetball, and they awarded the first prize to Guillermo Vilas, even though Khan and Vilas were tied in points.) Anyway, the squash televised quite nicely, and certainly Sharif struck a blow for squash. He also proved most convincingly that he's a world-class athlete.

But the significant thing about that contest, to me, was it brought home the point that when people are thinking about racquet sports, squash now gets considered. These days, when articles are written on racquet sports, squash gets mentioned as a good one. And when sports complexes are planned, thought is given to putting in some squash courts. The most publicized new courts are in commercial squash centers, but, squash courts these days are also being included in apartment buildings, health clubs, tennis complexes, and sometimes even in racquetball centers.

Squash has entered the public's vocabulary for racquet sports, and gone are the days of whenever the game was mentioned so was the vegetable. Now, when Tom Seaver breaks his nose playing squash, the reporter doesn't feel he has to explain to the reader what squash is.

Squash has entered the public's vocabulary, but the game has yet to "go public" the way I'd like to see it go public. In Australia and England squash has the mass appeal that bowling has over here. But in the U.S. and Canada the pay-and-play centers to date have only gone after people who are relatively affluent. As leisure activities go, squash can be quite inexpensive, but thus far nobody in the industry has sought to attract people with incomes in the middle to lower-middle range. Racquetball, which comes out of the handball tradition, has been quite successful with this market, and, in fact, this is the base on which they are building.

I'd like to see squash courts go up in public parks (perhaps made of cement and plexiglass and open to the sky), but I'm afraid it will be a while before that happens. In the meantime, I'm sure the game will get a lot bigger—now that commercial centers are on the scene—but so long as these centers cater only to the relatively affluent, the game will never get that big. Until the promoters start going after the mass market, I'd have to agree with the title Jim Kaplan of *Sports Illustrated* chose for a piece he did on squash several years ago. The title for his article was: "For the Many, If Not the Masses."

I love the game and I'd like to see more people discover the pleasures of playing it. I also enjoy being a celebrity, albeit a very minor one, in a growing sport, and I look forward to having my skills appreciated by a larger public.

But at base, squash remains a personal challenge for me. There's that old saw in sports: no matter who you're playing, the only real opponent is yourself. And it's true that you are trying to better your past performances, eliminate bad habits, and keep control of yourself under pressure. But I don't like to think of squash in terms of beating myself. That's too negative. Players who are continually fighting themselves end up losers, usually in terms of the score, always in terms of missing out on enjoying the game. No, I like to think about improvement and growth. Win or lose, whenever I compete, I have the chance to learn more about myself and the game. And the thought that I could always get a little better is one of the things that keeps me coming back.

Over the years I've never had to suffer the boredom of winning all the time. Looking back, I can think of matches I would have liked to have won but didn't. Yet I have no regrets. If you take on challenges, you're going to lose part of the time. And no matter how good you get, you have to take your share of defeats. Time and again, Niederhoffer, who ruled supreme in the amateur ranks, got whipped by the Khans before he finally cracked through. Even Sharif Khan, who wins almost everything over here, comes up against players he can't seem to beat in the soft ball game. And when Geoff Hunt, king of soft ball, went after the hard ball title in 1977, he found he couldn't go all the way, at least not the first time.

If you didn't lose part of the time, winning wouldn't be nearly so much fun. What separates the real competitors from the pack is not just the ability to win, but also the ability to learn from defeat and to not be too discouraged by it.

But enough on losing! I prefer to dwell on thoughts of victory. Down through the years the big thrill for me has been that at each stage of my squash career I have been able to get good enough to be able to beat everyone in my league on occasion. Maybe the odds were against me, but I had myself convinced before each match that I could end up on the winning end of the handshake.

Each time I moved into a new league, as I worked my way up from JV at Exeter to the pros, I was presented with a new set of challenges; but by working at it, I was eventually able to compete at the top of each league.

That for me has been the big thrill of competing, knowing that every time I stepped on the court I could win. I've been lucky to experience this at the top of the game, but I think having a shot at winning is something everyone who plays the game can experience.

A great thing about competitive squash is it's organized so that everyone can compete. Almost everywhere that squash is played, there are leagues, tournaments, ladders, handicap events, what have you, organized by age, sex, occupation, or level of skill; so everyone from Sharif Khan right down to the rank novice can find his or her level and have a shot at winning a real match.

Right now I still feel I can win matches at the top of the game. I used to think that when I could no longer play near the top, I'd probably quit. But as I've written this book I've come to realize that the game is too much a part of me to do that. This past summer, when I wasn't competing, I used squash as a way of winding down from a day of writing. I wasn't trying to prove anything, I was just playing for the fun of it and because I felt better after the workout.

No, as long as I can walk, I'll always be playing squash, and, if I get to heaven and find out they don't play squash there, I'm coming back.

Appendix A
THE GAME, HOW PLAYED, SCORED

Squash is a racquet game played by two or four people in an enclosed, rectangular, four-wall court. The singles court is 32 feet long and 18½ feet wide; the doubles court is 45 feet by 25 feet. What follows is a description of the singles game.

The racquet, which measures 27 inches in length, has a long thin neck and a small round head, which is strung with gut or nylon. It weighs between 7 and 10 ounces when strung, and is something like a heavy badminton racquet. The rubbery ball is hollow and squishy and is about the size of a golf ball (see The Racquet and Ball in Appendix C).

The players usually stand side by side, facing the front wall, about two-thirds of the way back in the court. The idea of the game is to hit the ball to the front wall in such a way that the opponent is unable to return it successfully. For a return to be good, the ball must be hit before it bounces twice on the floor, and it must make it to the front wall, clearing the 17 inch high "tin" that extends along the base of the front wall. The ball can hit any combination of walls to get there, but it must reach the front wall on the fly (that is, it may not bounce on the floor on the way to the front wall). The ball may not hit the ceiling, nor may it at any time hit above or outside of the out-of-bounds lines that surround the court (see The Court in Appendix B).

A point is begun by one of the players serving the ball to the front wall. The decision as to who will serve first is done by chance (usually by spinning the racquet), but thereafter, the winner of the previous point is the server for the next point.

To be good, a serve must hit the front wall before it hits any other wall and it must clear the service line on the front wall. The server must keep at least one foot in the quarter-circle service "box" as he strikes the ball, and if the receiver chooses not to volley the return, the ball must land within the service lines on the floor on his side of the court (see The Court in Appendix B). The server is allowed one fault. The receiver may not play a fault. If the server makes two faults he loses the serve and the point.

If the service is good, the rally continues until one of the players is unable to make a good return. The winner of the rally wins one point and the serve. A game is played to 15 points and a match is 3 out of 5 games. If the score is tied at 13 all, the player who got to 13 first may extend the game beyond 15 points. He may choose a "set" of 3 or 5 points, in which case the game is played to 16 or 18 points respectively. Or he may choose "no set," that is, 2 points, which means the game is played to 15. If the score is tied at 14 all and was not previously tied at 13 all, the receiver may extend the game to 17 points or keep the game to 15.

Play is meant to be continuous within each game. There are no time-outs permitted for players to recover their strength or review their strategy. There is, however, a two-minute break between all the games, except between the third and fourth games, when there is a five-minute break. In the case of an injury, a break in play is allowed, but if the injured player is unable to continue after an hour, he must forfeit the match.

As soon as a player hits the ball he must "clear" (get out of the way) and not interfere with his opponent's attempt to play the ball. If a player feels he has been interfered with in his attempt to get to the ball and/or stroke it, he may request a "let," which is a playing over of a point. When there is no referee, the point is automatically played over. But, if there is a referee, the referee decides if this is a legitimate request. The referee may decide that the striker was not interfered with or could not have gotten to the ball following the path he was taking before obstructed, in which case, the request is denied and the point is awarded to the other player. If the referee feels the request is legitimate, he awards either a let or a "let point." A "let point" is the awarding of a point to a player when his opponent unnecessarily or deliberately prevents him from reaching and/or stroking the ball. A let point may also be awarded when the obstruction was unavoidable, but the player interfered with was in a position of real advantage. If there are judges in addition to the referee, a player may appeal a referee's decision. For the referee's decision to be overturned, both judges must disagree with the referee's decision.

The above represents a brief summary of the basic playing rules. There are numerous technical points and elaborations of these rules not included here. Players who wish to resolve disputes should consult the official rules, published by the various squash associations and posted at most clubs. It should also be noted that these are the basic rules for North American or "hard ball" squash, which differs somewhat from English or "soft ball" squash.

Appendix B
THE COURT

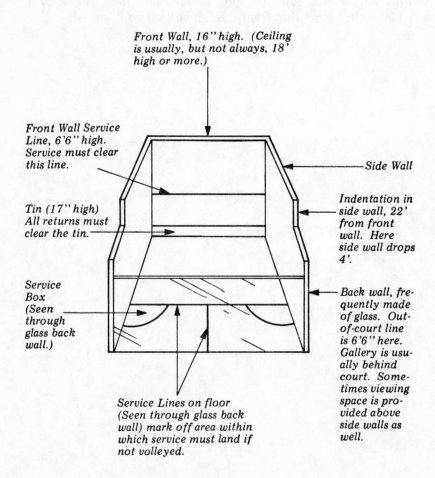

Front Wall, 16" high. (Ceiling is usually, but not always, 18' high or more.)

Front Wall Service Line, 6'6" high. Service must clear this line.

Tin (17" high) All returns must clear the tin.

Service Box (Seen through glass back wall.)

Side Wall

Indentation in side wall, 22' from front wall. Here side wall drops 4'.

Back wall, frequently made of glass. Out-of-court line is 6'6" here. Gallery is usually behind court. Sometimes viewing space is provided above side walls as well.

Service Lines on floor (Seen through glass back wall) mark off area within which service must land if not volleyed.

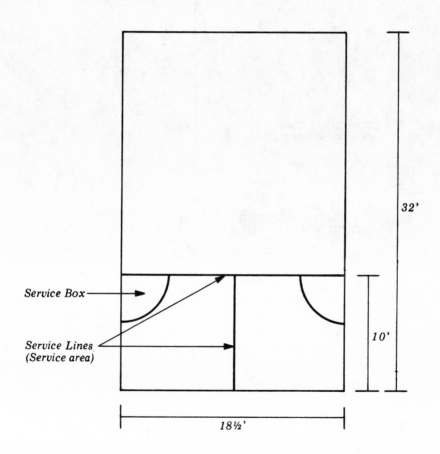

Service Box

Service Lines
(Service area)

32'

10'

18½'

Appendix C
THE RACQUET AND BALL

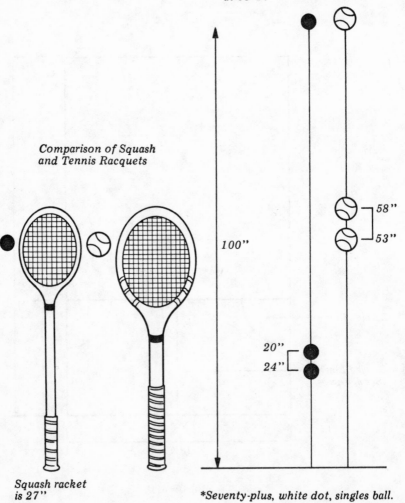

Bounce of squash ball*
compared to tennis ball
in a drop of 100" upon
a solid base. Ball's surface
at 68° F.

Comparison of Squash
and Tennis Racquets

100"

58"

53"

20"
24"

Squash racket
is 27"

*Seventy-plus, white dot, singles ball.

Appendix D
SHOTS DIAGRAM

The "T"
The Diagonal

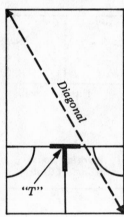

Rail Shot

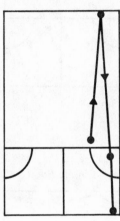

Cross-Court

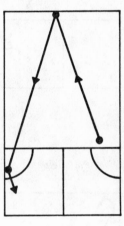

Roll Corner

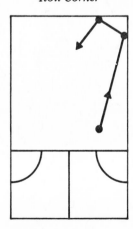

Reverse Corner

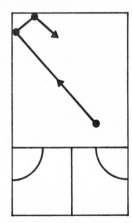

Drop Shots into
the Nick

Cross
Drop

Straight
Drop

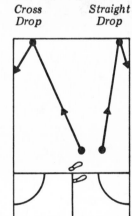

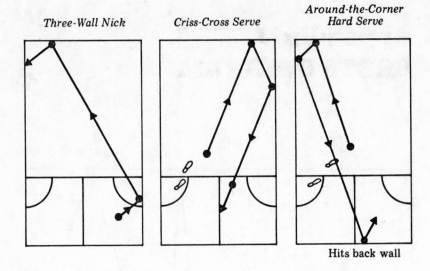

Three-Wall Nick

Criss-Cross Serve

Around-the-Corner
Hard Serve

Hits back wall

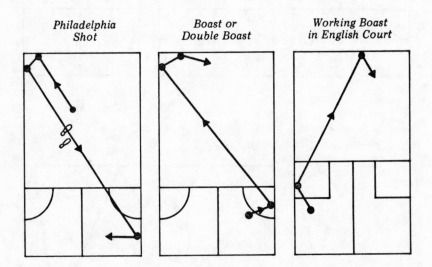

Philadelphia
Shot

Boast or
Double Boast

Working Boast
in English Court

Glossary
A SQUASH PLAYER'S GUIDE TO TERMS

"A" Player See RATING.

Alley Shot Same as RAIL SHOT. See Appendix D: Shots Diagram

An Amateur Makes his money from squash through the business contacts he develops playing squash. Compare with PROFESSIONAL.

American Ball The squash ball used in the AMERICAN GAME. See HARD BALL. Compare with ENGLISH BALL.

American Game The version of squash that is played in the U.S., Mexico, and Canada. Compare ENGLISH GAME; see HARD BALL.

Angle Shots A primarily British term for CORNER SHOTS.

Anticipation The ability to figure out where a shot is going well in advance so that it can be returned with ease.

Appeal A request by a player to the JUDGES that the REFEREE's decision be overturned. Both judges must agree for this to happen.

Around-the-Corner Serve A HARD SERVE that ricochets around the front corner, nearest the SERVER, and then cuts diagonally across the court. Very tricky. See Appendix D: Shots Diagram.

"B" Player See RATING.

Backhand A stroke made with the back of the hand moving forward. This is a more natural stroke than the FOREHAND, and most advanced players find their backhand more reliable than their forehand. Most beginners have a problem with the backhand because they tend to face the front instead of turning to the side wall and getting their shoulder around. A backhand blow is banned from boxing because it it too lethal.

Back Opponent Off A technique of backing up while preparing to play the ball, which enables the STRIKER to back his opponent out of the center of the court.

Backspin   Same as UNDERSPIN. Called backspin because spin is imparted by drawing OPEN RACQUET down and across the back of the ball. See UNDERSPIN, and compare with TOP SPIN.

"Bad" Loss   All losses. But particularly those to players who are obviously inferior, you think.

Beginners   Beginners should be greatly encouraged, but at a great distance, since they are likely to have untamed swings.

Best Build for Squash   There is no best build. If you're tall you can reach; if you're short you can turn quickly. However, all TOURNAMENT PLAYERS, whatever their size or shape, have big rear ends. It comes from all the stretching.

The Best Game   "There is no such thing. Know yourself, exploit your talents, use what you've got and don't waste time regretting what you haven't got. If you can hit—hit. If you're fast, be a retriever. If you have touch, use a lot of shots. If you have a quick wrist, stress the volley and rush your opponent. The best game is a theoretical rainbow. Find *your* game and forget the best game. Squash is a great leveller. Champions range from 5'5 to 6'5."

Jack Barnaby, famous Harvard coach, from *Squash Racquets in Brief*

Boast   A blast that goes side wall, side wall, front wall. Though blasted into the side wall, it just grazes the front wall, if it makes it at all. A very difficult shot to return because it's tough to read and because the ball comes out even less than a DROP SHOT. But it's even tougher to make, and, therefore, it's hardly ever used, even by top tournament players. Also called "double boast." See Appendix D: Shots Diagram.

Break   The rest period between GAMES. The break between the third and fourth games is five minutes; between all other games it lasts two minutes.

Break off the Wall   To rebound off the wall.

Broken Ball   If the ball breaks all the way through (squeeze it and check the seams), it is removed from play, a new ball is WARMED UP, and the point is replayed. If you think the ball may be broken, but have just won a POINT, proceed quickly to the SERVICE BOX.

Bury the Ball   To hit to perfect LENGTH, so that the second bounce is just before the back wall. A buried DRIVE is not easily exhumed.

"C" Player   See RATING.

Call   A decision by a REFEREE or JUDGE.

Calling a Ball Down   The decision (or admission) that a ball was not retrieved before it bounced twice on the floor, or that it did not clear the TIN. Playing with or without a REFEREE, the STRIKER is expected to call "double bounces" on himself. See PLAYING A DOUBLE BOUNCE.

Carry   A cradling of the ball on the racquet so that it is carried rather than hit. This is not permitted.

Challenge Match A MATCH to determine a position on a LADDER. The rules as to who can challenge whom vary, but the winner of a challenge match assumes the position on the ladder of the previously higher of the two players, and the loser takes the position just below him.

Choke Result of no PLAN.

Clear As soon as a player hits the ball he must "clear" (get out of the way), and not interfere with his opponent's attempt to play the ball. See LET and LET POINT. Compare with CROWDING.

Closed Racquet Racquet face is tilted forward. This is a technique used for imparting TOP SPIN and is ordinarily not recommended for squash because it makes the ball climb on the front wall and take a long, high bounce on the floor, with the result that it's difficult to BURY DRIVES or to make DROPS and CORNERS DIE.

Closed Stance Addressing the ball with the front foot closer to the side wall than the back foot is. This is the preferred technique, as it facilitates the proper transfer of weight.

Closed Tournament A tournament that is not open to PROFESSIONALS, or that is open only to players from a particular region.

Club Player A recreational player of more or less average ability, who may compete, but not in top tournaments. Compare TOURNAMENT PLAYER.

Club Pro A PROFESSIONAL employed by a club to teach and run the squash program. See TEACHING PRO.

Club Surgeon A guy with a wild follow-through. Has difficulty finding games.

Come Around To go after a ball that is breaking around you off the back wall by pivoting instead of backing up. Also called TURNING ON THE BALL.

Come Out A ball that takes a long bounce off the side or back walls, and is thus easy to play, is said to come out.

Commercial Center A squash facility where courts can be rented, or a squash club where the only criterion for membership is a good credit rating.

Competing More fun than not competing.

Conditioning A player's level of fitness.

Consolation Tournament A TOURNAMENT held for first-round losers. In other words, an opportunity to lose twice. Consolation events are a good way for an aspiring player to get some extra competition. (I at one time owned every consolation tournament title in North America.)

Continuity of Play The rule is that "play shall be continuous." Players are not permitted to interrupt the play during a GAME in order to recover their strength or wind, to review strategy, or to attempt to break their opponent's momentum. There are, however, BREAKS taken between GAMES. See STALLING.

Controlling the T The basic strategy in squash—keeping yourself in the center of the court, near the T, and your opponent not. See the "T."

Corner Shot Ball that ricochets around either of the front corners of the court, hitting the side wall first. See REVERSE CORNER, ROLL CORNER.

Courtesy Points Giving away points by purposely making errors or feeding opponent SETUPS. Well meant, but frequently patronizing and often backfires. Never give an opponent anything, unless you're thinking to give him the match. The greatest courtesy is to let your opponent know you're taking him seriously.

Court Running Doing wind sprints in the court to improve your speed and your ability to recover from tough points. Squash always hurts, but the more pain you take in practice, the less you take during a match. See STARS.

Cover a Shot To be ready to return a particular shot.

Covering the Court Retrieving.

Criss-Cross Serve A HARD SERVE that breaks in front of the RECEIVER. See Appendix D: Shots Diagram.

Cross-Court A DRIVE to the other side of the court. Also called "v" shot. See Appendix D: Shots Diagram.

Cross Drop A DROP SHOT that goes across the court and NICKS after hitting the front wall. See Appendix D: Shots Diagram.

Crowding Failure to CLEAR. In a squash court two can be a crowd.

CSRA Canadian Squash Racquets Association.

Customer's Game CLUB PRO keeps score close and drops a game or two to keep pupil coming back.

Cut On ball, see SLICE. On face, see doctor.

"D" Player See RATING.

Default Occurs when a player withdraws from or is disqualified from a scheduled match. His opponent advances to the next round in a TOURNAMENT. Defaults do not count for rankings unless the player who receives the default was leading at the time of the default. Defaults do count, however, in figuring team standings.

Dentist's Delight See CLUB SURGEON.

The Diagonal The longest distance in the court. See Appendix D: Shots Diagram. Better your opponent is made to cover this distance than you.

Die A ball that dies is one that is no longer in play because it has bounced twice on the floor or NICKED. A player is said to be dead when he's too tired to chase after balls that aren't dead.

Double Boast See BOAST.

Double Fault The loss of a point because both SERVES are ruled FAULTS. Since you can always use a safe, underhand SLOW SERVE for a second serve, you shouldn't double fault more than once every five years.

Double Hit To hit a ball twice in the same stroke. This is not allowed, but often hard to detect. Rarely called by REFEREE, but on your conscience.

Doubles A game of squash played by four people, two on a side. The doubles court is bigger (25 feet by 45 feet) than a SINGLES court, and the doubles ball is peppier than the singles ball.

Doubles Player Someone too old or out of shape to play competitive SINGLES.

Down NOT UP.

Down-the-Line Same as RAIL SHOT.

Draw The match-up of opponents entered in a TOURNAMENT. After SEEDED players have been placed, the rest of the match-ups are meant to be drawn by lot. But all too often, if the draw comes out of a hat, that hat is on someone's head.

Drill A one- or two-man practice routine intended to improve a shot or skill. To drill someone, however, may also mean to hit him with the ball, hard.

Drive A ball hit hard after it bounces on the floor. Usually hit for LENGTH. See RAIL and CROSS-COURT.

Drop Shot A ball hit directly to the front wall, in such a way that it DIES short in the court, or at least TAKES THE OPPONENT SHORT. The ideal drop shot clears the TIN by a safe margin and, using the side wall as a brake, NICKS. See Appendix D: Shots Diagram.

English Ball The ball used in the ENGLISH GAME. See SOFT BALL.

English Court Used for the ENGLISH GAME. Much like the American court except that it is 2½ feet wider, the TIN is 2 inches higher, and the out-of-court lines on the side walls are lower because they slope downward.

English Game The English version of the game of squash, using a softer, slower ball, a 2½ foot-wider court, and a scoring system of 9 POINT GAMES, with points scored only by the SERVER. It is played in many of the countries that were once part of the British Empire, including Australia, New Zealand, South Africa, India, Egypt, and Pakistan. It is also played somewhat during the summer in the U.S. and is becoming popular in Canada. Also called the SOFT BALL GAME. See ENGLISH COURT, SOFT BALL. Compare with the AMERICAN GAME.

Error A failure to make a good return in a situation where the mistake was not forced. Brilliant WINNERS are what people remember, but unforced errors are what determine the outcome of most close matches.

Excuses Rarely valid. A real competitor takes no excuse into the court, and accepts none afterward.

Exhibition A game put on for spectators that doesn't count for anything, but is meant to show off the game, the facility, or the skills of the players. Some players treat all games like exhibitions.

Expert There are many experts in the GALLERY, fewer in the court.

Fault A SERVE that is not good. See Appendix A: The Game, How Played, Scored.

Feather Drop A very soft DROP SHOT that dribbles off the front wall. Ordinarily not a PERCENTAGE SHOT.

A Fitness Freak Anyone in better shape than you are.

Fluke A lucky shot. Only opponents hit flukes.

Foot Fault While serving the ball, the SERVER must keep at least one foot within the SERVICE BOX, and not touching the line. Otherwise, it is a foot fault, and the SERVE is called FAULT.

Footwork The way in which a player lines up his feet when addressing the ball. Most racquet errors can be traced to improper footwork. See CLOSED STANCE, OPEN STANCE.

Forehand A stroke made with the palm of the hand moving forward. Compare with BACKHAND.

"Forty-Five Dollar Practice Stroke" Breaking your racquet in the process of mishitting a ball. The price is going up.

Gallery Space provided for spectators usually above back wall, though sometimes above sides also, and increasingly behind glass back wall. The spectators are also referred to as the gallery. It is considered bad form to look at the gallery after you hit a WINNER.

Game Fifteen POINTS make a game, though overtimes may be elected at 13 all and 14 all. The first person to win 3 games wins the MATCH. See Appendix A: The Game, How Played, Scored.

Game Plan See PLAN.

Gamesmanship Not as effective as good speed, strength, strokes, and strategy.

Get A difficult return of a ball that looked to be a PUTAWAY. A save.

Good Lessons Competent instruction. Very important for beginners, otherwise you practice your mistakes.

Good Sport Someone who takes so much pride in his game, he doesn't want to just win, he wants to prove he can beat his opponents when they were given every opportunity to play their best and so can have no valid excuses.

Grip The way in which the racquet is held. This is much more important than most players realize. The only way to compensate for an incorrect grip is with an incorrect stroke. To keep the racquet from slipping in my hand when it gets wet, I wrap gauze (sold at all pro shops) on top of my leather handle.

Gut More effective in racquet than on squash player. Most TOURNAMENT PLAYERS prefer gut strings to nylon because they grip the ball better than nylon. But some use nylon because the ball comes off the racquet sooner. Most CLUB PROS recommend gut, it's more expensive.

Hacker A player of modest skills, but don't tell him, he's having fun.

Handicap Your DOUBLES partner. Also, a system of giving and/or taking away POINTS at the start of a GAME, so that two players of different abilities might have a closer game. True, this makes the score closer, but it doesn't mean that the play will be more interesting.

Hand In In the SOFT BALL game, the SERVER is referred to as "hand in," and the RECEIVER, as "HAND OUT."

Hand Out The RECEIVER in SOFT BALL game. See HAND IN.

Hard Ball Another name for the AMERICAN BALL. Called the "hard" ball because it is harder than the squishy ENGLISH BALL, which is often referred to as the SOFT BALL. The hard ball, which is peppier than the soft ball, rewards fast reactions and the ability to make shots. The soft ball, on the other hand, because it is slower and tends to hang, places more emphasis on fitness and retrieving.

Hard Serve Any SERVE that is hit hard with an overhand motion. Compare with SLOW SERVE.

Headhunter A player who attempts to intimidate opponents with his racquet or shots.

Hitter A SLUGGER.

Hitting Down the Wall Hitting RAIL SHOTS.

Hold Shot To pause before hitting a ball in an attempt to get opponent to commit himself too soon.

Holy Roller A THREE-WALL NICK that rolls out of the crease, perfected by Reverend Bob Hetherington. It works best on Sundays.

International Ball Some SOFT BALL enthusiasts refer to their ball as the "international" ball. See WORLD BALL.

International Game There is no one international game. English ball players, however, sometimes refer to their game as the "international" game.

ISPA International Squash Professionals Association. An association of SOFT BALL-PLAYING PROS.

ISRF The International Squash Rackets Association, an organization that promotes and governs international amateur SOFT BALL events.

Judges Two officials, one at each end of the GALLERY behind the court, to whom players may APPEAL a REFEREE's decision. Both judges must agree to overturn referee's decision. In squash the expression "Sober as a judge" does not usually apply, since frequently, though not always, judges are found by clearing the bar.

Junk Seemingly nothing balls, hit at funny angles in order to put off opponent's timing and concentration.

Keep Eye on Ball Yes, but also keep face out of opponent's stroke. See WAFFLE FACE. If opponent is hitting from behind you, watch him from the corner of your eye or peek through the strings of your racquet.

Knee Brace Often disguises a perfectly healthy knee.

Knock-Out Tournament A TOURNAMENT in which once you lose you're out. Compare with ROUND ROBIN.

Knock-Up Not what you think it is. The British term for the WARM-UP.

Ladder   A continuous ranking of players. Once a ladder is set up, changes in position on it are determined solely by CHALLENGE MATCHES. Ladders are used to determine lineups for teams.

Length   Depth of DRIVE. Hitting to "good length" or "perfect length" means hitting the ball very deep, but without it coming off the back wall. The ball DIES just before reaching the back wall.

Let   The playing over of a POINT. Most frequently lets are called because one player is in the way of the other. See LET POINT.

Let Point   The awarding of a POINT to a player who was interfered with while attempting to get to or play a ball. Only awarded when interference denied the STRIKER a commanding advantage or when the obstruction was unnecessary or deliberate.

Lob   A ball hit high and soft. A more important shot than most people realize. The lob is an effective defensive maneuver when making a GET, as it gives you time to get back in position. The occasional lob is also a good way to change the pace when you are on the offensive.

Loose Ball   A SETUP. An opportunity to attempt a likely WINNER, or at least to hit a good, punishing shot.

Match   Three out of five games makes a match. Any formal competition is called a match.

Mixed Doubles   DOUBLES teams composed of a woman and a man. Some call it "mixed troubles."

Monkey Doubles   DOUBLES in a SINGLES court, played with sawed-off racquets. Good game for monkeys.

Nick   If ball lands in the crease where the floor meets the back or side walls and rolls unplayable, it is said to "nick" or "catch the nick."

No Set   Decision by RECEIVER who is tied at 13 all (or at 14 all, if the score was not first tied at 13 all) not to extend the game beyond 15 points. See SET.

Not Free   You, when player with a wild follow-through proposes a game.

Not Up   Decision that the ball was not returned before it bounced twice on the floor, or that it hit the TIN.

Old Ball   A mythical ball of old, which never existed, but is often referred to by persons who have just lost a match, as in, "Why don't they bring back the old ball?"

Open Racquet   Racquet face is tilted backward so that ball can be SLICED.

Open Squash   Permitting PROFESSIONALS to compete against AMATEURS in most events.

Open Stance   Not turning completely sideways when addressing the ball. Sometimes you don't have time to get around properly, but it is very difficult to hit with authority this way. Compare with CLOSED STANCE.

Open Tournament   TOURNAMENT open to PROFESSIONALS as well as AMATEURS.

Out of Court   Ball hitting on, above, or outside of the out-of-bounds lines that surround the top of the court. See Appendix B.

Pace   The tempo of the play. The faster the pace, the less time an opponent has to react. Pace is achieved not just by hitting the ball hard but also by taking it early. VOLLEYing is a way of picking up the pace. Most of the leading players play at a very fast pace.

Percentage Shot   A percentage shot is one that you are not likely to make an error on. When an opponent makes a WINNER on a nonpercentage shot, congratulate him with hopes that he'll try another one.

Philadelphia Shot   Trickiest shot in squash. Following the path of a *z*, it hits three walls. It picks up a SPIN off of the second wall, which makes it zig when you expect it to zag as it rebounds off the third wall. See Appendix D: Shots Diagram.

Plan   A game plan or strategy for a particular opponent, designed to bring out the worst in his game and the best in yours.

Platform Tennis   Not a sport.

Player   Curious term to use for someone who takes something so seriously.

Playing a Double Bounce   Playing a ball that has bounced twice on the floor. Something that is only done by opponents.

Playing Pro   See TOURING PRO.

Point   In HARD BALL whoever wins the RALLY wins the point, and 15 points make a GAME. In SOFT BALL a POINT is awarded only if the winner of the rally was the SERVER, and 9 points make a game. See Appendix A: The Game, How Played, Scored.

Practice Games   GAMES or MATCHES that are not part of formal competitions.

Professional   Anyone who accepts money or other valuable consideration for playing or teaching squash or who is paid for using his or her prominence as a squash player to endorse products or services. See TOURING PRO, CLUB PRO. Compare with AMATEUR.

Psych   (1) To try to psych an opponent is to attempt to put him off by using GAMESMANSHIP.

(2) To be psyched *out* is to be unable to function normally because you feel nervous, confused, and a general lack of confidence.

(3) To be psyched *up*, however, is to be loaded for bear. The best way to get yourself psyched up is to get yourself a PLAN for your opponent.

Public Courts   Courts that are open to the general public, but the public, in general, must pay to use them. See COMMERCIAL CENTERS.

Putaway   A WINNER. A shot that opponent is unable to return successfully, not because of an unforced error, but because it is too difficult to return.

Racquetball   Never heard of it.

Rage   When all else fails, the strategy of slamming the ball every which way around the court in an attempt to get opponent out of groove.

Rail Shot   A ball hit tight along one of the side walls. One of the basic shots of the game, good on both offense and defense. Also called ALLEY SHOT and WALL SHOT. See Appendix D: Shots Diagram.

Rally   A rally is an exchange.

Ranking Yours is never as high as it should be, unless you served on the ranking committee.

Rating A classification of a player's level of skill by his local association, based on his performance in local events. Ratings usually range from "A" to "D," with "A" highest. Competitions are organized for players at each level. Players may compete in leagues and TOURNAMENTS above their ratings, but not below. In other words, a B player may play in an A event, but not a C event.

Receiver The player to whom the ball is SERVED.

Referee An official in charge of a match. He decides on LETS, NOT UPS, etc. His decisions may be APPEALED to two JUDGES, if JUDGES are also assigned to match.

Return of Service The return made by the RECEIVER.

Reverse Corner A side wall/front wall carom around the opposite front corner, usually hit as an attempted PUTAWAY. See Appendix D: Shots Diagram.

Rip Corner Same as REVERSE CORNER.

Roll Corner Side wall/front wall carom around the near front corner. See Appendix D: Shots Diagram.

Rough or Smooth A thin string is often wound around the strings at the top or bottom of the racquet face in such a way that one side of this string is rough (knotty) and the other smooth. This is used to differentiate the two sides of the racquet in the SPIN FOR SERVICE. One player calls "rough" or "smooth" while the other spins the racquet on the floor.

Round Robin A TOURNAMENT in which every player plays every other player, or at least everyone else in his division.

Runner A player who relies primarily on his ability to retrieve. His offense is his defense. Runners are much disdained (and feared) by SHOOTERS.

Scoring See Appendix A: The Game, How Played, Scored.

Scrambling Making hurried, improvised GETS. A lot more scrambling goes on in top matches than the textbooks would have you believe. In squash defense it is as important as offense, and the ability to run your way out of trouble is a great asset. There's nothing more demoralizing to an opponent than having his best shot returned.

Seeded Players Prior to making DRAWS for most TOURNAMENTS, several players are designated as SEEDED, based on their RANKINGS and past performances. SEEDED players are placed so that they do not meet in early rounds.

Serve The method of putting the ball in play. See Appendix A: The Game, How Played, Scored.

Server Player who puts ball in play. See Appendix A: The Game, How Played, Scored.

Service Box The quarter-circle area within which the SERVER must keep

at least one foot, while serving. See Appendix B: The Court. Also see
FOOT FAULT.

Service Lines The line on the front wall that the SERVE must clear, and
the lines on the floor which delimit the area within which the serve
must land, if the RECEIVER chooses not to VOLLEY the ball. See Appendix B: The Squash Court.

Service Return See RETURN OF SERVICE.

Set GAMES are ordinarily played to 15 POINTS, but when the score is tied
at 13 all or at 14 all (if it was not first tied at 13 all), the RECEIVER has
the option of extending the game beyond 15 points. At 13 all he may
"set" 3 or 5 points, making the game go to 16 or 18 respectively, or he
may choose "NO SET," which means the game will be played to 15. At
14 all he may choose "no set," which means the next point will determine the game, or he may choose a set of 3 points, thereby extending
the game to 17.

Setup An easy chance for a PUTAWAY.

Seventy-Plus Ball The modern North American HARD BALL, smaller and
softer than the old American hard ball. Originally designed for summer play in courts over 70 degrees (hence called the "seventy-plus"),
but now used year round. The best ball ever made for squash.

Shooter A player who attempts a lot of finesse shots.

Shot Maker A player who makes a lot of finesse shots.

Side Wall/Front Wall A CORNER SHOT.

Singles Squash played by one person on each side, as opposed to DOU-
BLES, in which there are two on each side.

Also a description of the ambience of some new COMMERCIAL CENTERS.

Slice A stroke that imparts sidespin and/or BACKSPIN. See OPEN RAC-
QUET.

Slice Serve A heavily sliced sidearm SERVE that just clears the service
line on the front wall, and is angled to catch the NICK just after the
spot where the service line on the floor meets the side wall.

Slow Serve LOB serve hit softly, underhand. The standard SERVE in
squash.

Slugger Basically hits hard and uses few finesse shots. Someone who
thinks a DROP SHOT is a ball that NICKS off the back wall on the fly is
a slugger.

Smash An overhead blast. Smashing the ball is a better idea than smashing the racquet. But if you must do the latter, jam the butt of the
racquet into a side wall. The court can take it, and so can your racquet.

Soft Ball The ENGLISH BALL used in the ENGLISH GAME. Often called the
"soft ball" because it's squishier than the AMERICAN BALL, which is
sometimes referred to as the HARD BALL.

Soft Ball Game The English version of squash. See the ENGLISH GAME
and SOFT BALL. Compare with HARD BALL.

Spin   A rotation of the ball. Spin can be imparted by opening or closing the face of the racquet. See OPEN RACQUET, BACKSPIN, and TOP SPIN.

Spin for Service   Used to determine who SERVES first. One player twirls the racquet head on the floor, the other guesses which side will be facing up when it drops. See ROUGH OR SMOOTH.

Squash   Chasing a little green ball around a little white room. Defies explanation.

Squash Administrators   A necessary evil.

Squash Racquets   Traditional name for squash, which evolved from the game of "racquets," hence "squash racquets." The British spelling is squash rackets.

Stacking the Lineup   Putting someone who is low down on the LADDER high up on the team so that all the other players will have easier MATCHES. This is against the rules.

Stalling   An attempt to delay or slow down the play without explicitly violating the CONTINUITY OF PLAY rule. An art form involving numerous ploys, such as going to the wrong side to receive serve, requesting a towel to wipe a sweat spot off the floor, checking to see if the ball is broken, serving your first serve out of the court, etc., etc.

Stars   A COURT RUNNING exercise to improve speed and fitness. You start at the T and run to each of the four corners of the court and to each of the two spots where the service line on the floor meets the side walls. Each time you go to one of the points of this star, you return to the T and then set out for another point. After doing this for a minute or so, as fast as you can, you rest for thirty seconds and then do it again. You keep up this routine of a minute on and thirty seconds off as long as you can without losing speed. Don't overdo it the first couple of days. This is not a fun exercise and is recommended only for very serious players, perhaps too serious. You have to have a pretty good reason to put yourself through this kind of torture, and I use this exercise only when I want to improve my fitness for a major event.

Striker   The person who is in the process of playing the ball. Give him room or you'll be the "strikee."

"T"   Point of intersection of SERVICE LINES on the floor, considered a good strategic place to be. It's easiest to make shots and GETS from here, and to control the play in general. See Appendix D: Shots Diagram and CONTROLLING THE T.

Take Opponent Short   To hit a shot that makes opponent run up near the front wall.

Teaching Pro   A professional whose primary interest and/or source of income is in teaching the game. See CLUB PRO. Compare TOURING PRO.

Tell-Tale   The TIN. A strip of metal 17 inches high that extends across the base of the front wall and above which the ball must hit. If it doesn't, the sound of the ball striking the TIN "tells the tale."

Three-Wall Nick   A shot that is angled into a side wall so that after hitting the front wall it NICKS on the other side wall. See Appendix D: Shots Diagram. This is one of the principal WINNERS in top-level squash. "The Three-Wall Nick" is also the short title for the premier book on squash.

Tight Shots that hug the side wall and do not come out in the center.

Tin The TELL-TALE. To tin is to hit the tell-tale.

Top Spin A forward rotation of the ball as it approaches the front wall. This makes the ball climb on the front wall and take a long, high bounce off the floor. Ordinarily not recommended because it makes the ball sit up and come out off back and side walls. Compare with BACKSPIN.

The Toss The SPIN FOR SERVICE.

Touch Finesse, particularly on short, soft shots.

Touring Pro A professional without teaching responsibilities who makes his or her money in squash by competing for prize money, giving exhibitions, and endorsing products. Compare with TEACHING PRO.

Tournament A formal competition in which a winner is determined through a series of matches, either through elimination (a KNOCK-OUT TOURNAMENT) or by everyone playing everyone else and then comparing scores (a ROUND ROBIN). See DRAW.

Tournament Player All players, whatever their level of skill, can find TOURNAMENTS to play in, but a "tournament player" is usually taken to mean someone who plays in top-level tournaments.

Tournament Tough Hardened by much formal competition, so able to get the job done under pressure.

Training Attempts to improve one's CONDITIONING. See STARS.

Trophy Hunter Someone who just won a tournament you wish you'd known about.

Turning on Ball To COME AROUND.

Unconscious Playing out of one's mind.

Underspin A backward rotation of the ball as it approaches the front wall. This makes the ball rebound downward off the front wall and take a low bounce off the floor. Much recommended to make finesse shots sit down and to keep DRIVES off back wall. Same as BACKSPIN. Compare with TOP SPIN.

Up-and-Down Game A style of play characterized by many RAIL SHOTS, that is, by the ball going **up** and down the side walls.

Veterans Players who are forty or over can compete in veterans events. For this reason, unlike Jack Benny, squash players actually look forward to turning forty.

USSRA United States Squash Racquets Association.

Volley Any shot in which the ball is played before it hits the floor. Volleying is a good way to maintain control of the center of the court and to pick up the PACE.

"V" Shot Same as CROSS-COURT. See Appendix D: Shots Diagram.

Waffle Face Imprint of racquet strings on your face. Can happen if you get too close to opponent's follow-through.

Wall Shot Same as RAIL SHOT. See Appendix D: Shots Diagram.

Warm-Up (The) Before beginning a practice game or a real match, there is a period of rallying to permit the players to loosen up and practice their shots. In formal matches this period is limited to five minutes. It's bad form to hit to yourself the whole time during the warm-up.

Warm Up the Ball A new ball doesn't bounce properly until it has been heated up. Whenever a ball breaks and a new ball is, therefore, introduced into play, the game is interrupted so that the players may warm up the new ball by rallying with it until it has a lively enough bounce.

Winner A PUTAWAY. Anyone who plays squash is a winner.

Women Squash Players Frequently underestimated by male squash players, often with embarrassing results.

Wood Shot A lucky hit off the wood of the racquet.

Working Boast In SOFT BALL game, a wide-angled side wall/front wall shot that works the opponent because he has to run way up to the front to retrieve it. See Appendix D: Shots Diagram.

World Ball Another name for the HARD BALL. Copyrighted by the WPSA in response to the SOFT BALLers calling their ball the "international ball."

WPSA World Professional Squash Association. The association for HARD BALL PROFESSIONALS.

Wrist Overused by most beginners.

Wrong Foot To "wrong foot" someone is to fool him with stroke deception and/or shot choice so that he takes off in the wrong direction (that is, on the wrong foot). HOLDing the SHOT is a good way to wrong foot an opponent. Hitting an opponent with the ball during THE WARM-UP may get the match off on the wrong foot.